WEST INDIAN COOKERY

WEST INDIAN COOKERY

by

E. PHYLLIS CLARK

Formerly Lecturer in Domestic Science,
Government Training College for Teachers,
Trinidad and Tobago
and of Department of Education, Uganda

NELSON

THOMAS NELSON AND SONS LTD
36 Park Street London W1Y 4DE
P.O. Box 18123 Nairobi Kenya

THOMAS NELSON (AUSTRALIA) LTD
597 Little Collins Street Melbourne 3000

THOMAS NELSON AND SONS (CANADA) LTD
81 Curlew Drive Don Mills Ontario

THOMAS NELSON (NIGERIA) LTD
P.O. Box 336 Apapa Lagos

THOMAS NELSON AND SONS (SOUTH AFRICA) (PROPRIETARY) LTD
51 Commissioner Street Johannesburg

Fifteenth impression 1972

0 17 147341 8

PRINTED AND BOUND IN ENGLAND BY
HAZELL WATSON AND VINEY LTD
AYLESBURY, BUCKS

PREFACE

The *West Indian Cookery Book* was prepared by Miss E. Phyllis Clark, a former Lecturer in Domestic Science at the Government Training College for Teachers, at the express request of the Trinidad and Tobago Nutrition Committee, and the rights of publication have been secured by the Government of these islands, under whose auspices the book is published.

No pains were spared in making the book essentially West Indian and practical, and much valuable advice was received from local medical officers, dietitians, and teachers, as well as from educationists and others in the various West Indian Islands. To all of these ladies and gentlemen the Compiler would desire to tender her grateful thanks.

In view of the importance attached nowadays to nutrition and diet, it is hoped that the book will foster in the young a correct attitude towards these important subjects, and will eventually help to reduce the incidence of malnutrition in these Islands.

To cater for the requirements of the substantial proportion of East Indian population of some of the Islands, a special section on East Indian recipes has been included.

The book will, I am sure, fill a long-felt want, and should be of particular value not only in schools and colleges, but to the Girl Guides, the W.V.S., Red Cross Detachments, Social Workers, and home-makers generally. I wish it every success.

R. Patrick
Director of Education

Education Offices
Trinidad and Tobago

CONTENTS

PART ONE—FOOD

PART TWO—HOW TO COOK FOODS

WEST INDIAN COOKERY

PART ONE—FOOD

CHAPTER 1

PLANNING MEALS

IT is difficult to imagine a world where fire was unknown, but we presume that in the olden days man used only uncooked food, and that he ate whatever he could find. It is therefore probable that people living near the sea were fish eaters ; others living in countries where game was plentiful ate much meat ; and those in cold countries found that fatty foods helped to keep them warm. Thus for a long time it seems that different kinds of food were naturally eaten (by different people) in different parts of the world.

Nowadays, although most races have particular tastes in foods, it has been proved that to grow properly and keep healthy everyone of whatever race must use certain foods. Because of this, it is important that every housewife should know not only how to cook, but how to plan meals correctly.

Unfortunately when money is scarce, it is sometimes very difficult to buy the best and most nourishing food, but a wise housekeeper will begin by planning out her money. The amount of money to be spent on food naturally varies in different families, depending on the wages earned and the number and ages of the children ; but it is a safe plan for most working-class people to allow no less than half their wages for food. We might, therefore, plan a budget in this way :

Father's wages (labourer) . . .	$3.00 a week
Mother's earnings (washer) . .	$2.00 ,,
Total Income	$5.00 ,,
Allowance for food and fuel . .	$3.00
House or land rent	1.50
Clothing	0.24
Savings or clubs	0.12
Spending money	0.14
	$5.00

The money for food must be divided out for each day ; this works out at 42 cents for this budget. One-third of the total will be needed for food for the father if he is doing hard work.

Next we must consider on what kind of food the money can best be spent. All the food we eat can be divided into three chief groups, which are :

Chief Food Groups

Food Groups	Importance	Where Found
Building or Flesh-forming	To build and repair muscle and skin	Beef, mutton, fowl, fish, eggs, milk, cheese, legumes, nuts
Protective or Regulatory	To keep the blood healthy and the bowels working properly. To help growth and protect from disease	Green vegetables, fruit, coarse grains (wholewheat, bran, porridge oats), farine, milk
Energy-giving	To make us active and give the heat our bodies need	Ground provisions, sugar, molasses, figs, plantains, oil, and fats of all sorts

When planning meals, we must remember that we should not only try to make a person feel satisfied or " full." All these food groups are important, and to be healthy it is necessary to use at least one food from each group at the chief meals of the day. Unfortunately it is a common practice for people to use several cheap foods from the energy group, and to forget all about the other two. In many cases a smaller quantity of more expensive but really good food is better than a big meal which is cheap but less nourishing.

A meal which contains the right amounts of food from each group is generally described as *a balanced meal.* If the food we eat were to be weighed and divided into groups we should expect to find that we eat:

one-fourth flesh-forming foods
one-fourth protective foods
two-fourths energy food of which a good proportion is some kind of animal fat

Secondly, we should arrange to eat *fresh or new foods* in preference to those which have been salted, dried, tinned, stored for a long time, or much refined, as in the case of polished rice or white flour. Fresh foods have more of the important protective substances called vitamins. Because of this, fresh milk is better than tinned ; young pigeon peas better than dried split peas ; fresh sweet potatoes better than imported Irish potatoes ; and fresh mackerel better than salt fish.

Lastly, in planning meals, we should consider not only their cost and the balance of food from different groups, but also remember :

(1) the age of the people eating the meal, as young children while needing plenty to eat cannot digest the same foods as grown-ups

(2) their occupation—people doing hard manual work need more than those who sit all day

(3) their state of health—sick people and pregnant mothers must have special food

(4) the amount of time for preparing and cooking the meal

(5) the cost of fuel, and the pots, pans, etc., in our kitchen

If a home-maker plans her meals thoughtfully, she should not only give her family good nourishing food, but she will save herself worry and work.

Some Suggestions for a Balanced Midday Meal

1 Beef and vegetables stewed together
Cress
Coconut water or milk

2 Beef or chicken pelau
Salad

3 Rice and peas
Gravy
Mangoes

4 Stuffed breadfruits
Oranges

N.B.—All these meals need only one saucepan or pot, and can be cooked on one fire.

5 Steamed fish
Steamed pumpkin
Boiled provisions
Bananas

N.B.—One saucepan, a steamer (which can be made from a large butter pan), and only one fire will be enough for this breakfast.

6 Pigeon pea stew
Brown rice
Papaw or melon

7 Crab callaloo
Pounded plantain (foo-foo)
Sapodilla

8 Floats and accra
Rice and spinach (bhaji) boiled together
Sugar-apple

9 Roast mutton
Baked potatoes
Melongene au gratin
Stewed guava and coconut cream

10 Boiled, poached, or scrambled egg
Cassava or bran bread
Golden-apple (pommecythere)

CHAPTER 2

THE FOODS WE EAT

As well as grouping our foods as we did in the last chapter, we can group them by the things they have in them. These things are called Food Factors, and there are six of them.

(1) *Proteins*

Proteins are the flesh-forming factors found in meat, fish, eggs, and peas, and contain nitrogen which builds and repairs muscle and skin. Protein from animals is more easily turned into flesh than that in nuts, beans, etc., and is therefore called *first class protein.* If, however, money is scarce it is better to buy *second class protein* from a vegetable than to use none at all.

(2) *Fats*

Fats, made up of carbon, hydrogen, and oxygen, provide the body with heat and energy (or power to work and play). They are found in ghee, butter, cream, milk, pork, anchovy, eggs, nuts, friolene, sweet oil, etc. Again those from animals are better than the others. This is because they contain more of the useful vitamins which keep the body in proper working order.

(3) *Carbohydrates*

Carbohydrates, also made up of carbon, hydrogen, and oxygen, do the same work as fats and oils. They are obtainable in the form of sugar from honey, jam, fruit, or cane, and of starch from bananas, all grains, and ground provisions. The coarse grains are better than those that have been refined, because as well as being rich in vitamins, they contain roughage or cellulose. Cellulose is the fibrous part of plants and their seeds, and it is used by the body to keep the bowels working properly.

(4) *Mineral Salts*

The important salts are derived from calcium, phosphorus, iron, and iodine.

Salts	Where Obtained	Importance
Calcium	from milk	for teeth and bones
Phosphorus	from meat, eggs, whole wheat	for teeth and bones
Iron	from goat's milk, green vegetables, especially ochroes, spinach, and green figs	to purify the blood
Iodine	from salt-water fish	for the thyroid gland

(5) *Water*

This is needed by the body in large quantities. It is present in most foods, especially such things as milk, juicy fruit, tomatoes, cristophine, etc. Large quantities are also added in cooking.

Wherever it comes from, the water must be pure. If there is any doubt, it should be boiled. Impure water may cause typhoid, dysentery, and worms.

(6) *Vitamins*

As these are a particularly important food factor, they deserve a special chapter to themselves.

CHAPTER 3

VITAMINS

IMAGINE we have planned a journey from one end of the island to the other—our luggage is packed ; food for the journey prepared ; and so we start, full of confidence in our bus or launch and its driver. Imagine our annoyance, then, if after a short distance the engine fails and the driver has to stop to see what is wrong. Probably his first thought would be to make sure that there is plenty of gasolene, and he might also see that the works are clean and the screws and nuts properly tightened. This done, the engine may start, but only to fail again after another mile or two. This time a more thorough overhaul may show that there is a shortage of oil in the works, and of water in the radiator or battery, so that the engine could not run smoothly without getting very over-heated or even badly damaged.

The ordinary food factors used by the body are like the gasolene in the bus, and as the engine could not work properly without oil and water, so our bodies will fail to grow as they should and will not be healthy unless they have vitamins.

Serious " deficiency diseases " caused by lack of vitamins are not very common in the West Indies, but we know that some people do begin to get these diseases, and there is no need for this to happen. We shall therefore describe some of the early signs, so that a shortage of vitamins may quickly be seen and put right.

The following six vitamins are important to man :

Vitamin A

Vitamin A, the anti-xerotic vitamin, is found in liver, fish oils (*i.e.* cod-liver or haliver oil), animal fats (*i.e.* milk fat, butter, ghee), carotene (*i.e.* yellow colouring of plants in carrot, yellow sweet potato, avocado pear, mango, etc.; green vegetable colouring in cabbage, spinach, etc.)

These foods prevent xerosis or hardening of different parts of the body, including the part of the eye called the conjunctiva. It was found in various countries that babies having a poor quality of milk, short of cream (or milk fat), often suffered from a serious eye disease called xerophthalmia; in fact, in India this is the chief cause of blindness in children. The inner lining of the nose, mouth, and windpipe may also be affected by lack of Vitamin A, and will then be less able to withstand the attack of germs.

Do you know of people who find it difficult to see at night; others who constantly suffer from dry scaly sores, or throat and chest troubles? These conditions may be improved by including Vitamin A in the diet.

Vitamin D

Vitamin D, the anti-rachitic vitamin, is found in much the same foods as Vitamin A—*i.e.* in animal fats (butter, ghee, and fish oils), green vegetables, and liver. One of the chief differences is, however, that these foods can only supply Vitamin D if they have been grown in a sunny place, or if we ourselves live in healthy, sunny places, when we turn the foods into Vitamin D in our own livers. Some foods are specially treated with artificial sunlight, called ultra-violet rays; but these foods are, of course, very much more expensive, and we should do our best to get enough natural sunlight by taking outdoor exercise and letting the sun into our houses.

Rickets, the disease against which this vitamin protects us, is sometimes seen among bottle-fed babies, or in poor badly nourished mothers who are trying to feed their babies themselves. Signs of rickets are weak bones resulting in bandy legs, curved back, bulging forehead, and pigeon chest.

Lack of Vitamin D is bad for teeth, which may become misshapen and decay easily. It is well known that bad teeth are often the cause of bad health. Apart from the pain they cause, the decaying substances poison the body; we have difficulty in chewing our food, and are almost sure to suffer from indigestion in consequence.

Vitamin B

Vitamin B, the anti-neuritic vitamin, is sub-divided into B_1 and B_2. The former is found in varying degrees in many of our common foods (excluding the fatty foods), but particularly in the outer covering and embryo (or growing part) of grains (therefore in brown rice and wholewheat flour); yeast and home-made, freshly fermented drinks; internal meat, such as liver; and egg yolk. Vitamin B_2 occurs more rarely, a little being found in lean beef and fresh vegetables such as onions, melongene, cabbage, tomatoes, spinach, etc. The list of the common sources of both is found in the table on page 13. Complete lack of Vitamin B causes a disease called beri-beri, which attacks not only man, but animals and hens. In fact, the way to prevent beri-beri was discovered because a Dutch doctor in Java noticed that sick hens got well when they fed on the husk (over covering) removed from polished rice. Beri-beri, which in its worst form causes paralysis, has been very common in certain parts of the East. While few of us know of people suffering from it here, there must be many of us who have friends who are nervy, who suffer from digestive troubles or tired hearts. These are some of the early symptoms of beri-beri, against which Vitamin B will protect us.

Vitamin P–P

Vitamin P–P, another anti-neuritic vitamin, is very much the same as Vitamin B. It is found in fresh meat, liver, yeast, peas, cress, and cabbage. Lack of this vitamin causes another nervous complaint called pellagra, which is still common in Italy, Africa, and the southern parts of the U.S.A., where in 1930 over 7,000 people died from it. People suffering from pellagra generally go mad. Although it is not common here, there are probably a number of people who do not eat enough Vitamin P–P, and as a result they are liable to suffer from skin disorders and digestive troubles, which occur in the early stages of pellagra.

Vitamin C

Vitamin C, the anti-scorbutic vitamin, is a very old friend, although it only received its present name a few years ago.

In the olden days of sailing ships, voyages were very slow, food was difficult to keep, and sailors fed mostly on dried and salted food. Many of them died from a horrible disease called scurvy—in fact, Vasco da Gama (the famous explorer) lost 100 men out of 160 on one voyage alone. Later, sailors found that by drinking orange or lemon juice daily they did not get scurvy. More recently scientists have discovered that this disease can be prevented by giving not only citrus fruits, but pineapple, mango, papaw, tomato, fresh milk, and uncooked green vegetables such as cabbage, lettuce, and cress.

Unfortunately, Vitamin C is very easily destroyed by heat, so that all these foods should be eaten raw. For this reason it is better to wash and chop cabbage, and use it in a salad instead of boiling it, since this preserves all the vitamins.

We want, of course, to be able to recognize these diseases and deal with them as early as possible. Old ships' records tell us that some of the first signs of scurvy are " a loathsome sloath," irritability, bleeding under the skin, causing marks like bruises, swollen painful joints, swelling of the gums and loosening of the teeth.

Vitamin E

Vitamin E, the anti-sterility vitamin, is most plentiful in green leaves and the embryo or growing parts of seeds (*e.g.* wheat grain, peas).

It is thought that people not having enough of these foods may not have healthy babies.

The table given on pages 13 and 14 indicates the chief sources of vitamins generally acknowledged at the present time :

SOURCES OF VITAMINS

xxx .. plentiful
xx .. moderate
x .. little
VL .. very little

Food	Vitamins					
	A	B_1	B_2	C	D	E
Cow's Milk	xxx	xx		x	x	
Human Milk	x	x		x		
Goat's Milk	xxx	x		x	x	
Buffalo's Milk	xxx	x		x	x	
Condensed Milk	x	x				
Butter and Ghee	xxx				x	
Beef Fat	xx					
Mutton Fat	xx					
Pork Fat						
Lard	VL					
Cod-liver Oil	xxx	VL			xxx	
Haliver Oil	xxx				xxx	
Cheese	xx	VL				
Coconut Milk						
Coconut Oil	x				VL	
Cottonseed Oil	VL					
Edible Oil						
Margarine						
Olive Oil (sweet oil)						
Lean Beef	VL	x	x	VL	x	
Lean Mutton	VL	x		VL	x	
Goat's Meat		x		VL		
Pork		x				
Liver	xxx	xxx		x	x	
Kidney	xx	xx				
Brain	x	xx				
Oily Fish (*e.g.* mackerel)	xxx	x				
White Fish		x				
Fresh-water Fish		x				
Fowl	x	x				
Duck	x	x				
Pigeon	x	x				
Eggs (yolk best)	xxx	xxx			xx	xxx

SOURCES OF VITAMINS (continued)

Food	Vitamins					
	A	B_1	B_2	*C*	*D*	*E*
Wholewheat Flour						
White Flour						
Oatmeal	x	xx				
Corn	xx	xx				
Split Peas	x	xx				
Brown Rice	x	xx				
White Rice						
Coconuts	x	xx				
Ground-nuts (pea-nuts)	xx	xx				
Onions	VL	xx	xx	x		
Garlic	x	x		xx		
Carrots	xxx	xx		xx		
Yams		x		x		
Irish Potatoes		x		x		
Sweet Potatoes (yellow variety)	x	xx	xx	xxx		
Brinjal		x		x		
Avocado Pear				xxx		
Green Sweet Peppers	xxx	x		xxx		
Melongene	x	x	x			
Tomatoes	xxx	xxx	xx	xxx		
Cucumbers		x		xx		
Pumpkins	xx	x	x	xxx		
French Beans (salad beans)	xx	xx		x		
Cabbage	xxx	xx	xx	xxx		
Lettuce (salad)	xxx	xx	xx	xxx		xxx
Spinach (bush)	xxx	xx	xx	xxx		
Bananas and plantains	VL	x		x		
Lemons		x		xxx		
Limes				xx		
Oranges	xx	x		xxx		
Grapefruit		x		xxx		
Pineapple				xx		
Water-melon				x		
Papaws	x	x		xx		
Mangoes	x			xx		
Guavas		x		x		

CHAPTER 4

MILK

To be healthy, people need a balanced diet—that is, meals in which the food factors are eaten in the correct quantities. Babies and young animals often live on milk alone, so it must follow that milk is a complete food supplying all the things they need. A look at the vitamin table at the end of the last chapter shows that it provides Vitamins A, B, C, and D. It also contains valuable mineral salts such as iron, calcium (lime), and phosphorus. The proteins in milk, and the milk fat (cream) which is made up of very tiny drops of oil, are easy to digest, therefore milk is a particularly suitable food for young children and sick people.

Apart from this, milk is a very valuable food for healthy people of all ages, but it has, of course, to be used with other foods, otherwise a full-grown working man living on milk alone would need about twenty pints (40 nips) a day in order to get enough carbohydrate.

(For comparison of different kinds of milks see Chapter 40, Feeding Babies.)

Goat's milk should not be neglected, because :

(1) It is more like human milk than the others, and can therefore be more easily digested.
(2) Goats rarely suffer from tuberculosis.
(3) It is very rich in iron.

Many people dislike the idea of goat's milk because they think it has too strong a taste, but this can be avoided if the ram is not kept with the herd, and if the goats are kept clean.

Fresh milk is generally best, because tinned milk may not be so easy to digest nor so rich in vitamins. On the other hand, tinned milk is easy to keep and is carefully tested for purity. One or two firms now evaporate their milk by using artificial sunlight. This, of course, improves the value of the milk by increasing the quantity of Vitamin D.

Where a *pure* supply of fresh milk can be obtained, it is, however, preferable to buy this rather than tinned milk.

Diseases sometimes caused by impure milk are tuberculosis, Malta fever, diphtheria, scarlet fever, typhoid, dysentery. The first two may be caused by drinking milk from an infected animal. Milk becomes contaminated (or made impure) when handled by sick people ; or milk is infected by impure water used to dilute the milk or to wash milk cans, etc.

PURE MILK

To obtain pure milk the following precautions should be taken :

(1) Animals must be clean and healthy and free from tuberculosis. In some islands arrangements are made for the testing of animals used for milking; this should be done regularly.

(2) Sheds in which animals are kept, or places where they are milked, must be clean, otherwise the air is full of germs which find their way into the milk.

(3) The milkers, dairymen, or milk vendors must be healthy and scrupulously clean in their habits.

(4) Milk should be covered at all times to protect it from dust and flies. This applies to milk waiting to be delivered, during delivery, and in the home. For this reason it is better to buy milk in sealed bottles than from a vendor who measures it from a can. Germs may find their way into milk every time the can is opened, and the measure may easily be placed on some dirty surface or be contaminated by flies.

(5) Milk should be kept cool. People who have no ice chest should stand their milk in an airy place or stand the bottle of milk in a pan of cold water.

(6) The jugs, bottles, cans, etc. used for milk must be kept spotlessly clean. All milk receptacles should have wide necks so that they are easy to clean. They should first be washed with cold water to remove all trace of protein, and then scalded out with boiling water to remove the grease from the cream, and to destroy all germs. In large dairies they are often scalded in steam cabinets.

Purification of Milk

Even when all the above precautions have been taken, it is still wise for everyone to make sure that the milk has been thoroughly purified. There are various ways of doing this :

(1) *Boiling* is the method most commonly used. This is very thorough, but it has been thought that the high temperature (212° F.) tends to harden the protein and make it less digestible for babies, to kill the vitamins, and spoil the taste.

(2) *Pasteurization* is the method used in dairies where a large quantity of milk is being purified.

(3) A simple way to pasteurize your own milk is as follows. Put it into a double boiler with milk in the inner one and water in the outer one, or stand the bottle of milk on a piece of wood in a pan of hot water. Allow the water to boil for twenty minutes, or continue until the milk begins to look bubbly on top. Cool quickly by placing the pan in cold water. This way gives more trouble than boiling, but some people think that the milk is more nourishing and digestible.

Ways of Using Milk

Because milk is such a valuable food we should try to use it as much as possible. Here are some suggestions :

(1) A plain drink. Sip it slowly. If gulped down it will not be properly digested.

(2) Milk shakes or punches, *i.e.* milk mixed with syrup or iced fruit juice.

(3) In egg-nog (egg-flip), cocoa, custard, milk pudding, white sauce, or cream soups.

(4) Used for mixing cornstarch, jelly, coo-coo, porridge, etc.

Ways of Using Sour Milk

Clean milk which has only turned sour should not be discarded. It can be used for :

(1) Making cake, bread, or scones.

(2) Making cheese. To do this, collect the curd by straining the milk through muslin or a thin cloth, allow it to drip, and when firm, add salt to taste, and press into shape.

CHAPTER 5

CHEESE

CHEESE is prepared from either whole or skimmed milk in which the protein has been coagulated, or hardened, to form a curd. This may either be brought about by natural souring, souring by the addition of an acid such as lime juice or vinegar, or by the addition of rennet. (Rennet is a liquid obtained from the lining of a calf's stomach, and when added to warm milk it causes the protein to form a clot somewhat similar to the curd found in the human stomach when milk is digested.) The curd thus formed is strained from the whey, salted, pressed, and allowed to ripen for any period up to six months.

Composition of Cheese

The average cheese consists of equal parts protein, fat, and water, with a small quantity of mineral salts.

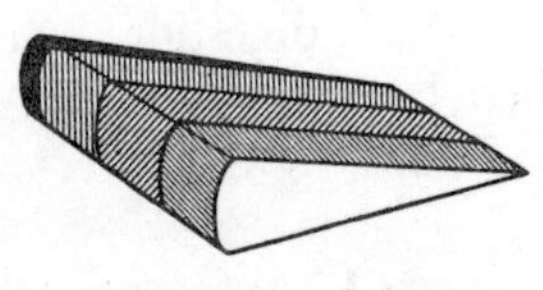

Composition of cheese

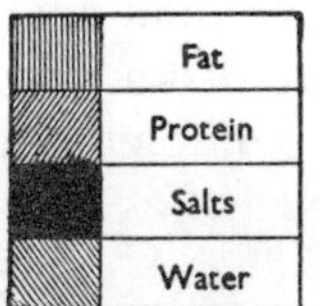

Key to shading

Cheese made from skimmed milk (from which the cream has been removed) has of course a much lower proportion of fat.

Food Value

One pound of cheese made from whole milk contains the protein and fat of a gallon (16 nips) of milk. It is therefore a cheap but good food.

Being rich in animal protein, cheese is a good flesh-forming food.

The large proportion of animal fat it contains also makes it rich in Vitamin A, and a good energy food.

Digestibility

Compared with most foods, cheese is very concentrated, and therefore somewhat more difficult to digest ; also, the large proportion of fat gives the protein a greasy coating, which prevents the digestive juices from coming in contact with it. On the other hand, a great deal of the protein is turned into a digestible form during the ripening stage, and provided it is well chewed, finely grated, or sliced, it can be easily digested by most people, including children. Hard cheeses which require more chewing are therefore better than soft creamy ones which clog together and form balls in the mouth. For the same reason raw unmelted cheese is more digestible than cooked cheese.

Apart from the question of digestion, cheese is almost completely absorbed by the body, and should be regarded as a valuable food.

(For ways of using cheese see Chapter 44, Diets for Vegetarians.)

CHAPTER 6

MEAT

UNDER the heading of " Meat," we include the flesh of any animal or bird. This flesh is composed of protein, fat, salts, and water in varying proportions. Lean meat is really the muscle of animals, and it consists of meat juice (or blood), and of bundles of very fine muscle fibres which can be seen when meat is rather overcooked and begins to fall to pieces.

Food Value of Meat

Lean meat provides us with mineral salts and valuable proteins belonging to the group called first-class proteins, because they are the kind best able to build up or repair our own flesh.

The fat from meat gives heat and energy, and in some cases a little vitamin.

The skin and bones of meat when boiled down yield a jelly which contains a substance called a " protein sparer." This cannot do the work of a true protein in building up flesh, but can help to save waste of protein from the body. Because of this, protein sparers such as cowheel are good for sick people who are too ill to eat meat, peas, etc.

Choice of Meat

(1) Good meat has no unpleasant smell.

(2) Meat should be firm and should have only a moderate amount of fat.

(3) Lean beef should be bright red ; if purplish or brown it shows either that the meat is dry and stale, or that it was cut from an old animal and is likely to be tough.

(4) Bones or skinny pieces of meat are only suitable for soup-making. Small pieces of meat should be used for stews. Good cuts of tender meat (which are generally more expensive) are the best for roasting, frying, or grilling.

Digestibility of Meat

The fibres in meat from smaller animals are finer than those from large animals, and they are therefore more easily digested.

Pork is rather indigestible owing to the large amount of fat it contains. Because pigs are such dirty eaters, it is sometimes found that pork is infected with different kinds of worms, and on this account it must be very carefully inspected and cooked rather longer than any other kind of meat.

Salt meat is usually tougher than fresh meat, owing to the effect of the brine in which it is soaked. For this reason, and because preserved foods are less nourishing than fresh ones, it is better to buy fresh rather than salt meat whenever possible.

Meat is easier to digest if soft, so that great care must be taken to prepare and cook it properly.

Preparation of Meat

(1) Paper must be removed from the meat directly it reaches the house, otherwise it absorbs the meat juice.

(2) Meat must be thoroughly cleaned. Small scraps of meat which have been exposed to dust and flies should be thoroughly but quickly washed. If allowed to soak in water much of the meat juice escapes, and the meat is less nourishing and inclined to be dry and tasteless.

Larger pieces of meat for roasting, etc., can easily be cleaned by thorough wiping with a clean damp cloth specially kept for the purpose.

(3) Salt meat should be washed and then left to soak in cold water. Small pieces are generally washed with lime and then soaked for half an hour, while larger pieces such as hams are scraped and soaked overnight.

(4) Frozen meat must be thoroughly thawed before cooking (that is, the ice in it must be allowed to melt), otherwise it will be very hard.

(5) Hard meat may sometimes be softened by wrapping it in papaw leaves or covering it with slices of pineapple. This is because papaw and pine contain pepsin, which starts to digest or soften food in much the same way as our own digestive juices. It must be remembered, however, that if left for any length of time, the meat goes bad just as easily as if unwrapped. Gentle pounding with a wooden spoon or pallet, which will bruise the fibres, also helps to soften hard meat.

(6) While it is obviously very dangerous to use bad or tainted meat, it sometimes happens that meat becomes rather strong-smelling even in the short time it takes to get from the market to the home. If this happens the meat should be washed with one pint of water containing a tablespoonful of vinegar, lime juice, or salt.

Some people have an idea that vinegar softens meat.

This is not the case ; in fact, the acid in vinegar tends to harden the protein in meat. When cooking for adults, however, it may sometimes be added to improve the flavour. Vinegar is not good for children.

(7) The method of seasoning and cutting up meat varies with the way it is to be cooked. Directions are given in the chapters on Stewing, Roasting, etc.

Cooking Meat

Most people now agree that meat which has been lightly cooked for only a short time is more nourishing than that which has been heated for long periods. Unfortunately short cooking is only suited to good quality tender pieces of meat, and as these are more expensive, many people cannot afford them. If this is the case, it is better to buy cheaper meat and cook it for a long time than to buy no meat at all.

When we are cooking meat we want either to :

(1) *Draw out all nourishment*, as when using cheap meat which is chiefly skin and bone. This is the case when making soup, and the meat should be cut up finely, placed in cold water, and cooked very gently for a long time.

(2) *Keep in all nourishment* when cooking fleshy pieces of meat, as when boiling a chicken or roasting beef, etc. In this case the meat should be in larger pieces, and enough heat should be used at the start to harden the outside of the meat as quickly as possible. In this way a thin covering is formed which will keep in the meat juices. The rest of the cooking should be slower, to allow the heat to cook the centre of the meat without overcooking the outer layers.

Grilling (also called broiling or toasting) is one of the best ways of cooking meat, because it is very quick and because the meat is made brown and tasty.

Roasting (baking) is also good.

Frying, although quick, is not so good, because the hot oil in which the food cooks makes it less digestible.

Stewing is fairly good ; no meat juice is lost, but it is a slow way of cooking.

Boiling is less good than the other ways, as it is rather slow and some of the meat juice and mineral salts are drawn out, so that unless the water is used for soup, these are wasted.

CHAPTER 7

FISH

MANY people who find it difficult to afford meat can buy plenty of fish. Fish are usually divided into the following groups or classes :

(1) *Oily or Dark Fish*—that is, any fish with dark-looking flesh such as cavalli and anchovy. This dark colour is due to the presence of oil in between the fibres of which fish is made.

(2) *Lean or White Fish*, such as moonshine, snapper (red fish), cod, grunt, flying fish, grouper. In this case the fish oil, instead of being mixed up with the fibres, is stored in the fish's liver. Because of this we can buy cod-liver oil.

(3) *Shell-fish*, which are of two kinds :

(*a*) Crustaceans—crab, crayfish, cascadura
(*b*) Molluscs—oysters, chip chip

(4) *Salt or Smoked Fish*, which is generally dried cod, salmon, or t'zare-salé.

FOOD VALUE OF FISH

FOOD	PROTEIN	FAT	SALTS	WATER
White Fish . . .	19·7	1·0	1·3	78·0
Oily Fish . . .	18·7	7·1	1·2	73·0
Oysters	6·2	1·2	2·0	86·9
Salt Fish . . .	28·6	0·3	14·7	54·8

We can see from the table that fish is a very valuable body-building food, owing to the large proportion of protein it contains.

Oily fish are specially good, because the fat they contain is rich in Vitamins A and D. In the case of

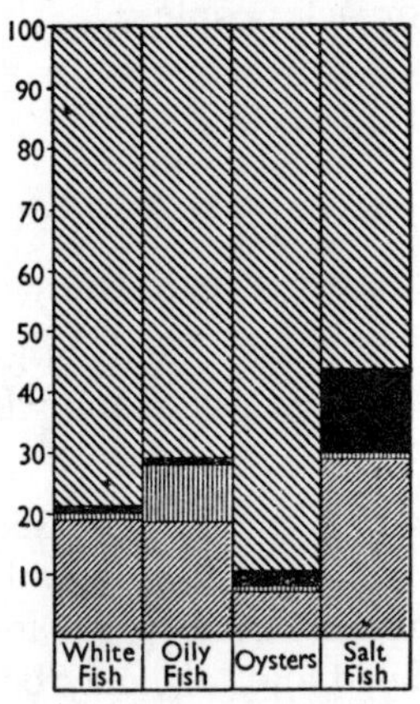

Composition of fish

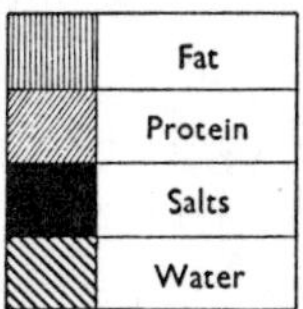

Key to shading

white fish, the liver in which the fat is stored is thrown away with the entrails (or guts), so that they provide no oil unless it is bought as medicine, *e.g.* cod-liver or haliver oil.

Digestibility of Fish

Fish, like meat, is made up of tiny fibres, but as these are finer than those in meat, fish is the more digestible food.

The digestibility of fish varies somewhat with the kind of fish : (*a*) White fish is the most digestible, and is therefore suitable in a light diet for people recovering from ill-health. Oily fish is digested by people in normal health. (*b*) Crustaceans (crab, etc.) have very coarse fibres and are difficult to digest. (*c*) Salt fish is less digestible than fresh fish because the salting and drying hardens the fibres.

The method of cooking also makes fish more or less digestible, and should be thought about when planning meals for young children or sick people.

Choice of Fish

(1) Good fish should have no unpleasant smell.

(2) It should be firm, not flabby ; with shiny scales.

(3) The eyes should be prominent and bright, and the gills vivid red. Never buy fish from which the gills have been removed.

(4) A short plump fish or a middle cut should be bought rather than a long thin fish or a tail cut, as these have more flesh and less bone piece for piece. The bony pieces, such as head and tail, may be bought when making fish broth (fish tea) or fish jelly.

Preparation of Fresh Fish

Handle the fish carefully. When prepared it should not look as though it had been dead for days.

(1) Spread a double layer of newspaper (Gazette paper).

(2) Cut off fins and spines and trim the tail. This can be done more quickly and easily with an old pair of scissors than with a knife.

(3) Scale thoroughly by scraping from tail to head in a deep basin of water—the water prevents the scales from flying about. Be sure to empty this water down an outside drain, not an *open* gutter, and not into a

sink. If the scales and water are poured down a sink drain, it is quickly choked, and will soon have a disgusting smell.

(4) Carefully slit open the under-side (belly) and remove all entrails, dark skin, and blood. Cut off the head or, if preferred, remove gills only.

(5) Collect all the waste in the newspaper and throw this away at once, as the smell quickly attracts flies.

(6) Wash the fish thoroughly but do not let it soak, as this makes it soft and tasteless. Examine the inside, if you can still see black skin scour it with salt.

(7) Season to taste. Lime juice is generally used, partly because it is antiseptic (*i.e.* purifying), and partly to improve the flavour of fish.

Do not leave the fish lying in seasoning for more than twenty to thirty minutes, otherwise it begins to smell and go bad.

To Fillet or Bone Fish

Filleted fish looks very attractive, and if suitably cooked is a good food for toddlers or people on a light diet. Scale it in the usual way and cut off the head, then instead of cutting it open along the under-side, take a sharp knife and, starting from the centre of the back, cut the flesh away from the backbone first on one side and then on the other. Lift out the backbone and entrails, and cut the flesh into two or four fillets, according to the size.

Wash the fillets, the head, and the backbone. The head and bones can be boiled to make soup or sauce, and the fillets can be steamed, grilled, or fried.

Preparation of Salt Fish

(1) Wash the fish well, place it in a small pan barely covered with cold water, heat it to boiling-point, and then throw off the water at once. This scalding purifies the fish, draws out some of the excess salt, and loosens skin and bone.

(2) Because it is concentrated and hard, salt fish should next be finely divided. Either pound or flake it with a fork.

Preparation of Crabs

(1) Crabs are foul feeders. On this account keep them for about a week in some place from which they cannot escape. Feed them on clean food, such as grass, bread, etc., and give them pepper leaves which act as a purge.

(2) When ready for use, plunge them straight into fast boiling water, as this kills them at once.

(3) As soon as they are dead, break off the legs, remove the body from the shell, and take out the little black sac, or gall. The eggs and fat may be used if liked, and the flesh should be picked from the legs and body shell.

Preparation of Oysters

Many people are rather afraid of eating oysters, because they may grow in dirty sewage-contaminated water, and because there is often no cooking which would help to destroy germs.

Oysters should not be easy to open, if they are it shows that they are stale or dead.

After opening oysters, wash them in salt water, and sprinkle each one with a little lime juice.

Cooking Fish

Whole fish are very good stuffed or baked.

Small pieces of fish may be grilled or fried. Fried fish is less digestible than that cooked in other ways. For young children or invalids fish should be steamed. Some people object to steamed fish because they think it is rather tasteless, but this difficulty can be overcome if an appetising sauce is served with it. Fish can also be boiled, but this is rather wasteful as much of the mineral salts is drawn out into the water and lost, and the fish is inclined to break. A better plan is to make fish soup or stew, and thus use the water in which the fish is cooked.

(For further directions see Chapters 20, 22, 23 on Stewing, Steaming, Frying, etc.)

CHAPTER 8

EGGS

In an egg there is everything that makes a chick, so it must contain all the food factors needed for building the body.

The edible part of an egg consists of sticky white stuff known as albumen enclosing a thicker yellow part called the yolk. The yolk is held in a very thin skin twisted at each end to suspend it in the white. This twisted part is often described as the speck, but should not be confused with the true ovum. The ovum found in fertilized eggs is the part which would develop into a chick, while the yolk and white only provide it with food and covering.

Composition of a Hen's Egg

Water	73·7	per cent.
Protein	14·8	,,
Fat	10·5	,,
Salts	1·0	,,

The eggs of most of the larger birds have much the same composition, that of the duck being slightly richer in fat than the hen's or the turkey's eggs.

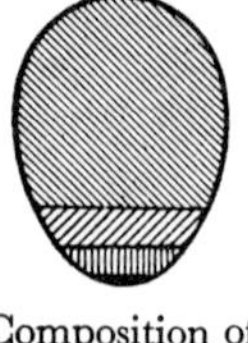
Composition of a hen's egg

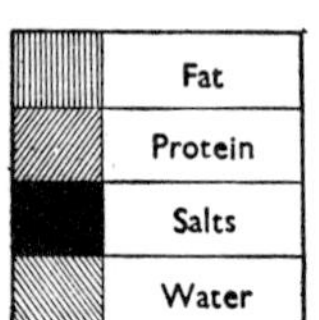

Key to shading

Food Value of Eggs

We see that eggs are a very valuable source of first-class protein, particularly as they are cheaper than meat.

The fat they contain not only supplies the body with energy, but provides Vitamins A, B, D, and G.

The salts in the form of calcium and iron are good for the blood and for bones.

Digestibility

Eggs are easily digested by most normal people. Raw or lightly cooked eggs, in which the protein is still semi-liquid, are more digestible than those cooked until hard.

The fact that eggs are both nourishing and digestible make them an excellent food for toddlers or invalids, as well as for grown-ups. The iron they contain makes them a valuable food for people suffering from anaemia (poor blood).

Tests for Freshness

(1) Good fresh eggs do not rattle when shaken.

(2) When held to a strong light, no dark patches are seen.

(3) If placed in a basin of cold water, fresh eggs sink, while stale ones rise to the surface and float, due to the gas formed as they go bad.

(4) Fresh eggs have no unpleasant smell when broken.

N.B. Tests (3) and (4) are the most reliable.

Preservation of Eggs

Keep eggs in a cool place in a rack or box filled with sand. Turn them daily.

Eggs often get scarce and expensive during November and December, so that many people buy a quantity before they become dear, and preserve them to use at these times.

The aim when preserving eggs is to keep out air ; this may be done in one of the following ways :

(1) Grease the shell thoroughly with saltless fat (tallow, sweet oil, mutton fat, vaseline), and wrap in paper.

(2) Grease or wrap in paper, and then bury in salt or sand.

(3) Soak in a bucket containing lime or isinglass solution.

CHAPTER 9

VEGETABLE FOODS

THERE are many different kinds of vegetables ; their use varies, and for this reason they are grouped or classified as follows :

(1) Ground provisions or root vegetables, *e.g.* tannia, potato, yam, etc.

(2) Green vegetables—the stems, leaves, or flowers of plants—*e.g.* cress, lettuce (broad leaf salad), cabbage, patchoi, googe, spinach (bhaji).

(3) Legumes or pulses—the pods and seeds of plants—*e.g.* split peas, red beans, gub-gub, chana peas, etc.

(4) Edible fungi—*e.g.* mushrooms. The Chinese buy these in dried form and use them for flavouring.

Choice of Vegetables

Vegetables should be free from mud and a good colour.

The skin should be smooth, unwrinkled, and firm, and the leaves unwithered and crisp.

Medium-sized ones are best, as very small ones are wasteful and troublesome to prepare, while large ones are often tough and fibrous.

The Aims in Cooking Vegetables

(1) To make them more digestible by softening the cellulose and the starch grains found in some kinds.

(2) To prevent loss of mineral salts and vitamins.

(3) To preserve their shape and colour.

CHAPTER 10

GROUND PROVISIONS

BECAUSE they have much the same food value as ground provisions, bluggers, green figs, and plantains are sometimes included with this group of vegetables.

Food Value

It will be seen that ground provisions contain a small amount of mineral salts ; these, especially the iron in green figs, makes them of use to the blood.

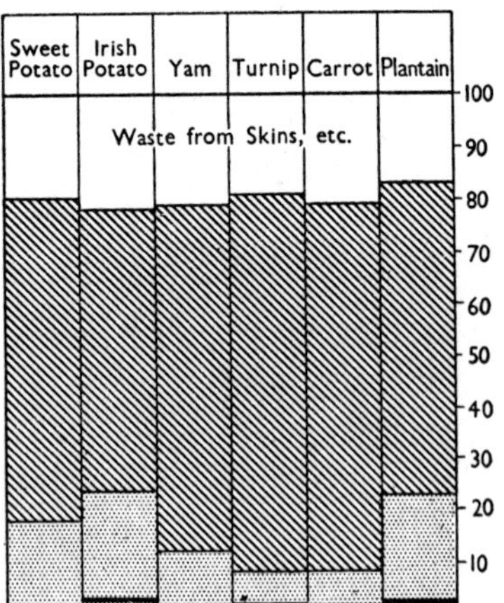

Key to shading

Composition of ground provisions

The plentiful supply of starch makes ground provisions a source of energy.

Those which contain the yellow colouring matter

called carotene (*e.g.* yellow sweet potato and carrot) also provide Vitamin A, while others such as yam and onion give a little Vitamin B. In this connection it should be remembered that fresh home-grown vegetables are richer than imported vegetables which, by being stored, have lost some of their vitamins.

Cooking Ground Provisions

Scrub all provisions thoroughly before cooking. As far as possible, choose those of the same size for cooking together, as they will all need the same time. Add salt in the proportion of one teaspoonful of salt per pound of provisions.

To prevent loss of mineral salts, stew, steam, or bake ground provisions (see chapters on these ways of cooking). If they are to be boiled, cook them, in their skins, for as short a time as possible. To shorten the time for boiling put them into boiling and not cold water. If, however, they are old and very fibrous, they will cook more evenly if put in cold water and heated slowly to boiling-point. Unfortunately, cooking in the skins tends to discolour a few provisions (*e.g.* Irish potatoes), so that some people sacrifice the mineral salts to their appearance, and peel thinly before boiling.

Boil ground provisions gently, as violent bubbling may break them, spoil the appearance, and cause loss of mineral salts.

Never leave provisions soaking in the water in which they have been boiled—this discolours them, makes them sodden and unappetizing, and causes further loss of mineral salts.

CHAPTER 11

GREEN VEGETABLES

THESE are largely made up of a framework of cellulose such as that seen in torchon (loofah) or a skeleton leaf; they also contain mineral salts and water.

Food Value

It is difficult to over-emphasize the value of this group of vegetables, and they should form a large part of everybody's diet.

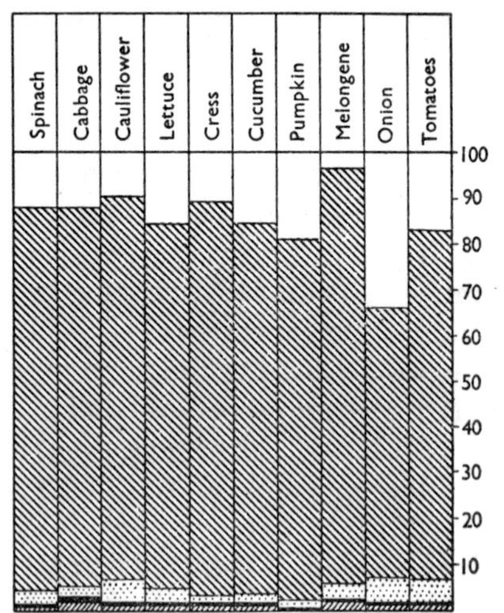

Composition of green vegetables

They are of great value for the mineral salts they contain—the iron being of use in purifying and maintaining the blood in a healthy state.

In addition to this, their rough framework helps to keep the bowels working properly.

Last, but by no means least, they are specially useful for their Vitamin C. Unfortunately, this vitamin is easily destroyed by heat, so that as many green vegetables as are digestible should be eaten in an uncooked state. This is why salads are important.

SALADS

(1) Cut away all useless parts such as withered leaves, long stalks, etc.

(2) Wash them either in running water or in at least three changes of water. Separate *all* leaves and examine every one.

(3) Soak in an antiseptic liquid—that is, one which will check the growth of germs. Salt may be used for this purpose when washing cabbage, but when washing lettuce and cress use Condy's fluid instead because salt withers them. (To make Condy's fluid dissolve one tablespoonful of permanganate of potash crystals in a pint bottle of hot water. Use enough of this in the washing water to colour it a bright pink. Permanganate crystals are cheap—1 oz. (4 tablespoons) costs only 24 cents and will last for weeks and weeks.)

The greatest attention must be paid to the preparation of salad foods as, if they are not thoroughly washed, raw green vegetables spread the germs of typhoid and dysentery and the eggs of hookworm and other parasites.

(4) Draw off all the water in which the salad has soaked. This can be done by using a strainer or by shaking very lightly in a clean pantry towel.

Raw cabbage : To make it more digestible shred finely or chop on a board. The flavour is improved if a small piece of onion or chive is chopped with it.

Raw carrots : Choose young ones. Scrape, wash, and grate them.

Tomatoes : Wash and soak with the lettuce and cress, or scald and peel them. The boiling water loosens the skin and destroys germs. Do not allow them to soak in hot water, otherwise it softens them and makes them difficult to slice.

Orange, banana, cucumber, and nuts may also be added to a salad. Wash, peel, and cut them into small pieces.

Pieces of hard-boiled egg, sweet pepper, cold cooked potato, beetroot, peas, or salad beans make a welcome change.

(5) Arrange the salad foods in a glass dish, remembering that this should only be done just before the salad is required ; otherwise it may go limp.

(6) Complete the salad by serving with one of the following dressings :

FRENCH DRESSING

4 Tbsp salad oil
2 Tbsp. vinegar or lime juice
½ teasp. salt
¼ teasp. white pepper

Mix oil and seasoning and add vinegar gradually. Beat well.

N.B.—For children, use lime juice or orange juice rather than vinegar, as vinegar has a slightly injurious effect on the blood. Melted butter may be used in place of oil ; butter, being an animal fat, is more nourishing.

ECONOMICAL MAYONNAISE

1 oz (4 level Tbsp.) flour
2 teasp. sugar
2 teasp. dry mustard
2 teasp. salt
2 oz (4 level Tbsp.) butter
2 eggs
1 gill (½ glass) milk
1 gill (½ glass) hot vinegar
1 gill (½ glass) salad oil

(To make about 1 pint)

Mix all dry ingredients to a paste with a little of the milk. Boil the rest of the milk, then stir in the paste and continue to boil for five minutes, stirring all the time. Cool a little, add eggs and butter, and beat well. Cook the mixture again, but without boiling, otherwise the egg will curdle. Next add the hot vinegar, beat well, then stir in the oil. Bottle the mayonnaise and shake before using.

N.B.—Use a double boiler if possible.

REAL MAYONNAISE

2 yolks of eggs
Approx. 1 gill (½ glass) sweet oil
1 Tbsp. vinegar (white preferably)
½ teasp. made mustard
Pepper and salt

Put the yolks with pepper, salt, and mustard in a small basin and gradually beat in the oil, adding a very small quantity at a time.

When the mixture looks like soft butter, thin it down to a sauce by gradually adding the vinegar. Lime juice may be used in place of the vinegar. Add more oil and vinegar to the yolks if a larger quantity of mayonnaise is required.

Cooking Green Vegetables

(1) Remove all eatable parts and wash very thoroughly.

(2) Cook them in some way which will prevent loss of mineral salts :

(*a*) by making into soup (*e.g.* callaloo) or stew

(*b*) by steaming or scalding. (This method is suitable if they are young and tender—*e.g.* young spinach)

(*c*) by boiling for *as short a time* as possible. (When boiling, preserve the colour by plunging them straight into fast boiling water and cooking without a cover)

Soften hard water by adding a half teaspoonful of bicarbonate of soda (baking soda) to every pint of water, and do not add salt until the vegetables are soft. Some people think that the addition of soda destroys the Vitamin C, but as this is probably already done by the heat, the use of soda is not likely to do much further damage, and it is a good way of hastening the cooking and preserving the colour. When soft, pour off the water at once and add butter and seasonings to taste.

Vegetables such as spinach can also be boiled or steamed with rice, so that the rice absorbs any mineral salts which come out.

CHAPTER 12

LEGUMES OR PULSES

Food Value

LEGUMES, being seed vegetables, contain all the food required for the development and growth of a young plant. They provide starch for energy; mineral salts,

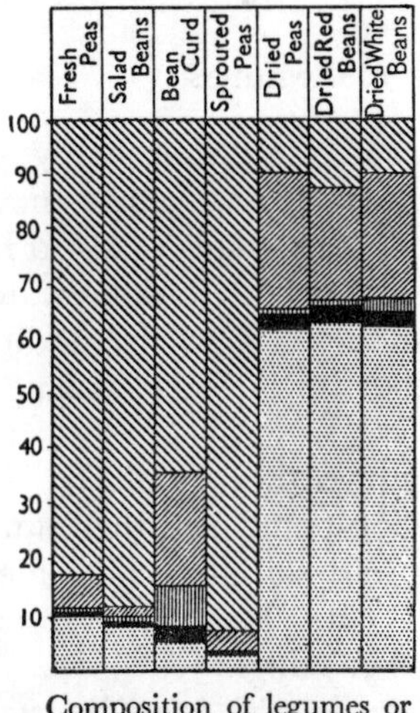

Composition of legumes or pulses

Key to shading

useful for our bones and teeth; Vitamin B in their outer covering; and unlike other types of vegetable are a good source of protein. Although this protein requires more change in the body than meat protein, it is a valuable food for people who cannot afford meat regularly—for this reason legumes are sometimes called "poor man's beef."

Legumes such as salad beans, waby beans, etc., where both seed and pod are eaten, provide a good deal of cellulose or roughage. They are also valuable for their mineral salts.

Digestibility

Legumes contain a certain amount of sulphur, which, with the large amount of cellulose, is a cause of indigestion to some people. If thoroughly cooked, however, they can be digested and absorbed by most people.

Cooking of Legumes

Dried peas and beans should be thoroughly soaked before cooking. This softens them so that they cook more quickly. Hard pipe (tap) water tends to harden the protein still further, so that both soaking water and cooking water should be softened by the addition of one teaspoonful of bicarbonate of soda (baking soda) to every pint of water.

When boiling dried legumes they should be put into cold water, heated to boiling-point, and then simmered till soft, when seasoning and salt may be added. If salt is added during the early stages it hardens the water and slows down the cooking.

Softer legumes, such as lentils, may be steamed, which although slow cooking is a good way as none of the nourishment is lost. (For this method see Chapter 22, Steaming.)

Fresh peas and beans, e.g. salad beans, pigeon peas, can be boiled in the same way as green vegetables (see previous instructions), or they can be stewed. (For this method see Chapter 20, Stewing.)

FUNGI

As many fungi are poisonous, very great care must be taken to see that only the good ones are used. One test is to place a small piece of silver (*e.g.* a clean shilling or 12 cent piece) with them while cooking. If this turns black some are bad, and all should be thrown away.

Fresh mushrooms should be peeled and washed before use.

Those which are bought in a dried state are very shrunken and should be soaked overnight and then thoroughly picked.

CHAPTER 13

FRUIT

FRESH fruits are just as valuable as green vegetables, and should be eaten every day.

COMPOSITION OF SOME COMMONLY USED FRUITS

FOOD	WATER	PROTEIN	FAT	SALTS	CARBO-HYDRATE AND CELLULOSE
Bananas	74·8	1·2	0·2	0·84	23·0
Oranges	89·9	0·6	0·1	0·3	9·1
Grapefruit	88·8	0·5	0·2	0·42	10·1
Limes	86·0	0·8	0·1	0·8	12·3
Lemons	89·3	0·9	0·6	0·54	8·7
Pineapples	85·3	0·4	0·2	0·42	13·7
Papaws	88·7	0·6	0·1	0·62	10·0
Mangoes	81·4	0·7	0·2	0·48	17·2
Guavas	80·6	1·0	0·6	0·7	17·1
Water-melon	92·1	0·5	0·2	0·27	6·9

Food Value

The water that fruit contains makes it refreshing and thirst-quenching, and both water and cellulose help the bowels to work properly. The mineral salts and vitamins keep the body healthy. Remember that raw fruit is more valuable than cooked fruit, because the heat of cooking destroys some of the vitamins.

Digestibility

Most people can digest raw fruit. It should not be eaten under-ripe or over-ripe, as in both cases it is likely to cause diarrhoea which may lead to dysentery. Under-ripe fruit which has fallen from the tree should be stewed and made into pies, etc. (See Chapter 30, Puddings or Desserts.) Over-ripe fruit should be thrown away.

Preparation

Wash the fruit as soon as it is brought into the house, and before it is put in a refrigerator, ice-box, or cupboard. This is not only to remove insects, etc., but because it may have been handled by dirty people.

Most fruits are improved by being chilled before serving.

CHAPTER 14

CEREALS

THE group of foods known as cereals includes most of the grains or seeds which are used for making bread, cakes, and puddings. Examples are : rice, wheat, oats, corn, etc. Although not true cereals, arrowroot, tapioca (obtained from the cassava plant), and sago (which is extracted from the pith of certain palms) are also frequently included.

Cereals may be bought in different forms :

(1) *Whole grain—e.g.* rice, corn

(2) *Fine grain—e.g.* flour, cornmeal, cornstarch, sago

Some of these fine or powdered grains are more thoroughly refined during milling than others. For example, white flour and cornstarch are more highly refined than wholewheat or cornmeal, and during this refining process many of the valuable parts are removed. The additional refining is usually done to make the grain keep better, and because some people prefer the appearance and taste.

(3) *Partly cooked or completely cooked grain—e.g.* Quick Quakies (rolled oats for porridge), Force, Kellogg's All Bran, etc.

Food Value

Cereals are useful for starch. As this energy-giving factor can easily be obtained in a number of other foods, clearly the best cereals to use are those that also give us mineral salts, vitamins, and roughage. These can only be obtained from the outer covering and from the embryo (or growing part) of the grain, so that we should buy brown rice in preference to white, wholewheat rather than white flour, and cornmeal rather than cornstarch (cornflour).

It will be remembered that fine grains such as flour do not keep well unless the embryo and covering have been removed, and because of this there is often waste from spoilt wholewheat, etc. To make good any loss, the manufacturers therefore increase the price, and as a result many people cannot afford to buy wholewheat. If this is the case, it is a good plan to buy ordinary white flour and to add bran (the outer covering of wheat) in the proportion of one part bran to three or four parts flour. Bran is the same price as flour, and although this mixture is not as good as wholewheat, it is better than white flour alone.

Cooking Cereals

The starch in food should be turned into a soft jelly-like form in much the same way as laundry starch is softened for stiffening clothes. This can only be done when it is properly moistened, and heated for a sufficient time.

The starch and mineral salts found in cereals are held together by a covering of cellulose. Unless cereals are thoroughly cooked, this covering is not softened, and the starch remains raw and indigestible.

Soaking hard cereals such as tapioca softens the starch and cellulose, and makes cooking quicker and more thorough.

Whole grains

Rice, sago, etc. should be picked, washed, and if necessary soaked. They should then be sprinkled into fast boiling milk or water, and sugar or salt added according to the use for which they are intended. If the grain is added by degrees the liquid will not stop boiling, so that the heat will quickly cook the grains and the bubbling of the liquid prevents them from sticking together. Some forms of rice grown in the West Indies are very sticky when boiled, and as most people object to rice which is not grainy, it is therefore wise to rinse it in cold water after cooking. This washes away excess starch, thereby separating the grains, which must be spread out on clean white paper or a clean towel and re-warmed before being used. It should be remembered that rice soaks up a great deal of water during cooking, so that for every cup of rice allow two and a half cups of boiling water and a half teaspoonful of salt. For sticky local rice allow a little extra water and drain this off before rinsing.

Rice may also be steamed (see Chapter 22, Steaming).

Fine grains

Fine grains such as flour will not mix with boiling liquid without forming lumps. They should therefore be blended (or mixed to a paste) with cold milk or water. This should then be stirred with the boiling liquid and thoroughly boiled for at least seven minutes. Small quantities must be stirred all the time the mixture is boiling. Large quantities are better boiled in a double cooker (this may be made by standing a medium-sized pan in a larger one containing boiling water), in which case the mixture cannot burn and need only be stirred occasionally. It should, however, be cooked twice as long.

Fine grains readily mix with hot oil, so that when making gravy or sauce there is no need to make a paste.

Patent or prepared cereals should be made according to directions given on the container. Be sure they are thoroughly cooked.

For ways of using Cereals, see the following recipes:

10 Cooo-coo
202 Rice Pudding
194 Blancmange (Cornstarch Jelly)
8 Paimi
21 Pelau
117 Bran Bread

CHAPTER 15

STORAGE OF FOOD

We have already learnt that food must be fresh and clean. When buying for a large family it is sometimes more economical and convenient to get enough food for several days, and where this is done care must be taken to see that it is kept in good condition. Stale food may cause vomiting, diarrhoea, and even poisoning.

When food is stale it goes bad because tiny living moulds, yeasts, or bacteria attack it. These are so small that we cannot see them without the help of a special magnifying glass. Many of them float about in the air, others are carried by flies, roaches, or other insects, and it is our duty to keep them out of food by storing it in a clean, cool, dry place. There should be plenty of room for everything, so that things can easily be looked at, and so that moist food does not affect dry food.

When planning the storage of food it is generally divided into two classes :

(1) Dry stores, *i.e.* flour, sugar, rice, baking powder, etc.

(2) Perishable foods, *i.e.* milk, butter, eggs, meat, fish, tomatoes, etc.

Dry Stores

Never leave food in paper bags ; they are untidy, they often burst, and the food which is then spilt attracts insects. Keep dry stores in covered jars or bottles, or in enamelled pans, as these are easy to keep clean.

Tins are sometimes used, but they are not so good because they often rust. Pans should be enamelled both inside and out.

Label all bottles or tins clearly, otherwise salt might be used in mistake for white sugar, or baking soda for baking powder, etc. Keep bottles and tins in a press which is free from insects. Dry foods are better kept in a press rather than in a safe with wire mesh, as the open mesh lets in dust. This is why some safes are made with wire mesh in the top half only, the dry foods being kept in the lower half.

If we can afford it, it is better to buy several pounds of dry stores at a time. When we spend only one cent or two cents the shopkeeper usually charges more, because he wants to make up for extra trouble and for the price of wrapping paper, etc.

In large houses or institutions, where a great deal of food is bought at a time, it is usually kept in a special store-room. This room must be clean, dry, and well ventilated. It is wise to keep it locked and to give out the food as it is wanted.

Perishable foods

These foods must, of course, be bought in small quantities. Keep them as cool as possible. The simplest way to do this is to keep them in an airy place. Country people sometimes make a hanging safe from two or three barrel hoops or a wooden box and wire mesh or cheese-cloth. To prevent ants from finding their way into the safe, pass the rope by which it hangs through a funnel or old cup. Plug up the hole with cement or soft candle and fill the cup with water. Hang the safe in a cool shady place.

In some cases more air will blow through a safe

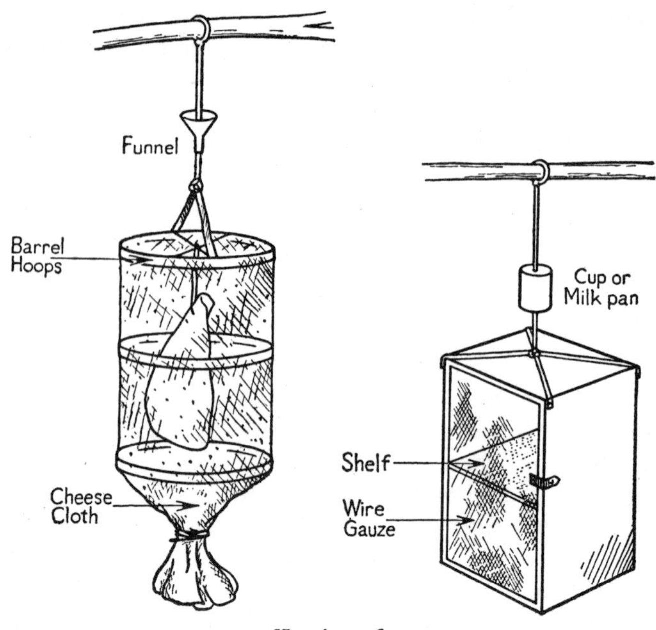

Hanging safes

which is hanging than through one standing on the floor in a small overcrowded house. This arrangement also leaves more room on the floor for other things.

An ordinary safe can, of course, be used where space permits. Put perishable foods on the upper shelf which is only surrounded by wire mesh. In this way more air will get to the food than if it is in a closed space. Cover or lightly wrap food to protect it from dust.

Keep ants out of these safes by standing the legs in antiformicas or double pans. The legs fit into the inner pans and water is put in the outer ones. To keep water pure and prevent breeding of mosquitoes, change the water regularly and add some sort of disinfectant. Some people use kerosene instead of disinfectant, but this is a bad plan, because it often forms a film over which ants can walk. Where there is no disinfectant, add plenty of salt to the water as this helps to stop breeding of mosquitoes.

The legs of safes can also be tied round with Hoodoo Tape. This is tape soaked in a strong chemical, and ants will not walk over it. It is obtainable at a drug store for 36 cents a roll, and can also be used round table legs or the legs of a baby's cot.

While both antiformicas and Hoodoo Tape are good ways of keeping ants away, remember that food will not be pure unless everything is kept clean. For this reason empty and scrub out the safe weekly, paying special attention to corners; then, when shelves are dry, re-line them with clean paper. Remove cobwebs between safe and walls or floor as soon as they appear —ants have been known to walk along cobwebs!

Milk is not kept cool enough just by standing it in a safe. Put the milk bottle in a basin of cold water to which salt has been added. Be sure the milk is covered.

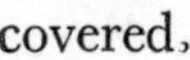

Wire Vegetable Rack

Ground provisions would take up too much room in a safe. Store them in a wire or wooden rack or a large basket with open mesh. If they are left in a sack (bag) or any dark damp place where the air cannot get to them, they often sprout or rot.

If it can be afforded an ice chest is better than a safe for storing perishable food. One can be made at home by lining a wooden packing case with galvanized iron and fitting it with shelves. A hole should be left at the bottom through which water can drain as ice melts. Better ice chests are enamelled inside and out. Either kind must be kept spotlessly clean ; wash them out regularly.

A refrigerator is ideal for storing perishable foods, but unfortunately both the refrigerator and the electric current or oil required for cooling it are still too expensive for a great many people. Care must be taken to prevent waste of electric current, so the refrigerator door should be opened as seldom as possible. Place food in special containers or cover or wrap all food in *greaseproof paper*, otherwise the smell of one food will affect another—milk, for example, may taste of fish.

Clean and de-frost the refrigerator weekly. To do this turn off the current and allow any ice to melt. Wash the refrigerator thoroughly, using hot water and soap, and pay special attention to corners.

Roaches and mice sometimes become a nuisance in a pantry or store-room. To get rid of roaches set traps made by mixing boric powder with cornmeal, tinned milk, or a little beer. Put the mixture in a small milk pan or cigarette tin which is covered but for a small hole, so that only insects and no puppies or cats will be poisoned by it.

Get rid of mice by setting traps, sprinkling shelves with plenty of black pepper, or by keeping a cat !

PART TWO

HOW TO COOK FOODS

INTRODUCTORY

Food is cooked for the following reasons :

(1) To make it more appetizing or tasty—*e.g.* meat, fish, eggs

(2) To soften it and make it more digestible —*e.g.* potatoes

(3) To extract nourishment from pieces too hard to eat—*e.g.* bones

(4) To purify it—*e.g.* milk

(5) To make it keep better

Food can be cooked in the following ways :

boiling	grilling	baking
steaming	stewing	roasting
	frying	

Each of these is dealt with in the chapters that follow.

CHAPTER 16

COOKERY APPARATUS

POTS AND PANS

POTS, pans, etc., are made of a number of different metals, and also of earthenware and glass ; most metals have some advantage which makes them particularly suitable for some special purpose.

Iron is very thick, strong, and durable, and is useful for slow cooking or for frying. Unfortunately it discolours some foods, so spoils the appearance, and in a few cases the flavour too. It should not be used for fruit, or any food containing milk. It also rusts easily unless care is taken to keep it dry when not in use.

Tin, which is a soft metal, is sometimes used to line iron saucepans, and for coating pot spoons, flour dredgers (sprinklers), pot covers, etc. It melts easily, and wears off if the covers, etc., are cleaned with too coarse a cleaning agent.

Enamel is also used for coating and lining iron pots and pans, which are then suitable for heating milk, cooking fruit, etc. Unfortunately the enamel does not expand at the same rate as the iron when the pan is heated. Because of this the enamel cracks, and in time flakes off. This is very dangerous, as the chips of enamel mix with the food, and may have some serious effect on the inside of the body. Never buy enamel-lined frying pans, and do not buy enamel at all unless you can afford a really good quality.

Stainless steel is now used in large institutions, hotels, factories, etc. It is expensive, but very strong and durable, and does not discolour the food or affect it in any way.

Aluminium is a very light metal which never rusts. Alminium pans look nice and are less tiring to lift than heavy iron ones. The food in them heats quickly, which is an advantage when fast cooking is required. Soda discolours aluminium, so that it is inconvenient to use aluminium frying pans from which it might be troublesome to wash the grease without the use of soda. Acid, on the other hand, removes stains from aluminium. This should be considered when using aluminium saucepans for cooking fruit, tomatoes, jam, etc.; or an aluminium fluting pipe for orange or lemon icing (frosting). Unless all tarnish is removed and the metal is bright before food is put in, the acid in fruit, etc., will polish the pan, and the tarnish may discolour food and spoil its appearance and flavour.

Brass is seldom used nowadays. It is durable but heavy and expensive. Many people avoid using it because of a poisonous substance called verdigris which forms on brass and copper when left damp or dirty. If it is used at all *very great care* must be taken to prevent the formation of verdigris.

Earthenware made in various colours is used for "canarees"—casseroles, pie-dishes, etc. Being thick, it is only suited to foods requiring long slow cooking such as stews. It has the advantage of being suitable both for use over a slow fire or in an oven. It should be heated gradually, and while hot must not come into contact with damp cloths, cold water, or cold surfaces. Because food can be served in these casseroles or pie-dishes, they save labour by reducing the amount of washing up.

Fireproof glass is only used for pie-dishes, because it can be used in the oven but not over an open fire. It is easy to clean, looks well, and should be treated with the same care as earthenware.

If when buying pots and pans money is scarce, it would be well to get one iron pot or saucepan for stewing, frying, and boiling provisions, and one really good quality enamelled pan for milk or foods which would be discoloured by iron. If a good quality enamel cannot be afforded, aluminium is next best. See that all pots and pans are provided with covers.

Ware or glass bowls are preferable to enamelled ones for beating eggs, mixing cakes, etc., because when whisking a mixture the enamel may be scratched or chipped off into the food.

Care of Pots, Pans, Knives, Pastry Boards, Troughs, etc.

Whatever the quality, style, or shape, the first and most important thing is to see that all cookery apparatus is spotlessly *clean.* Thorough washing is essential, and hot water is better than cold.

Pots, saucepans, cakepans, etc., are most easily washed when still warm, before any grease has hardened. Wipe out greasy things with waste paper, and soak any starchy pans in water.

Scour them with a stiff brush, coconut husk, or some gritty substance such as ash or Vim. Aluminium, tin, or enamelled articles must not be scoured with anything very coarse. If ash is used, it should be sifted to remove hard particles of stone or coal.

Dry the pans thoroughly on a towel, or put them near the fire; if left damp, metal either rusts or tarnishes. When not in use, store them in an airy place without the covers. The best plan is to hang them, or place them upside down on a shelf made of strips of wood between which air can pass. If the shelves are made of one piece of wood only, the pans should be placed so that they project a little over the edge.

Knives

These should be washed and dried as soon as possible after use. Unless made of stainless steel they quickly rust or tarnish when wet or if used for cutting tomatoes, etc. Knives should never be left with the handles soaking in water; this rots wooden handles and discolours white ones.

Wooden Pastry Boards, Bread Troughs, etc.

Wipe off all dry flour, etc., and if necessary scrape gently with the dull edge of a knife. Scrub thoroughly. Use hot water for pastry boards, otherwise the grease from the pastry will not be removed. Scrub the way of the grain, and pay special attention to the corners of troughs. Rinse well, wipe and leave in a current of air to dry. If very stained, use soda and scour with fine sand.

If the wood is left damp and is stained by mildew, sprinkle it with warm ashes. These dry out the mildew, and it can then be scrubbed in the usual way.

CHAPTER 17

FIREPLACES AND STOVES

Most people in the West Indies cook their food over either wood or charcoal (coal) fires. Both wood and coal are fairly cheap, but they are not the best kind of fuel to use because :

(1) They make a great deal of ash which blows about and makes things dusty, and because wood also makes pots very black.

(2) It is difficult to regulate the heat to just what is wanted, as one minute the fire is blazing, and soon afterwards it has died down and gives much less heat.

Fireplaces for Wood

These may be made of mud (clay) or brick. They should be built in such a direction that the wind will blow through them to draw up the fire. If the pieces of wood are all laid in this direction, the wind as it blows through will carry away the smoke which might otherwise spoil the taste of the food.

Brick Fireplaces

These get very hot, and if food which requires gentle cooking is stood on the hot bricks instead of over the fire it will cook slowly and evenly.

Mud Ovens

Mud ovens are often used in the country. A small oven gives the best results, as the food often fails to brown properly in a large one. There should be a small outlet for smoke and another one low down at the back through which hot ash can be brushed, so that it need not be swept out towards the person preparing the oven. Any gaps round the door should be blocked up with a clean bag (sack) as soon as the food is put in.

Coal-pots

It is convenient to have coal-pots of different sizes: a big one for irons and one or two to fit pots or saucepans. When buying them see that there is a good arch to allow for plenty of draught, and test them to make sure that they are uncracked.

Never pour cold water over hot coals while they are still in the coal-pot—this is bound to crack it. Grease coal-pots if they are to be stored away.

Fireplaces for coal-pots must be high enough to prevent stooping. Some people now have their coal-pots sunk into a concrete fireplace, or build a brick fireplace similar to those used for wood. These are, of course, an economy, as several pots can be simmered on the hot brick round one fire.

Coal-pot Ovens

Kerosene tin ovens can be obtained for about one dollar, but they do not last long. They are thin, so do not hold the heat very well, but can be successfully used for baking small cakes, small loaves, bakes, or custard. In order to brown the food, glowing coals should be put on the top of the oven.

Cement- or Oil-drum Ovens. These bake foods well, and can sometimes be cheaply made at home. The bottom

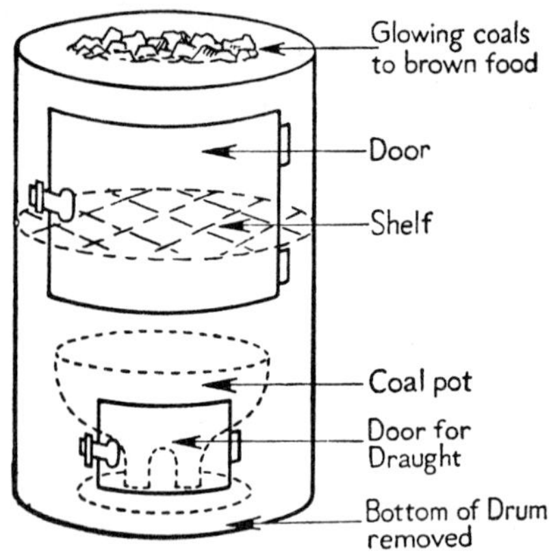

Cement- or oil-drum oven

should be cut out so that they can stand over the coal-pot, and holes must be made near the bottom to allow for draught.

Box Ovens are very good for roasting meat and for large cakes requiring long cooking. They are not so satisfactory for small cakes requiring quick browning. The oven should be lined with galvanized iron and packed with asbestos or sand mixed with clay. The packing helps to keep in the heat and to prevent the wood catching fire. Sand packing is cheap, but as it dries it crumbles and is apt to fall out. The door must be very closely fitting and should have a good latch. The oven should be fitted with two movable shelves which can be removed when the oven is washed out. There should be a movable circular shield hanging from the lower shelf to prevent the bottom of cakes burning.

All ovens must be washed regularly, and should be as clean as the inside of a saucepan.

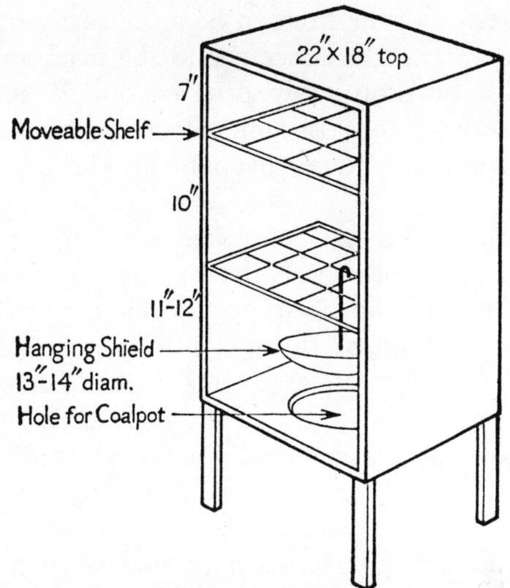

Inside of box oven

Cookers or Stoves

Those heated by electricity, gas, or oil are best, as they save time and labour and make no dirt.

The stove should be of a simple type without any complicated parts, which are difficult to clean and are inclined to get out of order.

The frame or stand should be high enough to prevent stooping, and should be coated with heat-resisting enamel which looks well and is easy to clean.

Fittings not covered with enamel should be made of stainless metal, which will not tarnish. A plate rack for warming dishes, etc., is convenient but not essential.

Kitchen Range or Caledonian Stove

This stove is still used by a number of people. The stove should have a movable bottom to the fire-box, so that the size of the fire can be more easily regulated. The " flues " (*i.e.* the space round the oven and at the back) must be thoroughly brushed out about once a week, otherwise they become blocked with soot, and there will not be enough draught for the fire to burn properly.

The fire should be controlled by " dampers " or regulators and not merely by opening or closing the door in front of the fire-box. When the door is left open the wood burns through much too quickly and the smoke which escapes makes the kitchen very dirty. The " ring " should not constantly be taken off the stove, as if saucepans are put right down over the wood, they become sooty and are troublesome to clean.

To obtain an even heat, particularly when baking, the fire should be made up regularly and frequently. Use good dry wood. Damp or green wood is not only difficult to light, but it produces more smoke and smell and this may affect the taste of the food.

To clean the stove, wipe off any grease while the stove is still warm. Protect the floor with newspaper or an old bag, etc. Rake out all ash and sweep down the stove, using a brush specially kept for the purpose. Apply stove polish and rub this well in, otherwise it will blacken the bottoms of saucepans. When necessary wash the stove with hot water and soda, paying particular attention to the oven. If the stove is not to be used for some time, grease or oil it with some saltless fat (*e.g.* cooking oil, linseed oil) to prevent rusting.

Oil-burning fittings are now used in some Caledonian stoves. They burn " range oil," which is very much cheaper than kerosene and is more labour-saving than wood or coal.

Care must be taken to heat the burners and stove very slowly, otherwise they smoke badly. Thorough weekly cleaning of both burners and "flues" is necessary.

Oil Stoves

Burners of oil stoves should be screened from wind, and should be made in such a way that the oil is turned from a liquid into a vapour or gas. Kerosene or "range oil" burning as oil has a smoky yellow flame, but when vaporized, the flame is blue.

When using an oil cooker, turn out the burner just before you have finished with it, as in most cases it takes 2–3 minutes to go out, and the oven keeps hot for some time.

If the stove flares, turn it out and look at the chimneys or burners; if these are not straight or do not fit properly, the stove is sure to smoke. Too much oil in a burner also causes smoking.

To clean an oil stove, remove and wipe or wash chimneys. Clean the wicks and their sockets by wiping with newspaper (Gazette paper). While still warm, clean the oven and stand, first with newspaper and then a damp cloth. When necessary wash or scrub with hot water, but avoid the constant use of soda, which removes gloss from enamel.

Gas Stoves

These must not be confused with the stoves burning gasolene, which are very like ordinary oil cookers. Real gas stoves burn either coal gas, natural gas, or petroleum gas conveyed to them in vapour form by means of pipes. They are commonly used in houses on oil fields or petroleum refineries.

The burners on gas stoves should have air regulators to enable the housewife to adjust air and gas mixtures correctly. There should be no iron bars immediately over the burners, as these waste heat. The taps should be so placed that the gas is not turned on by accident. The oven should be ventilated to allow for escape of fumes. A heat regulator, used to keep the oven at an even temperature, is attached to some types.

For use on a gas stove, buy saucepans with flat rather than rounded sides, as in this way two or three may be used over one burner.

The stove should be cleaned in the same way as an oil cooker.

Electric Stoves

These stoves are heated by an electric current carried by wires. The wires on the top of the stove are generally covered by a thick piece of metal called the boiling plate, and this has to get hot before foods begin to cook. For this reason it is best to choose a stove which has one " open element," that is, one set of uncovered wires which heat up very quickly and can be used when doing quick cooking as when boiling an egg. Once the hot plate has been heated, it remains hot for a long time, and several saucepans may be put over one hot plate. The oven, too, keeps its heat for some time, so that custards, meringues (soupirs), etc., can be baked after the current has been switched off altogether.

Only smooth-bottomed pans should be used, as the whole of the saucepan should touch the hot plate. Iron pots or old and wrinkled aluminium saucepans are therefore unsuitable. Flat-sided pans are an economy.

The stove should have a main switch which cuts off the whole supply of electric current. This must always be turned off before cleaning the stove.

The stove should be cleaned in the same way as an oil cooker, but great care must be taken to see that no water falls on an " open element." If food boils over on to these, it must burn itself off.

CHAPTER 18

THE PROPER WAY TO MEASURE

If *every* dish we cook is to be a success, and if we are anxious to avoid waste due to failures, we must *always* take the trouble to measure properly.

Many people cannot afford weights and scales, and some of the people who have them are too lazy to use them. On the whole the quickest and easiest way to measure is by using cups and spoons. Because cups and spoons are of different sizes, it is wise to buy the special kind sold for measuring.

Aluminium measuring cups for flour, rice, etc., are about the size of a teacup and cost 15 cents. Larger cups (the size of a breakfast cup) are for measuring liquids. As inexperienced cooks often get confused with the two sizes, it is better to buy the smaller size only, and to measure liquids in a glass (tumbler).

Sets of aluminium measuring spoons cost 20–24 cents, and should be bought whenever they can be afforded.

All measures should be absolutely level. This is because different people have different ideas about what is meant by a heaped spoonful. On the few occasions when you are told to use a heaped spoon, see that there is as much piled up as there is in the spoon itself.

Unless told to take a heaped measure, *always* take a knife and pass it across the top to remove any surplus food.

Abbreviations

teaspoon = teasp.
tablespoon = Tbsp.
ounce = oz.
pound = lb.
pint = pt.

Equivalents

Remember that measures should be level

4 saltsp. = 1 teasp.
3 teasp. = 1 Tbsp.
16 Tbsp. = 1 cup

1 pint = 2 brimming glasses or 2 breakfast cups
1 " bottle " = 1½ pts.
½ " bottle " = p ¾ t.
1 nip = ½ pt.

Food	*Cups per lb.*	*Tbsp. per oz.*
Flour	4 after sifting	4
Wholewheat	3½ approx.	3½
Cornmeal	3	3
Bran	6¼	5⅓
Rice	2 slightly heaped	2
White sugar	2	2
Brown sugar	3 approx.	3
Icing sugar	3¼	3
Cornstarch	3	3
Cocoa	3¼ approx.	3
Raisins, Currants	2⅔	1½
Butter, Lard	2	2

N.B.—If a half or a quarter cup of butter is required, put half a cup or three-quarters of a cup of water into the measure, and then add butter until the water reaches the top.

CHAPTER 19

BOILING

BOILING? Why, we all know how to do that, you say, but just let us make sure you really do.

Boiling is a quick easy way of cooking which makes food easy to digest, but unless the process is carefully carried out it may make food broken, unattractive, and tasteless.

Boiling is generally done for one of two reasons :

(1) To soften foods such as ground provisions, ham, etc.

(2) To extract nourishment from foods, such as cow-heel, etc.

When cooking to soften food leave the food in large pieces, and unless very hard place it in *boiling* water. Boil it very gently for as short a time as possible, so that it will not break, nor will nourishment be lost. Additional heat which makes the water bubble violently does not raise the temperature of the water nor hasten cooking. Fast cooking is therefore definitely undesirable ; it not only breaks the food, but is extravagant because more fuel is used.

When extracting nourishment from food cut it in small pieces to expose as much of the inside as possible. Place it in *cold* water, heat slowly to boiling-point, and cook for a long time.

In both cases there should be enough water to cover the food.

RECIPES FOR BOILED FOODS

1 CURRIED RICE

½ oz. (1 Tbsp.) butter or oil
1 medium sized onion
1 medium sized tomato
1 teasp. salt
1 Tbsp. curry powder or massala
½ lb. (1 heaped cup) rice
2¼ cups water (use the cup used for measuring rice)

PEEL onion, wash tomato, and slice both. Heat oil and lightly fry onion. Add tomato, salt and massala, and cook again without browning. Put in water and rice (previously picked and washed), and boil till rice is soft and grainy (see page 50). No water should be left, and care is needed to see that the rice does not burn.

2 RICE AND PEAS

1 cup split peas
½ teasp. bicarbonate of soda
1 clove of garlic
½ lb. of soup meat
1 pt. (2 glasses) water
1 oz. fat pork or 1 Tbsp. cooking oil
1 cup rice
1 or 2 blades chive
1 small onion
Thyme, parsley, tomato
⅛ teasp. black pepper or small piece green pepper
1 teasp. salt

PICK and wash peas, and soak them overnight in water (about 2 glasses) containing half teasp. bicarbonate of soda.

Next day wash the soup meat quickly, then cut it up. Boil peas, soup meat, and garlic in the water in which the peas were soaking. Omit the soda when using soft rain water. Boil gently so that the peas are softened without being turned into a soup-like condition.

Peel, wash the seasonings, and cut them up, then brown lightly in the fat pork or oil to develop the flavour.
When peas are nearly soft add 2 cups boiling water and all other ingredients. Cook until both rice and peas are soft but grainy.
If liked, the rice may be cooked in a separate pan and added when soft.

(For boiling Provisions and Green Vegetables, see Chapter 9, Vegetable Foods.)

3 HAM

To every medium-sized ham allow 1 cup brown sugar and 2 tbsp. vinegar. These improve the flavour.

Thoroughly wash and if necessary scrape the ham.
Soak it overnight to draw out excess salt.
Place in a large pan with sugar and vinegar. Cover with cold water and heat quickly to boiling-point. Simmer gently, allowing 20 min. to every lb. of ham and 20 over on the whole piece, *e.g.* 10 lb. ham—boil for $10 \times 20 + 20$ min. $=$ 220 min., or 3 hr. 40 min. Skim during boiling if necessary.
After removing from the fire, let the ham remain in the water for 30 min., then take it out of the water, and when nearly cold remove the brown skin.
Sprinkle top of ham with golden brown bread or biscuit crumbs, and place a paper frill round the knuckle bone. Although the idea is old fashioned, some people still like to decorate the top with a few cloves.

N.B.—Sugar and vinegar may be omitted when boiling good quality hams. The ham skin may be boiled up in stock or soup to give additional flavour.

4 SOUSE

Half a pig's head   1 pig's tongue   2 trotters

SCALD the meat, then scrape and wash thoroughly, using lime juice.
Tie meat in a floured cloth, place in a pan of cold water and simmer slowly till tender, about $1\frac{1}{4}$ hr.
Cool the meat in the water in which it was boiled.
Skin and slice the tongue. Slice the meat from the head. Cut open the trotters.
Place the meat in a deep dish, add 2 teasp. salt, juice of 4 limes, and cold water to cover. Soak overnight.
Next day wash meat, then serve in a good sauce made from juice of 2 limes, 2 teasp. salt, 1 fresh pepper, half a slice cucumber, 1 cup stock.

5 BOILED FOWL

1 fowl
Stuffing (Recipe 360)
1 pt. coating sauce (Recipe 250)
1 hard-boiled egg
Chopped parsley
Carrot, turnip, onion

AN old fowl can be made tender by careful boiling.

Preparation

Pluck and singe the bird.
Cut skin around the knee joints, twist and remove feet and lower leg, at the same time drawing out tough sinews.
Cut off the head, make a slit along the back of the neck to the body. Loosen the skin, cut off the neck close to the body, but leave the skin on the bird.

Cut the skin round the vent, then loosen and remove the internal organs. Remove gall from liver and stones from gizzard. These parts are called the giblets.
Cut out the oil sack just above the tail.
Thoroughly wash the bird inside and out.
Scald the feet and remove scales and toes.

To Truss the Fowl for Boiling

Put a finger in the neck end and loosen skin round the legs. Push the legs upward till they slip inside the skin. Draw the skin smoothly over the bird to make an even surface for coating it with sauce when cooked. Turn the wings in under the bird and tie in place. Stuff the bird and fold the skin over at the neck.

To Boil Fowl

Rub the breast with lime juice to whiten it. Wrap in greased paper.
Place it with breast down in boiling water, boil for 3 min. and skim well.
Add a small onion, piece of carrot and turnip, prepared giblets and half teasp. salt.
Simmer fowl gently till tender, allowing 2–3 hr. for an old bird.
Remove the string, dry the bird, and place on a hot dish.
Coat with sauce—a white sauce is generally used—and garnish with sieved or chopped hard-boiled egg yolk and chopped parsley.

N.B.—Reserve the liquid in which the fowl was boiled for soup, gravy, etc.

6 BOILED FISH

A large piece of fish	Parsley
Salt and vinegar	Lime
Water	Sauce

SCALE, wash, and trim the fish. Tie it into shape if necessary.
Boil enough water to cover the fish, add salt and vinegar in the proportion of 1 Tbsp. salt and half teasp. vinegar or lime juice to every quart (4 glasses) water.
Put in the fish to simmer very gently till cooked. For a large piece of fish allow 10 min. for every pound and 10 min. over on the whole. For small pieces allow 15–20 min.
When the fish looks white instead of watery, drain well, and place on a hot dish. Decorate with slices of lime. Serve with sauce.

N.B.—The vinegar is used to whiten fish. It need not be used when cooking dark oily fish.

7 EDDOES IN SAUCE

About 1 lb. small white (Chinese) eddoes	2 Tbsp. vinegar
	Juice of ½ lime
1 Tbsp. butter	Red pepper to taste

WASH and boil eddoes in their skins.
Melt butter, add vinegar, lime juice, and pepper.
When eddoes are soft, squeeze (pulp) them from their skins and pour over the sauce.
Serve hot with stewed salt fish or similar food.

8 PAIMI OR CONKIES

1 lb. cornmeal or grated fresh corn ($3\frac{3}{4}$ cups)
2 Tbsp. lard
2 Tbsp. butter or margarine
2 Tbsp. raising, if liked
$\frac{1}{2}$ a dried coconut ($1\frac{1}{2}$ cups)
$\frac{1}{2}$ cup grated pumpkin
2 teasp. salt
$\frac{1}{4}$ teasp. black pepper } or 1 cup sugar
$\frac{1}{2}$ lb. meat (fresh or salt) } or 1 cup sugar
about 1 nip (1 glass) water
2 bunch banana leaves
Cotton to tie

GRATE coconut and pumpkin. Clean the meat and brown in the lard or butter, then brown the seasonings. Chop or mince meat and add all dry ingredients. Stir in enough water to mix to a firm dough.

Wipe banana leaves and heat them to make them pliable. Cut them into pieces about 6 in. by 6 in. Place about 2 Tbsp. of the mixture in each piece of leaf, roll up, fold over, and tie the ends. Place in boiling water and boil for $\frac{3}{4}$ hr.

9 PASTELLES

4 cornballs or 3 cups grated fresh corn
1 lb. beef steak
1 lb. pork
12 olives, if liked
1 small bottle capers } if liked
$\frac{1}{4}$ lb. raisins } if liked
$\frac{1}{4}$ lb. onions
2 oz. fat pork
2 Tbsp. lard
2 Tbsp. butter
1 green pepper
1 Tbsp. vinegar
1 bunch chive
1 clove garlic
3 medium-sized tomatoes
1 teasp. salt
$\frac{1}{4}$ teasp. black pepper
2 bunches banana leaves
Cotton to tie

(Sufficient to make one dozen)

CLEAN and cut up the meat and prepare all seasonings. Melt the fat pork, add half the lard and all the butter.

Brown the meat and seasonings and stew for 15 min. Mince the meat and seasonings, and add all ingredients except corn and lard.

Wipe, heat, and cut the banana leaves into pieces 7 in. by 7 in. Crush the corn, adding salted water if necessary. Grease the leaves and spread corn mixture on them—about $\frac{1}{8}$ to $\frac{1}{4}$ in. thick and 5 in. square.

Add about 2 Tbsp. meat mixture. Roll, and fold over the ends of leaves. Place in boiling water and cook 1 hr. from the time it boils.

10 COO-COO

- 1 cup cornmeal
- 3 to 4 ochroes
- $\frac{3}{4}$ pt. (1$\frac{1}{2}$ nips) water or milk and water
- 1 teasp. salt
- 1 Tbsp. butter

Wash and slice ochroes, add salt, and boil them in half the liquid. When the ochroes are soft enough to be swizzled, mix the cornmeal with the rest of the liquid. Stir this paste into the boiling liquid and continue to cook, stirring all the time until the mixture is thick and smooth. Turn out into well-buttered mould or basin.

11 BREADFRUIT COO-COO

- 1 breadfruit
- $\frac{1}{4}$ to $\frac{1}{2}$ lb. cooked seasoned meat
- 2 teasp. salt
- About $\frac{1}{2}$ glass ($\frac{1}{2}$ nip) water or stock

Boil, peel, and pound the breadfruit. Mince or chop meat and seasonings. Mix all ingredients and re-heat. Stir continuously until all the liquid has boiled away. Shape in a well-buttered basin or mould.

12 CASSAVA COO-COO

2 cups grated and sifted sweet cassava	½ teasp. salt
	½ pt. (1 glass) water

Boil water, add salt, stir in cassava. Cook thoroughly at least 7–10 min., by which time mixture should be stiff. Stir all the time. Turn into a greased bowl and shape. Serve hot.

13 JUG JUG

1 pt. (2 glasses) pigeon peas	¼ lb. lean pork
10 Tbsp. or a good ½ cup guinea cornflour	1 small onion
¼ lb. fresh or salt beef	2 to 3 blades chive
	Thyme and parsley
	Salt and pepper

Clean, cut up, and season the beef and pork. If salt beef if used it should be soaked. Stew the pork for 20 min., then add beef and peas and stew for another half-hour or until peas are soft. Strain off, but reserve the water, and mince or chop meat and peas.

Take ½-pt. (1 glass) of the water in which meat was stewed, add meat and peas, and stir in the cornflour. Cook for 15–30 min., stirring all the time. The mixture should be of the same consistency as coo-coo. Shape in a buttered basin and serve hot.

14 DUMPLINGS

4 oz. (1 cup) flour	2 to 3 Tbsp. shortening (see footnote, page 110)
2 Tbsp. bread-crumbs, if liked	1 teasp. baking powder, or ¼ teasp. baking soda
⅛ teasp. salt	

(Sufficient for 8 medium dumplings)

SIFT flour, wash and chop suet or fat pork. Mix all dry ingredients and add enough cold water to mix to a stiff dough. Knead lightly, form into balls. Put in boiling water or soup, and cook 30 min.

15 SEASONED DUMPLINGS

1 teasp. chopped onion
1 blade chopped chive
1 teasp. chopped parsley
Piece of thyme stripped from stalk

ADD to dumplings before mixing with water.

16 CORNMEAL DUMPLINGS

½ cup flour
½ cup cornmeal
⅛ teasp. salt
2 to 3 Tbsp. shortening (see footnote, page 110)
½ teasp. baking powder

MAKE in the same way as ordinary dumplings.

17 CASSAVA DUMPLINGS

1 cup grated sweet cassava
½ cup flour
½ teasp. baking powder
¼ teasp. salt
Water to mix

MIX dry ingredients, add enough cold water to bind. Knead, shape into balls, and boil 20 min. in soup or boiling water.

N.B.—If bitter cassava is used, squeeze out all juice, then dry and sift the meal before mixing it with flour.

CHAPTER 20

STEWING

THIS is a favourite way of cooking with most West Indians, but many of them only make what they call "Beef Stew," with a Pelau every now and again for a change. This is a pity, because although stewing is a slow way of cooking, it is cheap and can be used for any kind of food.

It is cheap because tough pieces of meat having much skin and bone, old and fibrous vegetables, or hard under-ripe fruit can be softened and made tasty by long slow stewing. There is no waste when stewing, as any nourishment drawn out from bones, any mineral salts from vegetables or fruit, are all found in the gravy or syrup. Meat and vegetables can also be stewed together, so that fuel and work are saved.

To stew over wood fires or coal-pots is rather troublesome, because to be successful stewing *must* be done very gently. This means that you must keep a constant watch on the fire to see that it is low, but not in danger of going out. Where people have stoves or a brick fireplace, it is, of course, easy to keep the fire the right size, or simply to simmer the stew at the side of a larger fire.

Unfortunately the long slow cooking needed to draw out nourishment from bones, or to soften very hard food, destroys all the Vitamin C. Care should be taken to serve plenty of raw vegetables or fruit with a meal for which a stew is used.

GENERAL RULES FOR STEWING

(1) Cut food in small pieces in order to expose the inside.

(2) Having heated the stew to boiling-point, allow it to *simmer* (*i.e.* hardly bubble at all).

(3) Use a pot with a cover, or the food will lose its flavour and may dry up.

(4) Try to add enough liquid (water, stock, or milk) at the start to last throughout the cooking. Many people have a deep plate of warm water over the top of the pot and they add water from this from time to time. This method is not good, because the water often gets dusty and full of ash, and because it is a waste of time.

18 BEEF STEW

- 1 lb. stewing beef, (shin, aitchbone or shoulder)
- 1 teasp. salt
- ½ teasp. pepper
- Seasonings, (chive, onion, thyme, or tomato)
- 1 teasp. brown sugar
- 2 Tbsp. flour
- 1 Tbsp. vinegar, if liked (omit this when cooking for children)
- 3 Tbsp. oil or dripping, or 1 Tbsp. fat pork and 2 Tbsp. oil
- 1 pt. (2 nips) cold water

CLEAN the meat thoroughly and cut into neat ½-in. cubes, or joint according to the shape of the bones. Prepare the seasonings, add to the meat, and leave for 20–30 min. Choose a thick saucepan or pot, heat the oil, add the sugar, and cook just until it bubbles. While oil and sugar are heating remove seasonings from the meat, coat with flour, and fry in hot oil in *an uncovered pot*. This browning improves the appearance and the taste of the stew, and in the case of lean meat, forms a coating on the outside which prevents too much of the meat juice running out. Either draw meat to the side of the pot or remove it altogether, and then brown the seasonings. Mix meat, seasonings, and water ; cover, heat to boiling-point, and simmer for 1½–2 hr.

19 BEEF AND VEGETABLE STEW

To the ingredients used for beef stew, add about :

1½ lb. ground provisions, *e.g.* potato, carrot, eddo, yam
1 teasp. salt
½ pt. (1 nip) water

20 SALMI D'AGOUTI

1 agouti (about 4 lb. in weight)
2 teasp. salt
1 teasp. pepper
2 onions (medium)
2 to 3 blades chive
2 Tbsp. rum
¼ lb. fat bacon
2 pt. water or stock or part stock and part white wine
1 Tbsp. butter
1 Tbsp. vinegar, if liked

Skin, clean, and joint the agouti.
Make the stew in the same way as beef stew, adding rum and wine (if used) just before serving.

21 PELAU

1 fowl or 1 lb. stewing beef and 1½b. salt beef
2 teasp. salt
1 teasp. black pepper or 1 green pepper
Seasonings, *e.g.* chive, onion, thyme, tomato
A few olives
About 12 to 15 parched nuts or almonds
3 Tbsp. oil
1 Tbsp. butter
2 teasp. sugar
2 pt. (4 nips) cold water
2 cups or 1 lb. rice

PLUCK, singe, and joint the fowl or clean and cut up the beef. Make in the same way as beef stew. Simmer for $1\frac{1}{2}$ hr., then add the rice previously picked and washed. Boil until rice is soft. No water should remain, so care must be taken to prevent burning. Add butter and nuts roughly chopped. Serve on a hot dish decorated with olives.

22 PEPPER POT

- 1 oxtail or tough fowl or duck, or any game in season
- 3 lb. fresh lean pork
- 1 lb. pickled pork
- 4 peppers
- 1 bunch thyme
- 1 lb. onions
- 2 heaped Tbsp. brown sugar
- $\frac{1}{2}$ to 1 gill ($\frac{1}{4}$ to $\frac{1}{2}$ glass) casseripe

CLEAN and cut meat into small pieces. Put in a large canaree (casserole) and cover with plenty of water. Cover and simmer for 2 hr. Add peppers (tied in a net bag), thyme, sliced onions, sugar, and casseripe. Simmer again till meat is tender. Boil up every day to prevent food turning bad. Add fresh meat from time to time (the meat must be unseasoned, and nothing starchy may be put in, or pepper pot will turn sour).

23 CURRIED BEEF STEW

- 1 lb. beef
- 1 teasp. salt
- $\frac{1}{4}$ teasp. pepper
- 1 or 2 onions
- 1 or 2 blades chive
- 1 tomato
- 1 Tbsp. sultanas or raisins, if liked
- 1 small fruit, *e.g.* mango, golden-apple, etc., to thicken
- About 1 Tbsp. curry (the quantity varies with the kind)
- 3 Tbsp. oil
- 1 pt. (2 nips) coconut milk or water

Clean, cut up, and season meat. Omit sugar, because curry should not be brown. Lightly fry meat, curry, and seasonings in a *covered* pot, but do not let them brown. Add sultanas and sliced or chopped fruit and coconut milk. Simmer for 1½ hr., and serve with rice.

(For dry Indian curry see Chapter 45, Some East Indian Recipes.)

24 CURRIED CRAB

2 large crabs
1 teasp. salt
¼ teasp. pepper
1 onion
1 or 2 blades chive
1 tomato
About ½ Tbsp. curry powder or massala
2 Tbsp. oil
1 Tbsp. butter
Water

See Chapter 7, Fish for purging of crabs.
Scald crabs and wash very thoroughly. Limb crabs, remove body from shell and throw away the gall which clings to the shell. Lightly fry chopped seasonings in hot oil, curry and cook 5 min. without browning. Put in crabs and enough cold water to make a gravy—about ½ pt. (1 glass). Simmer ¾ hr., add butter, and serve on a hot dish.

N.B.—If time permits cut open claws, pick out crab meat, and return this to the curry, keeping only one or two claws to decorate the dish.

25 CRAB PELAU

2 large crabs
2 to 3 teasp. salt
½ teasp. pepper
1 to 2 onions
1 to 2 blades chive
1 tomato
About 1 Tbsp. curry powder or massala
3 Tbsp. oil
1 Tbsp. butter
1¾ cups (or about ¾ lb.) rice
3½ cups coconut milk

Make as for curried crab, using coconut milk instead of water. After simmering for ½ hr., by which time the coconut milk should have boiled down to 3 cupfuls, add the rice and cook until it is soft. Add butter, and serve piled up on a hot dish.

26 CRAB GUMBO

- 6 crabs
- 3 large tomatoes
- 1 onion
- 1 to 2 blades chive
- ¼ red pepper without seeds
- Piece of parsley or thyme
- 1 bay leaf
- 6 to 7 ochroes
- 2 Tbsp. butter
- Salt to taste
- Water

Purge, scald, and thoroughly wash the crabs. Remove claws and take body from shell, discarding the gall. Cut body into four. Scald and skin tomatoes, if liked. Wash and cut up seasonings and slice ochroes. Melt butter and brown crabs. Add seasonings, and when brown put in ochroes. When all are well browned add bay leaf and enough water to cover—about 2–2½ pt. Cover pot and simmer 1 hr. When cooked mixture should be like thick soup. Serve in a hot tureen with rice.

27 CURRIED SHRIMPS

- 1 lb. shrimps—about 2 large handfuls
- 1 teasp. salt
- ¼ teasp. pepper
- Seasonings—onion, chive, tomato
- About 1 Tbsp. curry or massala
- 2 Tbsp. oil
- 1 Tbsp. butter
- Water

SCALD shrimps, shell, cut open along the back, and remove black cord. Wash well with lime juice. Lightly fry seasonings (use a covered pot to prevent browning), add curry, and cook 5 min. Put in shrimps and enough cold water to make a gravy (about 1 cupful). Simmer till shrimps are soft—about 15–20 min. Add butter, serve on a hot dish with a border of rice. Decorate with pieces of red pepper.

N.B.—If no gravy is required, add only about 2–3 Tbsp. of water, cover closely, and allow shrimps to steam rather than stew. Use a low fire.

28 STEWED TURTLE

2 lb. turtle
1 teasp. salt
2 to 3 blades chive
1 medium-sized onion
2 Tbsp. brandy
1 glass sherry
  or dry white wine
Pepper
2 medium-sized tomatoes
1 Tbsp. vinegar or lime juice
½ teasp. ground spice
  and clove
3 Tbsp. olive oil
  or cooking oil
2 Tbsp. butter
1 Tbsp. sugar

BOIL bay leaves in 1½ pt. water. Pour liquid over turtle and soak for 10 min. Clean and wash turtle in this water. Sprinkle with vinegar or lime juice and season with salt, pepper, chive, tomatoes, onion, spice and clove, brandy, and wine. Allow to stand for 15 min. Heat oil and butter, brown the sugar, add meat without seasonings, and cook for about 45 min. on slow fire. Then add all seasonings, and allow to simmer gently till turtle is soft.

N.B.—If more gravy is needed add more wine or some stock.

29 STEWED FISH

1 lb. fish—sliced or if possible boned	1 teasp. chopped parsley
1 teasp. salt	1 blade mace
½ teasp. pepper	2 Tbsp. butter
1 or 2 blades chive	1 pt. (1 glass) water
1 onion—small	1 Tbsp. flour
	A little milk

(Suitable for young children or invalids)

SEE Chapter 7, Fish.

Clean and cut fish in slices or cutlets. Season for not more than 20 min. Fry fish and seasonings very lightly in a covered aluminium or enamel-lined saucepan. Add water and simmer gently for about 20 min. Mix flour to a paste with a little cold milk and stir this in to thicken the gravy. Add parsley and boil again for 5 min., stirring all the time. Serve on a hot dish decorated with sliced tomato.

30 CURRIED FISH

COOK in the same way as stewed fish, adding about 1 Tbsp. curry to the fish and seasonings. If possible, use coconut milk instead of water. Leave out the cow's milk, mace, and parsley.

31 STEWED SALT FISH

½ lb. salt fish	1 Tbsp. flour
2 tomatoes	About ¾ pt. (1½ glasses) water
Chive, onion, and pepper to taste	About ¼ teasp. roocoo to colour, if liked
1 Tbsp. cooking oil	
1 Tbsp. butter	

SCALD salt fish, remove skin and bone, and cut into 1–1½ in. pieces. Heat oil and butter and lightly fry seasonings. Stir in the flour, then add fish and enough water to make a good sauce. Cover and stew until fish is tender, about 20 min.

32 STEWED CASCADURA

- 6 medium-sized cascadura
- 1 bunch chive
- 3–4 medium-sized tomatoes
- ½ teasp. ground spice and clove
- 2 teasp. vinegar or lime juice
- 2 medium-sized onions
- 1½ teasp. salt
- Pepper
- 3 Tbsp. oil
- 2 Tbsp. butter
- 1 whole lime
- 1 Tbsp. sugar
- ¾ pt. (1½ nips) water

Put cascadura in a pail of water and rub from head to tail with a piece of cloth to remove mud. Rub with lime and salt to get rid of slime. Clean and season in the usual way (see Chapter 7, Fish). Heat oil and brown the sugar till bubbly. Brown cascadura in an uncovered pot (about 10–15 min.). Add seasonings, and when brown put in the water. Simmer till fish is cooked (about 20–30 min.).

33 SALT FISH IN CHEMISE

- ½ lb. salt fish
- 2 Tbsp. oil
- ¼ teasp. pepper
- 1 or 2 blades chive
- ½ onion
- 1 small tomato
- Thyme
- 2 eggs
- ½ Tbsp. flour
- ½ pt. (1 nip) water

Scald salt fish, remove skin and bone, and flake finely. Heat oil and lightly fry seasonings without browning. Add flour and water, then fish, and simmer for 10 min. Place the mixture in a greased fire-proof dish (*e.g.* enamel or Pyrex), and break the eggs over it. Bake or steam until the eggs set. Serve at once.

34 PIGEON PEA STEW

2 cups shelled peas
6 to 8 oz. salt beef
½ lb. pumpkin
(2 ¢ to 3 ¢ piece)
2 pot-spoons cooking oil
or 1 ¢ fat pork and
1 pot-spoon oil
Seasonings—chive, onion, tomato, thyme, garlic
½ teasp. pepper

SOAK salt beef for at least ½ hr., and then cut it into ½-in. pieces. Shell peas ; peel, wash, and chop pumpkin ; pound garlic ; chip seasonings. Lightly fry seasonings, pumpkin, and peas in a covered pot. Add meat and water, and simmer for 1 hr. When cooked the pumpkin should be mashed, and the peas must be soft but whole.

35 CURRIED BREADNUTS (CHATAIGNE)

1 full (but not ripe) breadnut
2 dried coconuts
1 Tbsp. curry
2 Tbsp. butter or fat pork
1 teasp. salt
Seasonings—onion, chive, thyme, tomato

PEEL chataigne and divide into natural divisions. Boil for 2 hr. then squeeze dry. Take out and peel seeds. Prepare and lightly fry the seasonings, add the curry powder, flesh and nuts from the chataigne. Make and add about 1 pt. (2 glasses) coconut milk, and stew till nuts are soft. Serve on a hot dish with a border of rice and a border of grated coconut. Decorate with pieces of fried salt fish.

36 STEWED FRUIT

1 lb. fruit (full but not ripe golden apples, pomerac, mammy apple, etc.)
½ pt. (1 nip) water
¾ cup sugar

Put sugar and water in an aluminium or enamelled saucepan and boil it without a cover for 10 min. Meanwhile wash, peel, and cut fruit into neat pieces. Put fruit in the syrup and simmer very gently till soft, the time varies with the kind of fruit. When cooked the pieces of fruit should still be whole and not a broken mash.

N.B.—This is a good way of using up under-ripe fruit which has fallen from the tree. It is served as a sweet or dessert, and should not be confused with jam or conserve.

37 STEWED DRIED FRUIT

Wash, then soak the fruit overnight. Cook in the same way as fresh fruit.

CHAPTER 21

SOUP

Most of us know and probably like pea or "pease" soup and sancoche. These and most other well made soups are economical, stimulating, and in many cases a nourishing form of food; economical because if suitably made they can replace meat in the diet, and stimulating if made either with bones or a little meat.

Soup may be included in a meal for the following reasons:

(1) To provide nourishment and replace meat. Such soups can be made from meat or fish and vegetables, or vegetables alone. If leguminous vegetables are used the quantity of protein is increased. These soups are easy to digest and suitable for small children. They may be made in two ways:

(*a*) A broth in which meat and vegetables are cut into slices or squares;

(*b*) a cream soup or purée in which the ingredients are cut up quite roughly, and when cooked are mashed, swizzled, or rubbed through a sieve. Little cubes (or croûtons) of fried bread or toast are generally served with it.

(2) To act as an appetiser or stimulant at the beginning of a large meal and so encourage the flow of the digestive juices. In this case the soup is strained, and only a very small quantity of clear, highly flavoured soup is served. If only lightly seasoned, these strained

soups or " teas " (*e.g.* beef tea) are given to sick people who are too ill to digest ordinary food. See Chapter 43, Diets for Sick People.

RULES FOR SOUP-MAKING

(1) Use an enamelled or aluminium saucepan. Iron pots discolour soup.

(2) Except for clear soups, which must be absolutely free from grease, lightly fry all seasonings and vegetables. This frying, or sautéing, as it is sometimes called, develops the flavour. It must be done *without browning* the food, so that a covered pan is often used.

(3) Carefully distinguish between sieving and straining. When sieving soup, everything except bones, hard seeds or skins, etc., must be pressed through the sieve. When straining, no crushing of vegetables or seasonings should be done.

(4) Always put bones or soup meat in cold water and cook for a long time. The foundation of most good soup is well-made stock—that is, the water in which meat or fish and vegetables have been boiled. People who have a refrigerator should make stock overnight.

38 FIRST OR BEST STOCK

2 lb. shin of beef for brown stock
or 2 lb. knuckle of veal or cow-heel for white stock
2 qt. (8 nips) cold water
1 carrot and onion or other seasoning
1 sprig parsley and thyme
1 teasp. salt

Wipe or wash the meat, cut into small pieces and remove *all* fat. Chop the bones, if necessary, and remove any marrow which is fatty. Put meat, salt, and water in a large saucepan. Cover and heat slowly to boiling-point. Skim well and add seasonings whole or cut in *large* pieces not slices, because stock must not be made cloudy. Simmer for 3–4 hr. to extract all nourishment, then strain into a basin which should stand on a wire grid or sieve so that air can pass underneath. When cold, stock should be in jelly form. Remove fat that has risen to the top and reserve it for frying, roasting, etc.

39 SECOND OR HOUSEHOLD STOCK

Scraps of cooked meat
Cooked or uncooked bones
Vegetables
Clear gravy
Salt
Water

MAKE in the same way as first stock. Avoid using any greasy or starchy scraps for the stock.

BROTHS

40 CREOLE PEA SOUP

1 lb. soup meat or salt beef
2 Tbsp. oil or butter
½ cup split peas
2 pt. (4 nips) water
1 lb. ground provisions (5 medium size)
2 teasp. salt (less if salt beef)
¼ teasp. black pepper
Small pinch baking soda
2 to 3 blades chive
1 onion
1 bunch "finity" (soup seasoning)

(Sufficient for about 6 people)

PICK, wash, and soak peas overnight. Wash and cut up seasonings and meat (soak salt meat for ½ hr. before cutting up). Heat oil till smoking, lightly fry seasonings and set on one side. Brown any lean meat but not bone or salt beef. Put water, meat, peas, and soda to cook in a covered pot. When boiling skim well and add prepared seasonings. Simmer till peas are thoroughly softened and broken down—about 1 hr.—and swizzle if necessary. Peel and wash provisions, cut into neat slices or dice, add to the soup with salt and cook till soft—about 30 min. Add dumplings, if liked (see Recipe 14). Serve very hot.

41 SANCOCHE

$\frac{3}{4}$ lb. pickled meat, *e.g.* thick slice salt beef, thick slice salt pork, pickled pig's tail
1 Tbsp. butter or oil
1 qt. (4 nips) water
About $1\frac{1}{2}$ lb. provisions, *e.g.* plantain, tannia, sweet potato, green figs, cassava, pumpkin, ochroes, kallaloo
Seasonings to taste
$\frac{1}{2}$ teasp. salt
$\frac{1}{4}$ teasp. pepper
Dumplings, if liked (see Recipe 14)

(Sufficient for 4 to 6 people)

Soak and cut up meat. Peel and cut vegetables into blocks or thick slices. Peel, cut up, and lightly fry seasonings in the butter. Mix all ingredients and simmer till soft—about 1 hr.

42 COW-HEEL SOUP

1 cow-heel
3 pt. (6 glasses) water
1 onion
1 strip celery
1 carrot
1 lb. mixed vegetables
1 Tbsp. sago
1 teasp. chopped parsley
Lime juice
2 teasp. salt
Piece of red pepper
Grated nutmeg

Scald, scrape, and thoroughly clean cow-heel. Cut it up and put to boil in salted water. Skim and add chopped seasonings. Simmer gently for 6–7 hr. Peel, wash, and cut vegetables into dice. Remove meat from bone, cut into neat pieces, and return to soup with prepared vegetables and sago. Boil soup again till vegetables are soft—about 30 min. Add parsley, few drops lime juice, and grated nutmeg just before serving.

43 MUTTON BROTH WITH YOUNG CORN

$\frac{3}{4}$ lb. scrag end of mutton
2 pt. (4 nips) water
2 to 3 ears of corn
2 teasp. salt
Onion, chive, parsley, and pepper

(Sufficient for 6 people)

Clean and joint mutton, removing excess fat. Put mutton in cold salted water, heat to boiling-point. Skim, add seasonings, and simmer about 1 hr. Remove covering from corn, wash, and add to soup. Cook till corn is soft—about $\frac{1}{2}$ hr.

44 FISH BROTH

1 fish or fish head—about $\frac{3}{4}$ lb.
1 qt. (4 nips) cold water
1 onion
2 Tbsp. butter or 1 ¢ fat pork
3 to 4 Irish potatoes
$1\frac{1}{2}$ teasp. salt
$\frac{1}{4}$ teasp. pepper
Seasonings, including a clove and a blade of chive

Cut up seasonings and fry lightly in the butter or pork fat—avoid browning; use a cover if necessary. Clean and add fish, water, and salt. Heat to boiling-point. Skim and add potatoes previously peeled, washed, and diced. Simmer 30–40 min. till soft. Remove fish, separate flesh from skin and bone and return it to the soup. If liked, thicken with 2 Tbsp. flour mixed to a smooth paste with $\frac{1}{2}$ nip milk. Boil this paste in the soup 5 min. Garnish with chopped parsley.

45 CASSAVA BROTH WITH SHRIMPS

1 lb. bones	1 tomato and onion
¼ lb. mixed pickled meat (*e.g.* salt beef, pig's tail)	Thyme
A few shrimps	2 to 3 sticks cassava
1 green pepper	2 pt. (4 nips) water

(Sufficient for about 4 people)

Wash and simmer bones for 1½ hr. Clean and cut up meat; peel and wash cassava. Add meat and cassava to stock. Simmer till cassava is soft, then remove and pound it. Scald shrimps and remove shell and the cord down centre back. Prepare seasonings and lightly fry them with shrimps. Add seasonings, shrimps, and cassava to soup and boil till thick. Serve with foo-foo (pounded plantain).

N.B.—Pieces of fried salt fish may be used in place of shrimps.

46 KALLALOO

1 doz. eddo or dasheen leaves	8 ochroes
Seasonings (including garlic) to taste	2 to 3 crabs (See Chapter 7, Fish)
¼ lb. pickled meat (*e.g.* salt beef) or a ham bone	1 Tbsp. butter
	1 pt. *boiling* water

Soak and cut up salt beef. Scald crabs and scrub well. Strip the stalks and midrib from leaves, wash and roll them. Wash and cut up ochroes and seasonings. Put all ingredients except butter in enamelled or aluminium saucepan. Pour on boiling water (this makes leaves a better colour than cold water), and simmer until everything is soft—about ½–¾ hr. Swizzle thoroughly, add butter, and serve when the whole is soft and well divided. If liked, remove crabs, pick out and return flesh to the kallaloo before serving. This makes it easier to eat, but it is not a popular arrangement with most West Indians! Serve with foo-foo (pounded plantain), see recipe 359.

47 CHIP-CHIP SOUP

- ½ pailful chip-chips
- About 3 pt. (6 glasses) water
- 2 tannias or other vegetables to thicken
- 1 onion
- 2 to 3 blades chive
- 2 teasp. salt
- Piece red pepper
- 2 Tbsp. butter
- 1 Tbsp. Worcester or tomato sauce
- Lime juice to taste

WASH chip-chips in running water to remove all traces of sand. Wash again with lime juice. Scald them by pouring boiling water over them. Put chip-chips in clean cold water, heat to boiling-point, and cook 10–15 min. Strain off but reserve this water and to it add prepared seasonings and peeled sliced tannias. Cook until tannias can be mashed to thicken the soup. Meanwhile shake chip-chips in a tray or sieve and remove all shells. Add butter, chip-chips, and sauce to soup and re-heat. Avoid overcooking chip-chips or they will be tough.

CREAM SOUPS OR PURÉES

48 TANNIA CREAM SOUP

- 1 lb. tannias
- 1 pt. (2 nips) water or light stock
- 1 onion
- 1 or 2 blades chive
- 2 Tbsp. butter or oil
- 1 teasp. salt
- Small piece green pepper or unground black pepper
- ¼ pt. (½ cup) milk
- About 4 Tbsp. fried dice of bread (croûtons)

(Sufficient for about 4 people)

Peel, wash, and roughly cut up tannias and seasonings. Melt butter in an enamelled or aluminium pan and lightly fry tannia and seasonings without browning (use a cover). Add stock and salt; heat to boiling-point, skim, then simmer till tannia is soft and broken down. Rub the mixture through a fine sieve (hair for choice), pouring only a little at a time. Add milk, re-heat and serve at once. Serve with fried croûtons.

49 POTATO CREAM SOUP

Make in the same way as Tannia Cream Soup (Recipe 48), using Irish potatoes instead of tannia. Flavour with a blade of mace.

50 EDDO SOUP

Make as for Tannia Soup (Recipe 48).

N.B.—Any ground provision may be substituted.

51 TOMATO SOUP

1 lb. tomatoes or 1 medium-sized tin
1 pt. (2 nips) water or light stock
1 oz. ham chips—cooked or raw
1 teasp. salt
Piece of carrot, turnip, and onion
Sprigs of parsley and thyme
Grated nutmeg
Blade of mace
Piece of green pepper or 5–6 unground black peppers
1 Tbsp. butter
1 Tbsp. starchy food for thickening—*e.g.* flour, cornstarch, sago, or crushed tapioca
½ cup milk, if liked
A little sugar, if liked

(Sufficient for about 6 people)

Wash and roughly cut up tomatoes and seasonings, except for parsley, thyme, and mace, which should be left whole. Cut up ham and heat slowly to melt any fat. Add butter, then lightly fry seasonings and tomatoes without browning (use a cover). Add stock, herbs, and salt, and simmer until tomatoes are thoroughly soft—about ½–¾ hr. Rub through a hair sieve. Mix cornstarch or flour to a smooth paste with cold water, add to soup, and boil for 5 min. When sago or tapioca is used instead, sprinkle it straight into boiling soup and boil 5 min. If milk is used, add it to the soup at the last and warm without boiling, otherwise the acidity of tomatoes will make it curdle. Finally, season to taste with a little nutmeg and sugar, and if necessary add red colouring, *e.g.* roocoo. Serve with fried croûtons.

52 PUMPKIN CREAM SOUP

1 lb. pumpkin—
  about 5–6 ¢ worth
1 tomato
Piece of carrot, turnip,
  and onion
Sprigs of parsley and
  thyme
1 bay leaf
Piece of green pepper
  or about
  5 whole black peppers

Grated nutmeg, if liked
1 teasp. salt
2 Tbsp. butter or 1 Tbsp.
  butter and a piece of
  bacon or ham
1 pt. (2 nips) water
  or light stock
1 Tbsp. flour
  or cornstarch
¼ pt. (½ cup) milk

(Sufficient for about 4 people)

Make in the same way as Tomato Soup (Recipe 51). Mix flour to a paste with milk and boil 5 min.

53 LENTIL SOUP

½ lb. (1 cup) lentils	1 Tbsp. butter or dripping or a piece of fat pork
2 pt. (4 nips) water or stock	1 teasp. salt
1 onion	¼ pt. (½ cup) milk
1 bunch soup seasoning	Dice of fried bread (croûtons)
1 bunch herbs	
1 green pepper	
1 potato to thicken	

PICK, wash, and soak lentils overnight. Peel, wash, and cut up vegetables and all seasonings except herbs. Heat butter and lightly fry vegetables (including lentils) and seasonings. Avoid browning. Add stock, salt, and herbs, and simmer till tender—about 1 hr. Swizzle well or rub soup through a wire sieve. Re-heat, add milk, and serve hot.

N.B.—Any legumes (*e.g.* fresh pigeon peas, split peas, red beans), can be used in place of lentils. If pigeon peas are used, double the quantity and leave out the soaking.

54 SPINACH SOUP

2 bundles (about 6 oz.) spinach	1 pt. (2 glasses) water or light stock
1 large Irish potato	1 Tbsp. butter
1 large onion	1 Tbsp. flour
1 teasp. salt	½ pt. (1 glass) milk
¼ teasp. pepper	

PEEL, wash, and cut up potato and onion, and put to boil with water and salt. Wash and strip spinach, and steam or scald it. Chop finely. Crush or sieve potato and onion, return to water in which it cooked and add spinach and butter. Mix flour with a little of the milk, add to soup with remainder of the milk. Stir and boil 5 min.

55 WATERCRESS SOUP

Use 2 large bundles cress (1 ¢ bunches). Wash in several changes of water and discard all stalks. Make in the same way as spinach soup.

56 AVOCADO PEAR SOUP

1 Tbsp. flour	½ a large pear
1 Tbsp. butter	1 teasp. salt
¼ pt. (½ cup) milk	Piece of green pepper
1 pt. (2 glasses) white stock	Dash of Worcester Sauce, if liked

Melt butter, stir in flour without browning. Add milk gradually, and cook mixture until like a thick white sauce. Stir in the stock. Just before serving stir in the pear, previously peeled, and either pounded or sieved. Warm soup for a few minutes, but avoid boiling, which causes a bitter taste. Season, strain, and serve at once.

57 CORN SOUP

8–10 fresh corn cobs	1 Tbsp. butter
1½ pt. (6 nips) white stock	1 teasp. salt
	5–6 whole black peppers
½ pt. (1 glass) milk	Pinch of sugar, if liked

(Sufficient for 6 people)

Wash and grate the corn. Lightly fry it in the butter without browning. Add stock and simmer till corn is soft—about ½–¾ hr. Sieve soup, re-heat, and add milk.

58 GROUND-NUT SOUP

1 lb. (6 ¢) ground-nuts (pea-nuts)	$\frac{1}{4}$ oz. ($\frac{1}{2}$ Tbsp.) butter
1 pt. (2 glasses) white or light stock	$\frac{1}{4}$ pt. ($\frac{1}{2}$ glass) milk
1 onion	$\frac{3}{4}$ teasp. salt
	Piece of red pepper

Parch the nuts, remove shell and brown skins, then mince or pound them finely. Peel and slice onion, and fry it in the butter without browning (use a cover). Add nuts, pepper, salt, and stock. Simmer for about 3 hr. Skim off oil which forms from nuts and remove pepper. Rub through a sieve. Add milk and re-heat without boiling. Serve with fried dice of bread.

59 BREADNUT SOUP

1 pt. (2 glasses) bread-nuts	$\frac{1}{2}$ Tbsp. sugar
1 pt. (2 glasses) water or light stock	$\frac{1}{2}$ oz. (1 Tbsp.) butter
1$\frac{1}{2}$ pt. (3 glasses) milk	$\frac{1}{4}$ oz. (1 Tbsp.) flour
	Squeeze of lime juice
	Pepper and salt to taste

Boil breadnuts about 15 min. in salted water, then peel and chop them.

Melt butter in a white lined pan, add nuts and fry lightly without browning (use a cover). Add sugar, salt, lime juice, and water, and simmer 1 hr. or until nuts are tender. Sieve, add flour mixed to a paste with the milk, and boil again for 10 min.

Serve with fried or toasted cubes of bread.

CLEAR AND STRAINED SOUPS

60 CONSOMMÉ JULIENNE

1 qt. (4 nips) best quality stock free from all fat
$\frac{1}{4}$ lb. lean beef
1 egg white and shell
1 small carrot, turnip, and onion
Small bunch of herbs (parsley and thyme)
6 black peppers unground or 1 greenpepper
Small blade mace
2 cloves

CLEAN, chop or mince meat finely, soak in cold stock for $\frac{1}{2}$ hr. Peel and cut vegetables into large pieces. Mix all ingredients, heat to boiling-point, whisking meanwhile. When mixture has risen almost to the top of the saucepan, stop whisking, cover and allow soup to simmer 20–30 min. Strain 2 or 3 times through a cloth. Re-heat, add 1 Tbsp. sherry and serve with suitable garnish, such as shreds of vegetable previously cooked.

61 CONSOMMÉ ROYALE

MAKE in the same way as Consommé Julienne (Recipe 60), but garnish with small pieces of savoury custard cut in fancy shapes.

62 CONSOMMÉ À LA CELESTINE

MAKE in the same way as Consommé Julienne (Recipe 60), but garnish with shreds of savoury pancake.

63 CREOLE TURTLE SOUP

1½ lb. turtle fin
2 qt. (8 glasses) water
Piece of mace and bay leaf
2 onions
2 or 3 blades chive
2–3 whole black peppers or piece of red pepper
Clove, garlic, thyme, parsley, tomato, sherry, if liked

WASH and scald turtle and remove any skin or shell. Cut up, add water and simmer for about 3 hr. Add seasonings (left *whole*) and simmer for another hour. Strain soup and add sherry to taste. Garnish with small squares of fin before serving.

N.B.—Some people think that the flavour is improved if the turtle is lightly browned in a little hot oil or butter before being simmered. This must be done after scalding.

CHAPTER 22

STEAMING

Steaming ? You have never heard of cooking this way ? Well, now is your chance to learn.

Steaming can be done in three ways :

(1) Using a proper steamer, which is a metal pan fitting over a saucepan. Sometimes these steamers have a perforated bottom like a strainer so that steam can rise through the holes to cook the food, sometimes they have a tube up the side to carry steam. A home-made steamer can easily be made by piercing holes in the bottom of an empty butter pan which will fit over one of your own saucepans.

(2) By putting food in a basin, jug, or carrier, and standing this in a pan half-filled with boiling water.

(3) Using a covered plate over a pan of boiling water.

Steaming is a good way of cooking, because when food is cooked in steam instead of being boiled it is much less likely to break, and very little of the nourishment is drawn out ; steamed vegetables therefore contain more mineral salts than boiled ones. Since steamed food such as fish is more or less cooked in its own juice, without the addition of water and with little fat, it is very easily digested, so that it is good for people recovering from sickness and for young children, etc. Steaming is also economical, as two or three foods can be cooked over one fire. For example, we might put provisions to boil in a saucepan, spinach in a steamer over them, and fish on a plate on top of that.

Unfortunately steaming is a very slow way of cooking. On this account it can only be used for soft or small pieces of food. It is well suited to the cooking of pumpkin, spinach, googe, cristophine, slices of fish, sweetbread, custard, etc. Some people have an idea that steamed food is somewhat tasteless and unattractive in appearance. These disadvantages can easily be overcome by careful seasoning and by covering the food with a thick sauce or garnishing with sliced tomato, etc.

RULES FOR STEAMING

(1) Allow about 1½ times to twice as long as for boiling, *e.g.* boil a large quantity of rice for 20 min. ; steam the same quantity for 40 min.

(2) Use half as much salt for steaming as for boiling.

(3) Boil the water in the saucepan fast, this makes more steam.

(4) Use a pan with a tightly fitting cover to prevent escape of steam.

64 STEAMED PUMPKIN, CABBAGE, SPINACH, OR OTHER GREEN VEGETABLE

Choose only young vegetables.

Remove all uneatable parts and wash the vegetables in the usual way. Cut up if necessary. Place in a steamer, sprinkle a *small quantity* of salt between each layer, and steam till the toughest part (*e.g.* stalks) are soft—about 30 min. for a small quantity.

65 STEAMED RICE

2 cups rice   1 teasp. salt   3½ cups water
(*N.B.*—Measure water with the same cup)

Pick and wash rice in the usual way. Put rice, water, and salt in a large enamel jug or other heat-resisting receptacle. Place this in fast boiling water, being careful that the water is not more than two-thirds up the outside of jug, otherwise it may bubble over into the rice water. Steam 30 min., or rather longer for a large quantity. (This method is often used by the Chinese.)

N.B.—The boiling water round the jug should be used for cooking provisions or some other food.

66 STEAMED CUSTARD

1 pt. (2 nips) milk   2–3 Tbsp. sugar
2–3 eggs   ½ teasp. essence or spice

Grease a pie-dish or enamelled basin. Lightly beat eggs (they need *not* be frothy) with sugar, and add milk and flavouring. Pour into pie-dish and cover with greased paper to keep out steam. Place in a steamer or large pot containing a little boiling water. The pie-dish should not rest on the bottom of the pot as this may make the custard cook too fast, and if it boils at all it will immediately curdle. For this reason, place two or three pieces of clean wood or an upturned saucer in the pot on which to stand the pie-dish. Cover the saucepan and steam gently for about 1 hr. or until custard sets. If liked, the top may be browned by placing a baking sheet with glowing coals over the pie-dish for the last 15 min.

67 CABINET PUDDING

3 sponge cakes or 3 slices stale bread
1 Tbsp. currants or cherries
Citron, if liked

CUSTARD

1 nip (½ pt.) milk
2 eggs
1 Tbsp. sugar
¼ teasp. essence or spice

REMOVE crusts from bread and cut bread or cake into neat squares. Wash and pick currants and chop citron. Prepare custard as for Steamed Custard, and mix all ingredients in a buttered pie-dish or bowl. Stand until bread is thoroughly soaked, then steam as for Custard (Recipe 66). Serve hot or cold. If served cold it may be turned out.

68 STEAMED PINEAPPLE PUDDING

2–4 oz. (¼–½ cup) shortening *
4 oz. (½ cup) sugar
4 oz. (1 cup) flour
2 eggs
2–3 Tbsp. diced pineapple
1 Tbsp. pineapple juice
½ teasp. baking powder

GREASE a pudding basin or mould and dredge with flour. Decorate bottom of basin with pieces of pineapple. Cream (beat) butter and sugar together till white and frothy. Whisk eggs, and gradually beat them into the mixture. Sift and lightly stir in the flour, about one-third at a time. Add baking powder with last spoonful of flour and stir in the rest of the pine and the juice. See that the mixture is soft enough to drop from the spoon—if too stiff add a little milk—and pour

* "Shortening" is another word for grease, such as lard, butter, cooking oil, suet or fat pork. The kind used will depend on the flavour required, and whether the pudding is to be sweet or savoury. See also pages 149–150.

into prepared mould, which should not be more than two-thirds full. Cover closely with greased paper. Steam 1½ hr. and serve hot.

69 PATRIOTIC PUDDING

4 oz. (1 cup) flour
2 oz. (4 Tbsp.) shortening
2 oz. (4 Tbsp.) sugar
1 egg
¼ cup milk
1 teasp. baking powder
2 Tbsp. golden syrup or molasses
1 teasp. grated orange rind or other flavouring
Pinch of salt

Grease a pudding basin or mould and a piece of grease-proof paper large enough to cover the top of it. Put the molasses in the bottom of the basin. Wash, dry, and grate the orange, being careful to use the coloured skin only and none of the bitter white pith. Sift flour and salt into a mixing bowl and, using finger tips or a fork, rub in shortening till it looks like fine crumbs. Add sugar, orange rind, and baking powder and mix well. Beat egg and add milk, and stir these into dry ingredients. Pour mixture into prepared basin, which should not be more than two-thirds full. Cover closely with greased paper. Steam 2 hr. Turn out and serve hot.

70 STEAMED FISH

2 or 3 slices king fish or grouper, or 1 small red fish
Seasonings to taste
Salt and pepper
Lime juice
1 Tbsp. butter

Clean and season fish in the usual way (see notes on Fish, Chapter 7).

Prepare a pan of boiling water and butter a plate or carrier. Put fish with its seasoning in prepared plate or carrier, with a small dab of butter on each piece. Add lime juice, cover closely and steam. Allow 25 min. for small slices of fish ; or 15 min. to each pound and 15 min. more if steaming a large fish. Use the liquid which collects round the fish to make a creole or white sauce. Garnish with slices of lime or tomato.

71 STEAMED CHICKEN

See Chinese Dishes, Chapter 46.

CHAPTER 23

FRYING

Mmmm—— What a delicious smell! What is it? Fried fish—chips—accra?

How much we look forward to the tasty meal which follows the appetising smell that goes with frying, and how wonderfully quickly we can cook that meal, be it salt fish fritters, beef balls, or fried egg! But at the same time some of us dismally remember the indigestion which followed our last meal of hot bakes or other fried food! In order to make fried food tasty and attractive in appearance the oil or fat must be made very hot, and this great heat changes oil into an indigestible form. For this reason it is unwise to give fried food to young children, invalids, or anyone with a weak digestion, and even healthy people should eat it only occasionally.

KINDS OF FRYING

(1) *Shallow frying:* Used for cooking small or thin pieces of food such as pancakes, bacon rashers, eggs, and sometimes fish and meat. Use just enough oil to prevent the food from sticking, or for fish, etc., take enough to reach half-way up the piece of food.

(2) *Deep frying:* Use enough oil to cover the food completely. Because of this the food cooks more quickly, and no turning is necessary, so that food browns more evenly and is less likely to break. Some people imagine that the use of so much oil is extravagant, but provided that care is taken to prevent the

oil from burning, it can be used over and over again, so that it is not more expensive in the long run. Deep frying should be used rather than shallow frying whenever cooking large quantities or large pieces of food.

Kinds of Fat for Frying

Butter. This gives food a delicious flavour, but it is expensive and burns very easily. It should only be used for frying omelettes or very small pieces of food.

Margarine. This is sometimes used instead of butter, but does not give as good a flavour.

Lard. Some people object to lard on the ground that it makes food greasy. This does not happen if the lard is hot enough when food is put in.

Dripping (from a roast) can be used after the gravy which collects at the bottom has been removed.

Fat pork can be used when frying small quantities of food. It should first be washed, cut into small pieces, and then heated very gradually to melt out the oil from the skin. It is often mixed with other fat to improve the flavour.

Edible oil gives excellent results and is best when frying large quantities. Some people find that lard gives a better flavour.

To make Oil or Dripping from large pieces of Meat Fat or Suet

Wash fat, remove any lean or pieces of thick skin. Cut into small pieces, cover with cold water and simmer until all the fat has melted. Strain into a basin ; cool and then skim off the fat and throw away the water.

To make Coconut Oil

2 very dry coconuts About ¼ pt. of water (½ nip)	This gives about ¼ pt. of oil

1st Method

Grate coconuts, add water and knead for about 5 min. to work out milk. Strain. Boil milk without stirring till it turns to oil—1–1½ hr. Strain, cool, and bottle.

2nd Method

Prepare coconut milk as above. Strain, and add 1 to 1½ teasp. lime juice and a pinch of salt. Stand for 12 hr., by which time oil separates from water and floats at the top. Skim off the oil and boil for 20–30 min., until all water has been dried off. Strain, cool, and bottle.

To clarify (or clean) Oil which has been burned

Allow the oil to cool, add about three times as much water as there is oil, and boil the two together for about 15 min. Pour into a basin, cool, skim off the fat, and throw away the water.

GENERAL RULES FOR FRYING

(1) Use an iron or steel frying pan or pot. Enamel frying pans crack very quickly with the great heat of the oil, and aluminium pans, which must not be washed with soda, are a nuisance to clean after frying.

(2) Use a deep pot for deep frying.

(3) Always see that the oil is *smoking* before putting in any food. Bubbling or boiling does not mean that oil

is hot enough for frying, only that there is water or gravy in it. The smoke should be in the form of a faint blue vapour—not a dark brownish smoke, which means that the oil is overheated.

(4) Do not put too much food into the oil at once; this cools the oil and is as bad as starting with cold oil. If the oil is not hot enough the food breaks, and becomes sodden and very indigestible.

(5) Dry food before frying it. If wet pieces of fish or wet potato chips, etc., are put into the oil they make it cold, and sometimes make it bubble so much that it boils over.

(6) Coat any protein foods, except eggs, before frying. This dries them, makes them brown more easily, and helps to form a crisp outside which will keep in any nourishment. The following coatings may be used:

Dry flour—a quick coating for meat, fish, ripe plantain, etc.

Bread-crumbs (fresh) Raspings (dried bread-crumbs) Farine Crushed vermicelli Oatmeal	Used with a thin paste of flour and water or beaten egg, which makes the bread-crumbs, etc., stick. These are good coatings for meat or fish cutlets, beef balls, rissoles, etc.

(7) Drain fried foods thoroughly. All foods except meat and eggs should be drained on a piece of clean crumpled absorbent paper.

(8) Do not cover fried foods closely while hot. This would make them lose their crispness.

(9) Strain any surplus oil after frying is finished. If pieces of meat or fish are left in it, they will go bad and spoil the oil.

(10) Wipe greasy pans or pots with waste paper before washing—they will then be easier to clean.

72 FRIED MELONGENE

Peel, wash, and cut melongene into lengths $\frac{1}{4}$ to $\frac{1}{2}$ in. thick. Sprinkle with salt, white pepper, and finely chopped chive (if liked). Allow to stand for 5–10 min., remove chive and fry in hot smoking oil. Sprinkle with powdered bread-crumbs or raspings and serve hot.

73 FRIED OCHROE

Wash ochroes, cut off stem and cut into four lengthways. Season with salt and pepper, roll in dry flour, and fry in smoking hot oil.

74 FRIED BREADFRUIT

If breadfruit is almost ripe, peel, wash, cut into six or eight slices, remove core, and treat in the same manner as Melongene. If breadfruit is green, boil or steam before frying.

75 FRIED POTATO CHIPS

Peel, wash, and cut potatoes into $\frac{1}{4}$ to $\frac{1}{2}$ in. slices. Cut into $\frac{1}{4}$ to $\frac{1}{2}$ in. strips, and soak in salt water for about 20–30 min. Dry *thoroughly*, and fry in smoking hot oil till golden brown and crisp outside and soft in the middle.

76 BAKES

½ lb. (2 cups) flour
1 oz. (2 Tbsp.) shortening
1 teasp. salt
2 teasp. sugar
2 teasp. baking powder or 1 teasp. bicarbonate of soda

Sift flour, salt, and baking powder together. Add the shortening, and using finger tips or a fork, mix thoroughly until it resembles bread-crumbs. Dissolve the sugar in one-third cup of water and use this to mix the flour to a soft dough. Knead lightly, cut into pieces the size of a small egg, and roll into balls. Flatten balls to ¼ in. thick and fry in smoking hot oil until golden brown.

N.B.—Bakes may be cooked on a hot baking stone, turning when one side has browned.

77 CORNMEAL BAKES

11 oz. (2 cups) fresh cornmeal
2 oz. (¼ cup) flour
1½ teasp. salt
1½ teasp. baking powder
2 oz. fat pork
½ oz. (1 Tbsp.) shortening—lard or butter
Water to bind

Chop fat pork finely, add to flour mixture, and make as for Ordinary Bakes.

78 CORNMEAL ARRAPE

1⅓ lb. (4 cups) cornmeal
2 oz. (½ cup) flour
1 oz. (2 Tbsp.) butter
1 oz. (2 Tbsp.) lard
2 teasp. salt
3 teasp. baking powder
Water to bind

Filling

½ lb. beef
1 oz. fat pork
½ teasp. salt
Seasonings to taste
2 Tbsp. oil

CLEAN the meat and brown it with the fat pork and seasonings. Cover and stew for half an hour, then mince or chop finely. Prepare the cornmeal mixture as for Bakes, and flatten the balls to $\frac{1}{8}$ to $\frac{1}{4}$ in., or roll out the mixture and cut into 2 to 3 in. circles with a cup or cutter. Put about 1 Tbsp. meat mixture on one circle, damp the edge and cover with a second circle. Squeeze the edges together and fry in smoking hot oil till golden brown. Drain and serve hot.

N.B.—Flour is sometimes omitted. In this case mix cornmeal with *hot* water.

79 CORN FRITTERS

- $\frac{1}{4}$ pt. ($\frac{1}{2}$ glass) milk
- 2 cups boiled corn cut from the cob
- $\frac{1}{2}$ lb. (2 cups) flour
- $1\frac{1}{2}$ teasp. salt
- $\frac{1}{3}$ teasp. pepper
- 2 teasp. baking powder
- 1 Tbsp. melted butter
- 1–2 eggs (if only 1 egg is used reduce the quantity of flour)

BEAT eggs and gradually stir in flour and milk. Add all other ingredients except baking powder and beat well. Stir in baking powder last of all. Fry spoonfuls in smoking hot oil. Drain on absorbent paper and serve at once.

80 TANNIA CAKES OR FRITTERS

- 2–3 small tannias or 1 cup grated tannia
- 1 Tbsp. flour
- $\frac{1}{2}$ teasp. salt
- 1–2 blades chive
- $\frac{1}{2}$ teasp. bicarbonate of soda, or 1 teasp. baking powder
- Pepper
- 1 egg (if liked)

WASH and peel tannias. Wash again and grate finely. Chop seasonings finely and mix all ingredients. Beat well. Drop spoonfuls in smoking hot oil. Fry till golden brown, drain, and serve at once.

81 PLANTAIN CAKES

2–3 small yellow plantains (not ripe enough to fry)
1 teasp. salt or 1 Tbsp. sugar } to every cup crushed plantain
½ teasp. baking powder }

Boil the plantains, peel, pound, or mash them. Mix all ingredients. Shape into little cakes slightly larger than a penny and fry in smoking hot oil.

82 PUMPKIN PANCAKES

½ lb. (4 c) pumpkin
1 oz. (¼ cup) flour } to every cup crushed pumpkin
½ oz. (1 Tbsp.) sugar }
¼ teasp. spice or essence }
½ teasp. baking powder }

Wash, peel, and steam the pumpkin. Mash thoroughly and stir in all other ingredients. Beat well and fry by dropping spoonfuls into smoking hot oil. Dry, sprinkle with fine sugar, and serve at once.

N.B.—Beaten egg may be added to the mixture. In this case increase the quantity of flour by half as much again.

83 FRITTER BATTER

2 oz. (½ cup) flour
4 Tbsp. water or milk
1 Tbsp. oil (if water is used)
1 egg white or ½ teasp. baking powder
Pinch of salt

Sift flour, and gradually beat in oil and water. Cover and set aside for 20–30 min. Whisk egg white until it is stiff enough to stand in a point, and fold it lightly into the batter. Use for fish or fruit fritters.

Important Note. If baking powder or soda is used in place of egg, use 2 extra Tbsp. water, and do not add the baking powder until after the mixture has stood.

84 BANANA FRITTERS

2–3 bananas according to the size	Fritter batter as given above

Peel the bananas, cut in half lengthwise, then cut into two or three across. Coat each piece with batter and fry in smoking hot oil till golden brown. Drain, sprinkle with sugar, and serve at once.

N.B.—Some people mash the bananas and make them in the same way as Pumpkin Pancakes. This is not so good, as the fritters are inclined to be heavy, indigestible, and unappetizing.

85 SALT FISH FRITTERS

½ lb. salt fish	Pepper to taste
2–3 blades chive	Fritter batter as above

Prepare the batter. While it is standing, thoroughly scald the fish, then bone, skin, and pound or flake it. Chop the chive very finely. Complete the batter, add fish and seasonings, and drop spoonfuls of the mixture into smoking hot oil. Turn as required, and cook until golden brown—about 2–3 min.

N.B.—Fresh *cooked* fish may be used in place of salt fish ; in this case add half teasp. salt.

86 JAMAICA AKRAS

TAKE any quantity of Black Eye Peas and soak them overnight. Pulp them out of the skins, add salt and green pepper, and pound them until creamy. Drop spoonfuls in smoking hot oil and fry till golden brown. Drain on absorbent paper and serve hot.

87 ACCRA

- ½ lb. (2 cups) flour
- ½ cake Fleischman's yeast (or ¼ oz. of other yeast)
- ½ teasp. salt
- 3 oz. salt fish
- 2 blades chive
- ½ small onion, garlic, and thyme
- Piece of red pepper or ¼ teasp. black pepper
- 1½ cups warm water

SCALD fish twice, then remove skin and bone. Pound fish, onion, garlic, thyme, and pepper together till fine. Sift flour and salt into a bowl. Mix yeast to a paste with a little of the water, then add the rest of the water and stir it into the flour until a soft batter is formed. Add fish and beat mixture for 2–3 min. Stand in a warm place to rise for 2 hr. Fry by spoonfuls in smoking hot oil. Drain and serve hot with Floats (see Recipe 88).

N.B.—A smaller quantity of yeast is sometimes used. In this case the mixture must be allowed to rise for a longer time.

88 FLOATS

- 1 lb. (4 cups) flour
- 4 oz. (½ cup) shortening, *e.g.* lard
- 1½ teasp. salt
- ½ cake Fleischman's yeast (or ¼ oz. other yeast)
- Warm water

SIFT flour and salt together. Add shortening, and using finger tips or a fork, mix thoroughly till it looks like fine crumbs. Mix yeast to a paste with a little warm water, then add to the flour and shortening, adding enough warm water to make a soft dough. Knead *well* until smooth. Put to rise in a warm place for 2 hr. or until mixture is twice as big. Cut into pieces the size of a small egg, and roll into balls. Put to rise again for 20 min. Flatten out to $\frac{1}{8}$ in. thickness, and fry in smoking hot oil. Drain and serve hot.

89 FRIED FISH

Fillets or cutlets of large fish, or a whole small fish
Seasonings to taste
Bread-crumbs or raspings or farine or flour
Oil for frying
Beaten egg or batter made from 1 Tbsp. flour and 3 Tbsp. water or milk
Sauce, *e.g.* creole butter sauce, parsley, or shrimp sauce

CLEAN the fish and season it for not more than 20 min. Beat the egg or prepare the batter in a *shallow* plate, and put bread-crumbs or farine on a piece of paper. Remove seasonings from fish, dip each piece in egg or batter, then drain well, using two forks; toss in the bread-crumbs, place on a board, and press the bread-crumbs in place with the blade of a knife.

(*N.B.*—If flour is used, no egg or batter is required.) Fry at once in smoking hot oil—if left to stand after coating, the flour or bread-crumbs become saturated and do not fry so well. Turn fish if necessary, and be very careful not to put too much in oil at once, otherwise this cools the oil, and this is bound to make the fish break. Drain well on crushed absorbent paper. Arrange on a hot dish. Use the seasonings for a suitable sauce.

90 FRIED BEEF

1 lb. beef—good quality *e.g.* steak, fillet, tenderloin	$\frac{1}{8}$ teasp. pepper
	6 Tbsp. oil (approx.)
	1 onion
1 Tbsp. flour for coating	1 blade chive, thyme
$\frac{1}{2}$ teasp. salt	$\frac{1}{2}$ pt. (1 nip) stock or water

WIPE meat thoroughly, then beat it gently with a rolling-pin or bottle to bruise the fibres, and so soften the meat. Cut it into neat slices not less than 1–1$\frac{1}{2}$ in. thick, then cut the slices into pieces about 3 in. square or more. If the meat is cut too thin or into too small pieces, so much of the inside is exposed that the meat juice runs out, and the meat is less nourishing and less tasty.

Prepare the seasonings (cutting onion into rings), and season the meat for about 20 min., or simply rub the meat with the onion before cutting it up. Mix the flour, salt, and pepper, and coat the meat. Heat the oil till slightly smoking, put in the meat, cook quickly for the first 2 min., turning as soon as one side has browned. Then decrease heat slightly and cook meat for 10–12 min. in an *uncovered* pan.

When cooked the beef should be well browned and look puffy. When pressed it should dent easily but regain its shape at once. If it is not puffy and does not dent easily when pressed, this is a sign that it is overcooked.

Keep the meat hot and make a sauce. Fry the seasonings, add the rest of the flour, and brown evenly. Stir in the stock or water gradually and boil for 2–3 min.

CHAPTER 24

GRILLING

"GRILLING! Why, that is a really excellent way of cooking," says the doctor or dietitian as he looks at our tongue or questions us about our indigestion. "Why don't you eat more grilled and less fried food?"

Well, what is this grilled food? Let us be sure that we know what grilling is.

Other names for grilling are broiling or toasting, and it is done over, under, or in front of a glowing fire—for example, we can hang a piece of meat or a fish over glowing wood when we are out camping, we can put it on a grid over glowing coals, or under an electric or gas griller if we are lucky enough to have one.

Grilling is a convenient way of cooking, because it is quick, and doctors think grilled food is good, because this short cooking does little to spoil the food value. Little oil or fat of any kind is used, so that it is more digestible than fried food.

On the other hand many people cannot afford grilled food. Because it is a quick way of cooking, only small tender pieces of food can be grilled, and young birds and tender meat cost more than old or tough and bony cuts.

RULES FOR GRILLING

(1) Use a hot glowing fire to brown food quickly—quick browning cooks the protein on the surface of the meat, and this forms a thin covering which prevents meat juice from running out.

(2) Heat the grid before using—this also helps food to brown quickly.

(3) To prevent food from sticking, grease the grid before heating it.

(4) Grease the food too. This prevents it from drying up and becoming unpalatable.

91 GRILLED MEAT

Suitable meats for grilling are mutton cutlets, beef steak or fillet (undercut), kidneys, sausages.
Seasonings to taste, Maître d'hôtel Butter (Recipe 92).

Mutton. Trim off excess fat which would simply melt. Do not remove the meat from the bone.

Beef. Pound or beat the beef lightly to soften it. Cut into 1–1½ in. slices, and then into rounds or squares about 2–3 in. across.

Kidneys. Wash, scald, and skin the kidneys. Cut them open along the hollow side and cut out all tubes, etc.

Sausages. Wash and prick.

Season the meat. Usually nothing but salt, pepper, and a little vinegar or sauce are used, but the meat may be rubbed with onion or other seasonings, if liked. Brush over with oil or butter, place on a hot grid, and brown quickly. Turn as soon as one side is well browned (about 2–3 min.). Avoid pricking meat with fork or knife when turning, otherwise meat juice will escape through pricks. Turn by holding between two spoons or the flat blades of two knives.

When both sides are brown, raise the grid a little from the fire and complete cooking more slowly. When cooked, meat should be brown and puffy, and if pressed the hollow made should immediately fill up again. Put a pat of Maître d'hôtel Butter (Recipe 92) on top of both mutton cutlets and beef. Serve at once.

92 MAÎTRE D'HÔTEL BUTTER

1 Tbsp. butter	1 teasp. lime juice
2 teasp. finely chopped parsley	¼ teasp. salt
	Pinch of white pepper

Wash, thoroughly dry, and finely chop the parsley. Mix all ingredients. Form into small pats and place on grilled meat just before serving. The meat must be hot enough to melt the butter. This is used instead of sauce or gravy.

93 MIXED GRILL

This is a substantial dish consisting of a variety of foods grilled and served together. Follow general rules for grilling and include such things as kidneys, sausages, ham or bacon, chops, steaks, mushrooms, and tomatoes.

94 GRILLED FISH

Use small fish or slices or cutlets from a large one. Scale, trim, and clean the fish (see Chapter 7, Fish). Butter both sides, season with pepper and salt, and, if liked, put finely chopped chive, tomato, etc., in the cavity left by cleaning.

Grill for a few minutes on both sides, turning very gently. Allow about 5–7 min. in all, depending on the size. When cooked, fish should look " set " like hard-boiled egg, and should be golden brown. Serve with creole butter sauce or a white sauce.

95 GRILLED POTATOES OR OTHER GROUND PROVISIONS

Scrub and boil the potatoes. Peel and place on a greased grid. Grill over a glowing fire, turning constantly to ensure even browning.

CHAPTER 25

BAKING AND ROASTING

BAKING is cooking in an oven or covered pot. In the old days people used both to bake and roast foods, but now very little roasting (which is cooking in front of a large open fire) is done. Many foods which are called roast are really baked, *e.g.* roast chicken, potatoes, etc.

Baking is a favourite way of cooking because crisp, brown baked foods both look and taste well. It is a better way of cooking than frying, because the food is more digestible.

Unfortunately baking is not a cheap way of cooking, because the food is likely to shrink and become dry, so only good pieces of tender and more expensive meat, young chickens, etc., can be baked.

Not only meat, but fish, vegetables, puddings, and cakes are all baked. An oven will, of course, give the best results (see Chapter 16, Cookery Apparatus), but small pieces of food can be baked in an iron pot or kerosene tin.

GENERAL RULES FOR BAKING

(1) See that the inside of the oven is as clean as the inside of a saucepan.

(2) Heat oven to correct temperature before putting in the food.

(3) Dry food such as vegetables or fish before putting in oven.

(4) If possible, save fuel by using your oven for more than one food at a time.

OVEN TEMPERATURES

(a)	*Moderate Oven*	220°–350° F.
	Large cakes	300°–350° F.
	Egg dishes, meringues (soupirs)	220° F.
(b)	*Hot Oven*	350°–375° F.
	Biscuits	350°–450° F.
	Fish	350° F.
	Plain cakes	370° F.
(c)	*Quick or Very Hot Oven* . .	375°–500° F.
	Sponge sandwich . . .	375° F.
	Pastry	420° F.
	Bread and Scones . . .	450° F.
	Meat (first 15 min. only) .	500° F.

If no thermometer is obtainable use the "bread test." Put a small piece of bread in the oven; if at the end of exactly 5 min. it is—

biscuit colour—the oven is moderate
golden brown—the oven is hot
dark brown—the oven is quick or very hot

96 ROAST BEEF OR MUTTON

1 joint good quality beef, *e.g.* undercut (fillet), sirloin, rolled ribs, aitchbone, topside
1 joint good quality mutton, *e.g.* leg, shoulder, or loin
2–3 oz. (4–6 Tbsp.) fat, *e.g.* dripping, lard, or oil
Salt and pepper

WIPE meat thoroughly with a damp cloth. If liked, rub it with seasonings or pack seasonings into any crevices —none should be left on the outside as they will burn. Using metal skewers (meat pins) and clean twine, tie joint into shape if necessary.

Put meat on a grid in dripping-pan with dripping or oil—if potatoes are to be cooked with meat, use the full 3 oz. oil. Put meat in a very hot oven, so that the outside will quickly brown and form a coating which will keep in the meat juice. Lower heat after the first 15 min. ; the dripping should sizzle gently. For large joints, allow 20 min. for every lb. and 20 min. over for the piece ; *e.g.* 4 lb. joint—time allowed $4 \times 20 + 20$ min. = 1 hr. 40 min. For small joints of under 3 lb. allow 1¼ hr. for thin pieces and 1½ hr. for thick pieces.

Baste meat (*i.e.* pour a spoonful of hot oil from the dripping-pan over the meat) every 20 min. This keeps meat moist and juicy and helps it to brown. Some people use a covered dripping-pan—in this case no basting is necessary, but remove cover 15 min. before meat is done, so that outside may be made brown and crisp. When cooked, put meat on a hot dish and keep hot while gravy is made.

97 PLAIN GRAVY FOR ROASTS

Strain dripping from pan in which meat was cooked, keeping back the brown semi-solid substances (meat juice) on the bottom of pan. Sprinkle in 1 teasp. flour and allow it to brown evenly. Add ½ pt. (1 glass) water or stock, ½ teasp. salt, and ⅛ teasp. pepper. Heat to boiling-point, and strain into a gravy tureen.

N.B.—This gravy should be clear and free from fat.

98 ROAST POTATOES COOKED WITH MEAT

Peel and wash potatoes, cut in halves or quarters if large. Soak in salted water for half an hour. Dry well and put in dripping pan round meat when it is about half cooked—allow 45 min. for potatoes. Baste and turn them as they brown. When cooked they should be soft inside and crisp and brown outside. Serve in a hot vegetable dish or round the joint.

99 ROAST PORK

CHOOSE leg, loin, or spare rib. Cook in the same way as beef, but for a longer time—allow 25 min. to every lb. and 25 min. over for the piece, *e.g.* 4 lb. joint, allow $4 \times 25 + 25 = 2$ hr. 5 min. When it is cooked the pork should be white-looking right through. It is dangerous to eat undercooked pork. Pigs are sometimes infected with tiny worms which lodge in their muscles (the lean of the meat). If we eat the meat with the worms still alive, we may contract the disease called trichinosis. It is very painful and may cause death. The worms cannot be seen without a microscope, so the only thing that we can do is to cook the pork thoroughly to make certain that the heat has completely destroyed any that may be present.

100 ROAST CHICKEN

- 1 young fowl
- About 4 Tbsp. stuffing or forcemeat (Recipe 360)
- About 10 rashers (slices) bacon
- Gravy (this should be paler than the gravy served with beef)
- ½ pt. bread sauce (Recipe 253)

PLUCK and singe the bird. If the bird is not very young pour hot water over it before plucking to loosen feathers and kill lice. Cut off head; make a long slit at back of neck, loosen skin and cut off neck close to body leaving skin on the bird. Cut round vent to free entrails, remove gullet, crop, windpipe, and all internal organs. Cut out oil sack above tail. Wash and dry inside and outside of bird. If liked, rub with lime juice and salt. Break legs above spur, twist and draw out sinews. Stuff the bird and fold skin over at neck. Press legs forward close to breast and turn wings in close to the sides. See that bird will sit flatly without wobbling, and tie legs and wings in place. Cover breast with one or two slices of fat bacon and place on a grid in a dripping-pan. Bake in a hot oven for 1¼–1½ hr., depending on size. Baste frequently. To brown the breast remove bacon 15 min. before fowl is cooked, dredge (sprinkle) with flour, and baste. Remove string and serve on a hot dish garnished with bacon rolls.

To make Bacon Rolls

Remove rind and flatten bacon rashers with the blade of a knife. Cut into strips about 1–1½ in. wide and roll up. Arrange several rolls on a skewer, put it across corner of dripping-pan, and bake with chicken for last 10 min.

To Prepare Trimmings or Giblets

Remove gall from liver and sac of stones from gizzard. Scald feet and remove toes and scales. Soak feet, liver, heart, neck, kidney, and gizzard in warm water for 20 min., then wash well. Add about 1 pt. (2 glasses) water and ½ teasp. salt, and simmer for 1 hr. to make stock for gravy, soup, etc.

101 ROAST SUCKING PIG

1 sucking pig, not more than 3 weeks old
Butter or oil to baste
Stuffing containing olives, capers, petits pois, spice, etc., if liked

Stab the pig in the throat and allow blood to run into a vessel. Put the pig straight into cold water, then after a few minutes, plunge it into boiling water, and leave for 2 min. Take it out of the water, pull off any hair as quickly as possible and thoroughly clean mouth, nostrils, and ears. Slit open a small hole in the belly and remove entrails. Wash thoroughly in cold water and wipe dry. Loosen and fold back skin round the feet. Cut off the feet and turn skin back over ends. Either rub the pig with seasonings or stuff it and sew up the opening. Draw legs well back and tie them in place. Brush all over with oil or melted butter, wrap it in several folds of greaseproof paper and bake in a hot oven for 2½–3 hr., according to size. Remove paper ½ hr. before pig is ready, dredge with flour and baste well. The pig should be crisp and brown when cooked. Place a baked potato in the mouth and serve with plain gravy and apple (or mango) sauce.

102 POT ROAST

Choose a small tender piece of meat weighing not more than 1 lb.

Wipe and season meat in the usual way, but before roasting remove all seasonings from the outside. Put about 4 Tbsp. oil or dripping in a small thick iron pot or saucepan—the oil should be about ½ in. deep. Heat till oil is smoking. Put in meat, cover, and brown quickly. Turn as required. When brown all over, reduce the heat and cook gently for about 50 min. Keep closely covered. Serve on a hot dish with gravy or creole sauce.

N.B.—Some people add a little water when pot-roasting. This should not be necessary if the cover fits well. If oil is overheated a little water may be added, but care must be taken to avoid scalds from the steam which rises when the water is put in.

103 BAKED STUFFED FISH

1 large red fish or mackerel
2–3 Tbsp. stuffing (see Recipe 360)
1 Tbsp. raspings (dried bread-crumbs)
2–3 Tbsp. oil, dripping, or butter

SCALE, trim, and clean fish in the usual way. Wash and dry it, but omit seasoning as it is to be stuffed instead. Prepare stuffing and fill cavity. Secure edges with a small skewer or sew them together, taking great care that the needle is not left in the fish ! Put oil in a dripping-pan and heat till smoking. Put in fish, dredge top with plenty of raspings, and baste at once. Cook for 20–30 min. in a moderate oven, basting frequently. Serve on a hot dish with gravy or creole sauce.

104 CRAB BACKS

READ in Chapter 7 the part dealing with Shellfish.

1 doz. crabs
2–3 Tbsp. butter
1 chopped onion
1 tomato
2–3 blades chive
1 Tbsp. Worcester Sauce or vinegar
Salt and pepper to taste
Raspings (dried bread-crumbs) for the top

For good results the meat of 12 crabs should be used for not more than 8–10 finished crab backs. For the sake of economy fresh bread-crumbs or cooked fish is sometimes added to the mixture to make it go further. Obtain crabs at least one day before they are required and keep them feeding on wholesome food, *e.g.* bread, pepper leaves, etc., till purged. Place in a large pan and pour on enough boiling water to cover. Throw away this water, wash crabs, and boil for half an hour to loosen flesh. Remove claws, cut open and pick out meat. Remove body from shell, carefully preserving any eggs and fat, but discarding the gall which clings to the shell. Scrub shells thoroughly. Prepare seasonings, and brown them in the butter. Add flaked crab meat, Worcester Sauce, salt, and pepper. Refill shells, sprinkle with raspings and a small dab of butter, and brown in a quick oven.

105 SALT FISH PIE

½ lb. salt fish	1 large onion
¾–1 lb. Irish potatoes	½ teasp. black pepper
3–4 blades chive	About ½ pt. (1 glass) milk

Soak fish well, then scald it and remove skin and bone. Boil potatoes and parboil onion. Pound fish with chopped chive and onion, and add pepper. Slice half the potatoes and mash the rest with a little milk. Arrange alternate layers of sliced potato and fish in a greased pie-dish. Moisten with the rest of the milk. Put the mashed potato on top, smooth with a wet knife and decorate. Add one or two dabs of butter and brown in a quick oven (about 20–30 min.). Garnish with slices of tomato or hard-boiled egg.

N.B.—Some people prefer to make a little white sauce to mix with the fish.

106 SALT FISH SOUFFLÉ

½ lb. salt fish	¼ pt. (½ glass) milk
2 oz. (½ cup) flour	White pepper to taste
2 oz. (4 Tbsp.) butter	1 teasp. lime juice

SCALD salt fish, and remove skin and bone. Flake or pound finely. Melt butter, stir in flour without browning. Add milk, and stirring continuously cook until a thick white sauce is obtained. Add all ingredients except egg whites, and beat well. Whisk egg whites very stiffly and fold into mixture. Pour into a greased pie-dish or basin, leaving enough space for mixture to rise. Bake in a quick oven till mixture is well risen, set, and golden brown (about 25–30 min.) or cover and steam till set (about 45–50 min.). Serve at once.

107 MELONGENE AU GRATIN

1 melongene
Pepper and salt to taste
1 Tbsp. butter or oil
Onion, chive, tomato, etc., if liked
Raspings (dried breadcrumbs)

WASH and boil melongene whole, or prick it and roast over a slow fire. Lightly fry the seasonings in the butter. When melongene is soft, cut in half lengthways, scoop out the centre and mix all ingredients. Refill the shells or pile mixture in a pie-dish. Sprinkle top with raspings, add dabs of butter, and brown in a quick oven.

108 PAPAW AU GRATIN

CHOOSE a green papaw, wash, cut in half and remove seeds. Boil till soft and then prepare in the same way as melongene. Seasonings may be omitted if liked.

109 MELONGENE ROMA

1 medium-sized melongene
1 egg
1 teasp. salt
4 Tbsp. butter or oil
¼ lb. grated cheese
4 Tbsp. chopped onion or onion and chive
1 cup tomato sauce or 3 large tomatoes

WASH and peel melongene, and cut crosswise in ¼–½ in. slices. Beat egg, add ½ teasp. salt and coat melongene. Heat butter and lightly fry melongene till brown but not quite tender. Arrange slices in stacks of three with cheese between and on top, and place in a shallow fireproof dish. Fry onion (and tomatoes if used) and put them with sauce and balance of salt round melongene. Add ½ cup water if no tomato sauce is used. Bake in a moderate oven till cheese browns (about 25 min.).

110 EDDO SOUFFLÉ

1 lb. eddoes
1 oz. (2 Tbsp.) butter
¼ pt. (½ glass) milk
2 eggs
1 teasp. salt
¼ teasp. white pepper

PEEL and wash eddoes with lime juice. Cook till soft in boiling salted water. Crush thoroughly, and mix with all ingredients *except egg white.* Beat well. Whisk egg white very stiffly and fold into eddo mixture. Pour into a greased pie-dish allowing room for the mixture to rise. Bake in a quick oven till well risen and golden brown—about 20–30 min. Serve at once before mixture falls.

N.B.—Other ground provisions may be used in the same way. 3–4 oz. grated cheese may be added, if liked.

111 AVOCADO PEAR SOUFFLÉ

1 medium-sized pear	½ teasp. salt
1 oz. (2 Tbsp.) butter	½ teasp. white pepper
1 oz. (4 Tbsp.) flour	2–3 eggs
¼ pt. (½ glass) milk	

PEEL and grate the pear. Melt butter, stir in flour, then milk, and make a thick white sauce. Cool mixture, stir in egg yolks and beat well. Whisk egg whites stiffly, fold them into sauce mixture with grated pear. Season to taste. Pour into a greased pie-dish, allowing room for mixture to rise. Bake in a quick oven till well risen and golden brown—about 30 min. Serve at once before mixture falls.

N.B.—The mixture may be steamed instead of baked; in this case, allow about ¾–1 hr., cover and steam till set.

112 CREAMED BREADFRUIT

1 ripe breadfruit	1 Tbsp. butter
About ½ cup hot milk	Pepper and salt to taste
1 egg	

WASH and boil breadfruit. Peel and mash with salt, pepper, and butter. Add enough hot milk to make to a thick creamy consistency. Beat egg thoroughly (white may be whisked separately if liked) and stir into mixture. Pile in a greased pie-dish and brown in a quick oven or fry spoonfuls in smoking hot oil.

113 STUFFED BREADFRUIT

1 breadfruit—full but not ripe	1 small onion
½ lb. fresh beef or pork	2–3 blades chive
1 thick slice raw ham or ¼ lb. pickled meat	1 Tbsp. butter or oil (more if no pork is used)
1 tomato	Salt and black pepper to taste

Peel and parboil breadfruit whole in salted water. Clean meat and seasonings, lightly fry them in the butter, then mince or chop. Cool breadfruit, and from the stalk end cut out core and a little fruit. Fill hole with prepared meat mixture. Bake in a moderate oven till soft and brown—about 45 min. Butter crust and serve hot.

Alternative Method

Use unpeeled raw fruit, scoop out centre, and after filling in the usual way, roast over a wood fire. Peel and butter before serving.

114 TANNIA MEGAN

3–4 tannias	1 tomato
¼ lb. salt beef (or cooked meat)	1 small onion
	1 Tbsp. butter or dripping

Wash and soak salt beef. Wash and peel tannias and onion, and cook in boiling salted water. Mash tannias, and chop or mince salt beef, onion, and tomato. Mix all ingredients, beat well, and pile in a greased pie-dish. Score the top, add a few dabs of butter, and bake till top is brown and crisp—about 45 min.

CHAPTER 26

BREAD

BREAD is something we all use daily, and because well cooked home-made bread is nicer and often cleaner than the bread we buy, it is something we should all know how to make.

Bread is different from other mixtures such as those used for cakes, because yeast or leaven (dough) is used instead of baking powder, and for this reason practically all the rising has to be done before baking. Baking-powder bread can, of course, be made, but it does not have such a pleasant flavour, and it dries more quickly.

Yeast

Yeast consists of tiny little plants, each made of a single beadlike cell. They are so small that we cannot see them, and so light that they are blown about in the air. When their surroundings are comfortable they grow and give off new cells by a process called " budding " —that is, they give off little shoots or buds which gradually develop into new cells, which break away from their parent. The things they need for growth are :

(1) Food—generally obtained from sugar, or starch changed into sugar.

(2) Moisture.

(3) Warmth—bloodheat (98·4° F.) is best for them ; great heat kills them, and cold stops their growth.

When mixed with food or liquid containing sugar or starch, the yeast cells feed on the sugar and split it up into alcohol and carbon dioxide. This is what gives bread, ginger beer, or mawby its taste and its bubbly appearance.

Kinds of Yeast

(1) Wild yeast collected from the air by leaving sour flour paste or potato mixture uncovered. This method is unreliable because it is impossible to tell whether the flour or potato pastes contain many or few yeast cells, so that results are very varied.

(2) Baker's leaven or dough. This is simply flour paste containing yeast. It is cheap, but somewhat unreliable, because here again we cannot tell how strong or weak the yeast is.

(3) Liquid yeast from a brewery—this often turns sour.

(4) Pure compressed or dried yeast, which is a mass of yeast cells unmixed with anything else. It can be bought by the ounce or by the packet. It costs more, but gives the best results.

GENERAL RULES FOR BREAD-MAKING

(1) Allow about 1 oz. yeast to 4 lb. flour, but always increase the proportion of yeast when using less flour, *e.g.* use $\frac{1}{4}$ oz. yeast to $\frac{1}{2}$ lb. flour.

(2) Add 1 teasp. sugar to yeast if bread is required quickly.

(3) Keep the mixture warm the whole time, so use warm water, and stand the bowl in a warm (not hot) place.

(4) Knead bread very thoroughly or the yeast will not be spread all through the mixture, and the bread will rise unevenly, and have large holes when baked.

(5) Allow bread to rise to twice its size before shaping into loaves—the time will vary with the quantity. Bread that is not given time to rise is heavy.

(6) Never over-rise bread. This often causes it to turn sour, because as yeast cells get weaker, they are attacked by other living cells in the air.

(7) Bake bread in a hot oven so that the yeast cells are killed, and the bubbles of gas made by the yeast are fully expanded. Lower the heat after the first 15 min., and bake bread until it is crisp and brown outside and sounds hollow when rapped on the bottom.

To make pan loaves crisp, bake them without a tin for the last 10 min.
Allow 45–60 min. for a large loaf, and 35–40 min. for small loaves.

115 WHITE BREAD

1 oz. yeast or 1 packet Fleischman's yeast or 2 ¢ dough
2 teasp. sugar
$\frac{3}{4}$ Tbsp. salt
4 lb. (16 cups) flour
$\frac{1}{4}$ lb. ($\frac{1}{2}$ cup) shortening, if liked
About 2 pt. (4 glasses) warm water

Crush yeast and sugar together and add warm water. Sift flour and salt, and add about $\frac{1}{4}$ of the total amount of flour to the yeast mixture. Cover and leave in a warm place to set the sponge (*i.e.* until mixture is bubbly), about 1 hr.
If shortening is used, rub it into remainder of flour, using finger-tips or a fork.
Add flour to yeast mixture and knead well until a

smooth elastic dough is formed. Add some more warm water if necessary, for a hard dry dough does not rise well.

Put bread in a greased or floured bowl, and grease or cut across the top to prevent a hard crust forming. Cover and leave to rise till twice as big.

Knead lightly to avoid bursting any bubbles and, without using extra flour, mould (shape) into loaves.

Cover and prove (*i.e.* put to rise again for 20–30 min.). Proving improves the shape of loaves, but may be omitted if time is short.

Bake in a hot oven, following general rules for baking.

116 WHOLEWHEAT OR BROWN BREAD

2 lb. ($6\frac{1}{2}$ cups) wholewheat flour
2 lb. (8 cups) white flour
2 teasp. salt
$\frac{1}{4}$ lb. ($\frac{1}{2}$ cup) shortening, if liked
1 oz .yeast, or 1 packet Fleischman's yeast, or 2 *c* dough
2 teasp. sugar
About $2\frac{1}{2}$ pt. (5 nips) warm water

NOTICE that there is less salt and more water than in the recipe for white bread. Wholewheat flour contains more mineral salts and is more absorbent.

Make in the same way as white bread—the mixture will probably take longer to rise. Increase the proportion of yeast for smaller quantities.

N.B.—Some people like their bread browner than this, in which case use more wholewheat and less white flour.

117 BRAN BREAD

WHOLEWHEAT flour does not keep well, and partly on this account it often costs more than twice as much as white flour. People who cannot afford it should use bran instead, as although it is not as good as wholewheat, bran bread is better than white bread.

3 lb. (12 cups) flour	1 oz. yeast
1 lb. (6 cups) bran	¼ cup molasses or 2–3 teasp. sugar
2 teasp. salt	About 2 pt. (4 nips) water
Shortening, if liked	

Make in the same way as wholewheat bread.

118 CLOVER LEAF ROLLS

Prepare a small quantity of bread mixture in the usual way. After it has risen, shape it into a number of *small* balls and brush the sides with melted butter. Grease deep pie pans or small cake tins and drop three balls into each.

Prove, and bake in a hot oven for about 10 min.

119 ORANGE BREAD OR BUNS

1 oz. yeast	2 oz. (¼ cup) sugar
1 Tbsp. sugar	1 egg yolk
1 pt. (2 nips) warm water or milk	Grated rind of 2 oranges
2 lb. (8 cups) sifted flour	¼ cup of orange juice
2 oz. (¼ cup) shortening	½ teasp. salt

Dissolve yeast and 1 Tbsp. sugar in warm water. Add 1½ cups flour, beat well, cover, and leave to rise in warm place until twice as large. Cream butter and sugar, and beat in egg yolk. Add to yeast mixture with remaining ingredients. Mix well, knead lightly, and shape as required. Half-fill greased pans, and leave to rise again till double in size.

Follow general rules for baking—loaves will take about 45 min ; buns about 20 min.

120 HOT CROSS BUNS

1 lb. (4 cups) sifted flour	½ lb. (1 heaped cup) currants
¼ lb. (½ cup) sugar	¼ teasp. salt
½ oz. yeast	½ teasp. mixed ground spice
½ pt. (1 nip) warm milk	1 egg, if liked
¼ lb. (½ cup) shortening	

(Makes 12 buns)

MIX yeast, a little of the sugar and the milk. Add 2 cups flour, cover, and leave until the sponge has set—about ½ hr. Clean the currants, melt and cool the shortening, and add all ingredients to the yeast mixture. Knead well, cover, and leave to rise until double in size. Shape into round buns, place at least 3 in. apart on a greased baking sheet. Cover and prove for 20–30 min. Mark a cross on the top, brush with melted sugar, and bake in a hot oven for 15–20 min.

121 RAISIN ROLL BUNS

½ oz. yeast	2 oz. (4 Tbsp.) shortening
2 teasp. sugar	4 oz. (½ cup) sugar
½ pt. (1 nip) warm milk	About 6 oz. (¾ cup) raisins
1 lb. (4 cups) sifted flour	½ teasp. ground spice
A pinch of salt	

(Makes 12 buns)

DISSOLVE yeast and 2 teasp. sugar in warm milk. Add 2 cups flour, cover, and leave until spongy—about ½ hr. Add salt and the rest of the flour, mix well, and knead thoroughly. Cover and leave in a warm place to rise until double in size. Knead lightly and, using as little flour as possible, roll out to a piece about 8 in. by 12 in. and not more than ½ in. thick.

Spread with the butter and sprinkle with raisins, spice, and sugar.

Roll up tightly from the longer side and cut into slices not more than 1 in. thick. Pack these into a greased sandwich tin with the cut edge upwards. Bake in a hot oven about 20–30 min.

122 POTATO BREAD

1 lb. (5 medium) Irish potatoes
½ lb. (2 cups) sifted flour
1 teasp. sugar
1 packet Fleischman yeast

PEEL, wash, boil, and mash potatoes, saving the water in which they were cooked.
Add ¾ cup of this water to potatoes. Dissolve yeast and sugar in another ½ cup water, and add to potatoes. Stir in flour, beat well, leave in a warm place till double the size.
Shape into small balls, prove, and bake in very quick oven or fry in smoking hot oil.

123 CASSAVA BREAD

4 cups finely grated cassava
2 teasp. salt

PEEL and thoroughly wash cassava. Grate very finely, and pound as well, if liked. Add salt and mix well. Taking only 1 or 2 cupfuls of wet meal at a time, hold it in a strong cloth or piece of flour-bag and wring out all the juice. Crumble the meal between the palms of the hand and pass it through a fine sieve. Put a baking stone on an evenly glowing fire and sprinkle a little cassava meal on it. When the meal browns, brush the stone and put the hoop (about 5 in. in diameter) in place. Spread about ½ cup meal evenly in the hoop—thin bread is crisper and more digestible than thick bread.
As soon as steam rises shake and remove the hoop,

then flatten and press the bread into shape, using a wooden palette or large knife. As soon as the bread is firm enough turn it frequently. When thoroughly dry and stiff, stand it on edge in the sun or near a fire —this improves the flavour and prevents the bread losing its crispness.

Brown or toast, and butter before serving.

124 BAKING-POWDER BREAD

1 lb. (4 cups) sifted flour	$\frac{1}{4}$–$\frac{1}{2}$ pt. ($\frac{1}{2}$ to 1 nip) water or milk
4 teasp. baking powder	
1 teasp. salt	

Sieve flour, salt, and baking powder together. Add enough milk to mix to a soft dough, but one which is firm enough to handle. Knead lightly and quickly on a floured board. Shape, put in a greased bread tin and bake in a hot oven for $\frac{3}{4}$–1 hr. Test with a skewer or knife when firm and golden brown.

N.B.—All rising is done in the oven

125 CORN BREAD

(Using Baking Powder)

5½ oz. (1 cup) cornmeal	½ teasp. salt
4 oz. (1 cup) sifted flour	1 egg
2 teasp. baking powder	¾ pt. (1½ nips) milk
1 Tbsp. sugar	4 Tbsp. melted shortening

(Makes one 8-in. square)

Sift together cornmeal, flour, baking powder, sugar, and salt. Beat egg and add with milk. Melt and cool shortening, add to mixture and beat well. Pour into a greased shallow pan (*i.e.* dripping or roasting pan). Bake in a hot oven for about 25 min. Test with a skewer or knife when golden brown and firm. Cut into slices when cold.

CHAPTER 27

PASTRY

There are about seven or eight different kinds of pastry, but because many beginners find it somewhat difficult to make, and because space is limited, we shall deal only with the better known kinds, such as short-crust, flaky, and puff pastry.

RULES FOR PASTRY-MAKING

(1) Use as large a quantity of shortening as you can afford.

N.B.—Remember that although plenty of shortening improves the flavour and lightness of pastry, it also makes it richer and less digestible, and at the same time much more difficult to handle, particularly in a hot climate.

(2) Add baking powder (1 teasp. per cup of flour) *only* when using less than half the weight of shortening to flour.

(3) Keep pastry very cool while mixing, to avoid melting the shortening. For this reason handle it as little as possible ; use china, glass, or enamelled apparatus rather than wood (*e.g.* use a large bottle rather than a wooden rolling-pin and a glass or enamel topped table rather than a pastry board). Glass, china, or enamel is also easier to keep clean, and is, therefore, more labour-saving and hygienic.

(4) While mixing, work in as much air as possible,

both to keep pastry cool and to make it light, as air expands and raises the mixture during the baking.

(5) Start cooking pastry in a *hot* oven (400°–420° F.). Unless flour starts cooking at once it cannot absorb or hold the shortening. Unabsorbed shortening quickly melts out and the pastry is spoiled. When cooking large pies, etc., the heat can be reduced after the first 15 min.

Kinds of Shortening

Fresh butter gives the best flavour, but is too expensive for regular use.

Lard makes good light pastry, but does not give such a good flavour.

Margarine gives quite a good flavour, but because it contains a lot of water it does not make pastry so light.

Dripping (from stock or a roast) is only suitable for savoury dishes and after all gravy has been scraped from it.

Prepared shortening, such as *crisco*, etc., gives good results.

For ordinary household purposes a mixture of lard and margarine or lard and butter is recommended.

126 SHORT CRUST PASTRY

	Example
Use half the weight of shortening to flour	8 oz. (2 cups) sifted flour
½ teasp. salt per lb. of flour	4 oz. (½ cup) shortening
Iced water or beaten egg and water to bind	¼ teasp. salt
	Iced water or egg and water

SIFT flour and salt to aerate them. Rub shortening into flour, using tips of fingers and lifting mixture high in the bowl to work in more air. If hands are very hot use a fork.

Continue till mixture looks like fine crumbs. Using a knife, stir in enough liquid to bind to a *stiff* dough. If too soft the pastry is sticky when rolled and hard when baked.

Knead very lightly till free from cracks and turn on to a floured surface. Roll out with short sharp strokes, rolling forwards only and turning pastry round to obtain the required shape. Keep the same side uppermost throughout, as this always has the best appearance for the outside. Roll until $\frac{1}{8}$–$\frac{1}{4}$ in. thick. Use as required, and follow general rules for baking.

127 FLAKY PASTRY

8 oz. (2 cups) flour	Iced water
6 oz. ($\frac{3}{4}$ cup) shortening	Half a beaten egg white, if liked
$\frac{1}{2}$ teasp. salt	
1 teasp. lime juice	

SIFT flour and salt. Add lime juice to about 1 cup iced water. Wash shortening to remove excess salt, wrap it in a floured cloth and dry well. Divide it into *four* equal parts, and using one part only, rub it into flour as when making short pastry. Mix to a stiff dough and roll out to a long narrow strip about $\frac{1}{4}$–$\frac{1}{2}$ in. thick. Keep corners square. Take another portion of shortening and spread it in dabs over two-thirds of the strip, leaving about half an inch unspread at the edges, so that shortening is less likely to ooze out after folding. If beaten egg white is used, put dabs of it between the dabs of butter. Dredge lightly with flour. Fold in the small unspread border, then fold into three with the unspread part between the other two. Lightly press edges with the rolling-pin—this seals them so that air and shortening are less likely to work out. Put pastry aside in a refrigerator for 10 min., or wrap in greaseproof paper and put on ice. Place pastry on board so that folded sides are to right and left, roll out to a long narrow strip, being careful not to burst bubbles or force air or butter out at the ends. Continue to spread shortening, fold, seal, and roll until all shortening has been used up. Put in the refrigerator between each rolling. Use flaky pastry about ¼–½ in. thick. After cutting to required shape, gather scraps carefully, do not knead them, but arrange in layers, fold, and roll out. If kneaded, the pastry loses its flakiness. Glaze pastry just before baking, by brushing with beaten egg or milk if a savoury dish, and with milk or sugar and water for a sweet dish. Do not glaze cut edges because it stops their rising. Follow general rules for baking. When cooked, pastry should be golden brown, and firm on top and along cut edges.

128 PUFF PASTRY

8 oz. (2 cups) sifted flour	½ teasp. salt
6–8 oz. (¾–1 cup) shortening	1 teasp. lime juice
	Iced water

WASH and dry shortening as for flaky pastry and cut about 2 Tbsp. from the piece. Sift flour and salt, and rub in the 2 Tbsp. shortening. Mix to a stiff dough and roll out to a strip 6 in. long and ¼–½ in. thick. Put the rest of the shortening all in one large piece in the centre of the strip. Fold over both ends, turn in sides and seal all edges. Give pastry a half-turn so that folded sides are now to left and right. Roll out, fold, seal, and chill as for flaky pastry until it has been rolled and folded at least three times. Glaze and bake as for flaky pastry.

129 COCONUT PIE

6 oz. short crust pastry (*i.e.* using $1\frac{1}{2}$ cups flour	Pinch of salt
	$\frac{1}{2}$ pt. (1 cup) milk
1–2 eggs	$\frac{1}{2}$ cup freshly grated coconut
2–4 oz. ($\frac{1}{4}$–$\frac{1}{2}$ cup) sugar	

(Sufficient for 3 to 4 people)

MAKE pastry, roll out and line a pie-dish or deep plate. Prick the bottom and set on ice till required.

Grate coconut. Boil milk. Lightly beat egg (it need not be frothy), add sugar and salt and stir in hot milk and coconut. Pour filling into pastry case, bake at once in fairly hot oven (400° F.). Reduce heat after first 10 min., otherwise custard mixture will boil and curdle. Cook until pastry is golden brown and mixture set—about 30–40 min.

130 CUSTARD PIE

MAKE as for coconut pie, but omit coconut and add an extra egg and flavouring such as vanilla or nutmeg.

131 PUMPKIN PIE

6 oz. short crust pastry (*i.e.* using $1\frac{1}{2}$ cups flour)	1–2 eggs
	$\frac{1}{2}$ teasp. salt
	$\frac{1}{2}$ teasp. ginger
2 cups steamed or stewed pumpkin	1 teasp. cinnamon
	$\frac{1}{2}$ teasp. allspice
1 cup sugar	

(Sufficient for about 4 people)

Make pastry, roll out, and line a greased plate or shallow sandwich pan about 9 in. across. Prick the bottom and set on ice if possible. Strain off water and mash pumpkin. Beat eggs. Mix all ingredients and beat for another 2 min. Pour into pastry case, place in very hot oven. Reduce heat after the first 15 min. and bake for another 45 min. Pastry should be golden brown and pumpkin custard mixture set and uncurdled.

132 LIME MERINGUE PIE

8 oz. short crust pastry

Filling

2 cups water	3 egg yolks
4 Tbsp. cornstarch	4–5 Tbsp. lime juice
2 Tbsp. flour	2 teasp. grated lime peel
1 cup sugar	1 teasp. salt

Meringue

3 egg whites	1 teasp. baking powder, if liked
3 Tbsp. very fine sugar	

(Sufficient for about 6 people)

Make and roll out the pastry, and line a large greased enamelled plate or pie-dish. Prick the bottom and bake in a hot oven till crisp and brown, about 20 min.

Filling.—Put water to boil. Mix cornstarch, flour, and sugar with an extra half cup of water, mix in egg yolks lightly beaten and add *slowly* to boiling water. Cook 5 min. (using double cooker if possible) ; stir constantly. Remove from fire, add lime juice, peel, and salt. Pour into baked crust.

Meringue.—Beat egg whites until very stiff, then beat n sugar *only* 1 *teasp.* at a time. Add baking powder, if liked. Spread thickly over filling. Bake in a moderate oven until light brown and slightly crisp—about 10–15 min.

133 ORANGE PUFF PIE

6 oz. short crust pastry	3 egg whites
½ cup sugar	½ cup fine sugar
3 egg yolks	⅛ teasp. salt
3 Tbsp. hot water	½ teasp. baking powder
Juice and peel of 1 orange	

Make pastry, roll out, and line a greased plate or pie-dish. Prick the bottom and bake till crisp and golden brown—about 20–30 min. Mix half cup sugar, egg yolks, and water, and cook in a double saucepan until thick and smooth. Add orange juice and finely grated peel.

Beat egg whites till very stiff, gradually beat in fine sugar 1 teasp. at a time, so that mixture remains stiff throughout. Add baking powder and combine with first mixture. Pour into baked pastry shell and bake in a moderate oven till set and slightly brown—about 20 mins. Serve at once before the mixture falls.

134 GROUND-NUT MOLASSES PIE

6 oz. short crust pastry	¼ pt. (½ glass) milk
½ cup molasses	¼ teasp. salt
¼ oz. (½ Tbsp.) butter	¾ cup chopped parched nuts
1–2 eggs	
4 oz. (½ cup) sugar	½ teasp. vanilla essence, if liked
¼ oz. (1 Tbsp.) flour	

Make pastry, line a large enamelled plate or a pie-dish and set aside on ice. Heat molasses and butter to boiling-point, and leave to cool. Whisk eggs, and gradually beat in sugar and flour. Stir in the milk and salt, and then the molasses. Add chopped nuts and essence, and pour into pastry case. Put in a hot oven. After 10 min. decrease the heat and cook until filling is set and pastry is crisp and golden brown—about 20-30 min.

135 GUAVA TART

6–8 oz. short crust pastry (1½–2 cups flour)
About 1–1½ lb. guavas
½ cup sugar
Lime juice

Make the pastry and set aside on ice. (If no ice is available make pastry after preparing filling.)
Wash and peel guavas ; cut in half and remove seeds. Put a pie-crust raiser or egg cup in centre of pie-dish, then fill dish with alternate layers of fruit and sugar, beginning and ending with fruit.
Roll pastry to an oval a little larger than dish and about ¼ in. thick. Cut off a strip (about ½–¾ in.) from all round the pastry, damp rim of pie-dish and cover with strip of pastry. Moisten again and cover top of pie with pastry. Lightly press the two layers of pastry together, raise the pie-dish in left hand, and holding a knife with the handle slanting under the dish, trim off spare pastry. Holding edge in position with first finger of left hand chop edges of pastry to give a flaky appearance. Make small scallops with left thumb and blunt edge of a knife. Bake in a hot oven for 20 min. ; lower the heat and continue to cook for about 15 min. Pastry should be crisp and brown. Serve with coconut cream (see Recipe 129).

N.B.—Many other fruits can be used in place of guava, *e.g.* apple, golden apple, pomerac, etc. As these are rather tasteless, add 2 or 3 cloves, 1 teasp. spice or a piece of ginger.

136 BUTTERSCOTCH PIE

4 oz. short crust pastry	1 cup milk
1 egg	Pinch of salt
½ cup brown sugar	1½ Tbsp. butter
2 Tbsp. cornstarch	½ teasp. vanilla essence

MAKE the pastry, roll out and line a greased plate or pie-dish. Prick the bottom and bake till crisp and brown—about 20–30 min.

Separate yolk and white of egg, beat yolk and sugar. Mix cornstarch with enough cold water to make a smooth paste and add to egg yolk. Boil and stir in the milk and salt. Cook mixture in a double saucepan until thick—about 7 min. Remove from fire, add butter and vanilla and cool. Whisk egg white stiffly, fold it lightly into cornstarch mixture, pour into baked pastry shell, and bake in a moderate oven till well risen and slightly brown—about 15–20 min.

137 CREAM HORNS

8 oz. flaky or puff pastry
Jam
White sugar

MAKE the pastry and set on ice. Prepare about 8 cones—these may be of tin or stiff white paper. Brush over with oil or butter. Roll out pastry to about ⅛–¼ in. Cut strips about 1 in. wide and 20 in. long. Wind them around the prepared cones, starting from the point. Brush with milk or egg white and sprinkle with sugar. Bake in a hot oven till crisp and pale brown—about 20–30 min. Cool, put a teasp. jam in each and fill with real or mock cream (see Recipe 138).

138 MOCK CREAM

3 cups icing sugar	1 teasp. essence
½ cup fresh butter	1 egg white

Cream the butter and gradually work in the icing sugar. Stiffly beat the egg white and fold it into the butter mixture. Flavour and freeze before using.

139 BEEF PIES

8 oz. short crust pastry (*i.e.* using 2 cups flour and other ingredients in proportion)

FILLING

¾ lb. beef	1 teasp. salt
2 Tbsp. oil	¼ teasp. pepper
Onion, chive, thyme, tomato to taste	Worcester Sauce, if liked

MIX pastry and put on ice while preparing filling. If no ice is available, prepare filling first.

Clean and cut up meat and seasonings. Brown seasonings to develop flavour, and stand on one side. Brown meat, cover and simmer for 10–15 min. (This makes it very much easier to mince.) Chop or mince it with seasonings; add sauce, if liked. Roll out pastry $\frac{1}{8}$–$\frac{1}{4}$ in. thick, cut in circles about 3 in. across and reserve the best eight for covers. Put the others in greased pie-pans, add about 2 teasp. filling, damp round edge of pastry and put on cover. Press edges of pastry together and using the sharp edge of a knife parallel with edge of pie, chop the two layers together to give a flaky look. Make a small hole to let out the steam. Bake in a hot oven till firm and golden brown—about 20–30 min., or fry in smoking hot oil (in this case use less shortening for the pastry).

140 STEAK AND KIDNEY PIE

8 oz. flaky or puff pastry	$\frac{1}{2}$ Tbsp. flour
1 lb. beef steak	1 teasp. salt
1 sheep's kidney or $\frac{1}{4}$ lb. beef kidney	$\frac{1}{3}$ teasp. pepper
	$\frac{1}{2}$ cup stock or water

WIPE meat; skin, wash, and dry kidney. Cut meat into large thin slices, and kidney into small pieces. Season meat, then roll pieces of kidney and fat in slices of beef. Coat with flour, brown, add water or stock and stew for $\frac{3}{4}$ hr. Put meat in pie-dish and cool.

Make pastry, cut a narrow strip and line damped rim of pie-dish. Damp this strip of pastry, then cover top of pie. Press layers of pastry together, trim and decorate as for guava tart, but making large instead of small scallops. Make a small hole to let out steam. Brush with egg or milk. Bake in a hot oven about 1 hr. Add stock if necessary.

141 VEAL AND HAM PIE

8 oz. flaky or puff pastry	1 teasp. chopped parsley
1 lb. fillet of veal	$\frac{1}{2}$ teasp. grated lime peel
4 oz. bacon or ham	1 teasp. salt
1 hard-boiled egg	$\frac{1}{3}$ teasp. pepper
	$\frac{1}{2}$ cup white stock

MAKE in the same way as Steak and Kidney Pie, but cut meat into cubes and arrange filling in layers. Bake $\frac{3}{4}$ hr.

142 RUSSIAN FISH PIE

8 oz. flaky or puff pastry (2 cups flour)	$\frac{1}{8}$ teasp. white pepper
$\frac{1}{2}$ lb. skinned and boned fish	$\frac{1}{2}$ teasp. lime juice
1 hard-boiled egg	SAUCE
1 teasp. chopped parsley	1 Tbsp. flour
$\frac{1}{2}$ teasp. salt	1 Tbsp. butter
	$\frac{1}{4}$ cup milk

Make pastry and set aside to cool. (If no ice is available, prepare filling first.)
Melt the butter for the sauce and stir in flour without browning. Gradually add milk, stirring all the time, and boil till thick and smooth. Set aside to cool. Clean, bone, and skin fish. Cut into small neat pieces and add to sauce with chopped parsley, sliced egg, pepper and salt. Roll out pastry to about 8 in. square and about ¼–½ in. thick. Turn pastry so that best side is downwards, place filling in centre, damp around edge of pastry and fold in envelope shape. Decorate, brush with egg, make a hole to let out steam. Bake in a hot oven for ¾ hr.—reduce heat if necessary after first 10 min.

N.B.—Salt fish or cooked fresh fish may be used in place of fresh raw fish. When using salt fish, scald it first, then skin, bone, and flake it. Omit salt from the filling.

143 SHRIMP PATTIES

12 oz. flaky or puff pastry (3 cups flour)
½ lb. shrimps

Thick Sauce

3 Tbsp. butter
4 Tbsp. flour
½ pt. (1 cup) milk
1 egg yolk
½ teasp. salt
⅛ teasp. pepper

(Sufficient to make 8 medium-sized patties)

Make pastry and set on ice. Roll out to ½ in. thick and cut out 8 rounds about 2–2½ in. across. With a smaller cutter cut a circle out of the centre, leaving rings only. Fold small circles inside uncut pastry and roll out again. Cut 8 more circles of the larger size, damp tops and put a ring on each one. Brush top only with beaten egg or milk, and bake in a hot oven till brown on top and firm at the cut edge—about 30–35 min.

Wash and scald the shrimps. Shell them, cut open along the back and remove black thread. Melt the butter, add shrimps, cover and cook for about 7 min. without browning; shake pan to prevent sticking. Remove shrimps from pan, add flour, and gradually stir in the milk, about $\frac{1}{3}$ at a time, boiling the sauce after each addition of milk, and cooking about 7 min. in all. Cool slightly, add egg yolk, and cook again without boiling until egg thickens. Add shrimps (cut into pieces if necessary) and fill hollows in pastry cases. Garnish with parsley or cayenne. Serve hot or cold.

CHAPTER 28

CAKES

Many people prefer home-made cakes to bought ones, and even those who don't are sometimes unable to buy what they like, so that recipes for cakes are always useful. It is not necessary to know a great many cake recipes, because if we have a few standard (or master) recipes, we can make a number of different cakes simply by changing the flavouring.

It is also possible to provide a greater variety by mixing the ingredients in different ways. There are four chief ways of making cakes :

(1) *The Rubbing-in Method*

Flour and shortening (butter, etc.) are mixed together till crumby. This method is good for rather simple buns and cakes, and is also used for pastry.

(2) *The Batter or Gingerbread Method*

Shortening is melted and cooled before being mixed with flour. This method is used for fairly plain cakes and muffins, etc.

(3) *The Creaming Method*

Shortening and sugar are beaten together till creamy. This is a favourite way of mixing cakes—it is excellent for rich Christmas and wedding cakes, and just as good when used for plain butter sponge or Madeira cake.

(4) *Whisking or Sponging Method*

Eggs and sugar are beaten until stiff and frothy. This method is used for plain sponges which are very light and digestible, but because they contain little or no shortening they get stale very quickly.

GENERAL RULES FOR CAKE-MAKING

(1) Before starting work, collect all the bowls, spoons, and other apparatus needed. It is inconvenient to go back to a drawer or press with floury hands, and a cake mixture should not stand about after beating.
Grease cake pans with a saltless fat, *e.g.* fresh butter, sweet oil, lard, or margarine which has been melted and skimmed. Flour cake pans if liked, or if to be used for very rich cakes line them with greased paper.

(2) Use good quality ingredients—one bad egg or a little musty flour will ruin a cake.

(3) Prepare all ingredients carefully before mixing them together :

Wash salt butter. Margarine (which is only about half the price) can be used for small buns and economical cakes. Sift flour several times—this not only removes impurities, but mixes air with the flour. Air will help to make the cake light.
Pick and clean currants, sultanas, etc. They may be cleaned by washing and then drying in a clean towel or in the sun, or by rubbing in a little flour which must afterwards be sifted from the currants and thrown away. If wet fruit is used it may make a cake heavy, and the cake will not keep well.

(4) Measure ingredients carefully. Do not use too much baking powder (or soda)—this spoils the flavour of a cake. Remember that all measures must be *level.*

(5) Try to work plenty of air into a cake. Do this by thorough sifting and beating. Air expands when the mixture is baked, and this makes the cake rise well.

(6) Bake the cake immediately the mixing is finished. If allowed to stand, the air bubbles gradually fall and the baking powder may lose some of its strength.

(7) See that the oven is properly heated before putting in the cake. (See Oven Temperatures in chapter on Baking, page 130.) Small buns need a hot oven to brown them quickly.
Large cakes need a moderate oven, otherwise the outside is overcooked before the middle is done.

(8) Open the oven door *as little as possible,* and never bang it. Constant opening cools the oven and makes the cake fall.

(9) When cooked the cake should be well risen, golden brown (dark brown for a rich fruit cake), firm on top, and slightly shrunken away from the side of the pan. When it looks like this and not before, test the *centre* with a clean warm skewer (meat pin) or knife. If no soft uncooked mixture sticks to the skewer, the cake is done.

(10) Do not leave the cake in a draught when it is first taken from the oven. Leave it in the tin for about 5 min., then turn it upside down. Loosen with a knife if necessary. Remove any paper and place right side up on a wire tray. Protect from flies.

The Rubbing-in Method

144 STANDARD RECIPE FOR SIMPLE BUNS

½ lb. (1 cup) sifted flour	Pinch of salt
3 oz. (6 Tbsp.) shortening	2 teasp. baking powder
3–4 oz. (about ½ cup) sugar	1 egg
	2–3 Tbsp. milk or water

(To make about 10–12)

GREASE small cake tins (pie pans) and prepare ingredients. Measure and sift flour and salt into a mixing bowl. Add shortening, and using the finger-tips (or a fork if the hands are hot) rub them together till they look like fine crumbs. Lift the flour high in the bowl while doing so—this works in more air. Stir in baking powder and sugar. Beat egg thoroughly, and use to bind mixture to a *stiff* dough. Add milk or water if needed. Knead lightly and divide into buns. Bake in a very hot oven for 15–20 min.

145 ROCK BUNS

To standard recipe (144) add :

3¾ oz. (4½ Tbsp.) currants	½ teasp. ground ginger or mixed spice
1 oz. (4 Tbsp.) chopped citron or other peel	

MAKE in usual way. Arrange in rough-looking heaps and sift over with sugar before baking. If liked, rock buns may be made richer by adding extra shortening and a larger quantity of currants.

146 COCONUT BUNS

To standard recipe (144) add :

1 cup grated coconut and 1 extra egg

147 RASPBERRY (STRAWBERRY) BUNS

MAKE 10 or 12 buns as in Recipe 144. After shaping, press a hole in the centre of each, fill hole with ½ teasp. raspberry (or strawberry) jam and close it up again. Brush over with milk, sprinkle with sugar, and bake in the usual way.

148 CHOCOLATE BUNS

To standard recipe (144) add :

- 2 Tbsp cocoa powder
- ½ teasp. vanilla essence
- 2 oz. (4 Tbsp.) extra sugar

SIFT cocoa powder with flour, add essence to egg, and bake in the usual way.

149 ECONOMICAL SULTANA CAKE

- ½ lb. (2 cups) sifted flour
- 4 oz. (½ cup) shortening
- 4 oz. (½ cup) sugar
- 2 teasp. baking powder
- Pinch of salt
- ¼ lb. (⅔ cup) sultanas
- Grated rind of 1 lime
- 2 eggs
- Milk or water to mix

MAKE in the same way as standard recipe (144), adding enough milk to mix to a very stiff paste or batter. Beat well with a wooden spoon. Turn into a greased floured cake pan and bake in a hot oven for 1–1½ hr. Decrease the heat after the first half-hour. Follow general rules for cake.

150 SCONES

- 4 oz. (1 cup) sifted flour
- 1 teasp. baking powder, or ½ teasp. bicarbonate (baking) soda, ½ teasp. cream of tartar, or some sour milk
- ½–1 oz. (1 or 2 Tbsp.) shortening
- ½ oz. (1 Tbsp.) sugar
- Pinch salt
- Milk to mix
- Currants or sultanas, if liked

(To make 9 small scones)

Make in the same way as simple buns (Recipe 144). Mix to a dough which is just stiff enough to roll out. Roll to ¾ in. to 1 in. thick. Cut into small rounds, brush the top with milk and bake in a very hot oven for about 10 min. Serve hot or cold. Split open and butter.

151 STANDARD RECIPE FOR ECONOMICAL BISCUITS

½ lb. (2 cups) sifted flour
2 teasp. baking powder
Pinch salt
1 egg
1–2 oz. (2–4 Tbsp.) shortening
About ¼ pt. (½ glass) milk or milk and water

(To make 12–14 biscuits)

Make in the same way as simple buns, using enough milk to mix to a dough which can be rolled out. Roll to about ¼ in. to ½ in. thick. Cut into rounds with a cutter or glass. Bake in a hot oven for 10–12 min.

152 WHOLEWHEAT BISCUITS

Make in the same way as standard recipe (151), but use only 1 cup white flour and add 1 cup wholewheat flour and 2–4 Tbsp. sugar.

153 CHEESE BISCUITS

Omit shortening from standard recipe (151), and add to the flour 8 Tbsp. finely grated cheese.

154 BROWN SUGAR BISCUITS

Mix and shape the biscuits in the usual way. Spread the top with butter and sprinkle thickly with brown sugar mixed with a little spice. Bake for about 15 min.

The Batter or Gingerbread Method

155 STANDARD RECIPE FOR CAKES

- 12 oz. (3 cups) sifted flour
- 8 oz. (⅔ cup) treacle or molasses
- 4 oz. (½ cup) shortening (lard is often used)
- 2 eggs
- 4 oz. (½ cup) sugar (brown sugar is generally used)
- 1 teasp. bicarbonate (baking) soda, or 3 teasp. baking powder
- ½ gill (¼ glass) milk or water

Gently heat shortening, sugar, and molasses together till liquid—cool but do not allow them to harden again. Sift flour and soda together. Beat eggs well. Gradually stir treacle, eggs, and milk into flour. Beat lightly for not more than 1 min. Pour into a lined cake pan and bake in a *moderate* oven for 1½–2 hr.

Follow general rules for cake-making.

156 GINGERBREAD

To standard recipe (155) add :

- 2 teasp. finely ground ginger
- 2 oz. (or about ½ cup) chopped candied peel
- 1 oz. (about 2 Tbsp.) chopped nuts, if liked

Sift ginger with the flour. Add peel and nuts with eggs, etc. Bake as for the standard recipe (155).

157 PARKIN

Use 12 oz. (2½ cups) oatmeal instead of flour and add 2 oz. (½ cup) chopped peel to Recipe 155. Divide into pieces the size of a walnut, place on a greased tray, and bake.

158 STANDARD RECIPE FOR MUFFINS OR SCONES

½ lb. (2 cups) sifted flour	Pinch salt
2 teasp. baking powder	1 or 2 eggs
½ oz. (1 Tbsp.) sugar	Milk or water to mix
4 Tbsp. melted shortening	

(To make about 14–15)

MELT and cool shortening. Sift flour, salt, and baking powder together. Beat eggs well. Mix sugar, shortening, and eggs with flour and add enough milk to mix to a stiff batter. Half fill greased muffin pans and bake in a moderately hot oven for about 20 min.

159 CORNMEAL MUFFINS

¾ cup cornmeal	4 Tbsp. shortening
1¼ cups flour	Pinch salt
2 teasp. baking powder	1 egg.
2 Tbsp. sugar	Milk or water to mix

(To make 12)

SIFT cornmeal with flour and make as for standard recipe (158).

160 BRAN MUFFINS

⅔ cup bran	4 Tbsp. brown sugar or molasses
1⅓ cup flour	4 Tbsp. shortening
2 teasp. baking powder	Pinch salt
1 egg	

MIX bran with flour, heat molasses and butter together, and make as for standard recipe (158).

161 CRUMB MUFFINS

FOLLOW standard recipe (158), and use 2 cups stale bread-crumbs and only 1 cup flour.

162 COCONUT MUFFINS

FOLLOW standard recipe (158), and add ½ cup grated coconut, use 1 egg (the shortening may be left out).

163 MOLASSES COOKIES

- ½ cup molasses
- 2 oz. (¼ cup) shortening
- 5 oz. (1¼ cup) flour
- ½ Tbsp. finely ground ginger
- 1½ teasp. bicarbonate (baking) soda
- 1 Tbsp. warm milk
- ½ teasp. salt

(To make about 20)

HEAT molasses and add shortening. Sift flour, ginger, and salt together. Gradually stir flour into molasses. Dissolve soda in warm milk and add to mixture. Drop spoonfuls of the batter on a greased baking sheet, leaving at least 1 in. between each, or thoroughly chill the mixture and when firm shape into a roll and cut slices. Bake in a moderate oven (325° F.) for about 10–15 min.

164 SWEET POTATO BISCUITS

- ¾ cup mashed sweet potato
- ¼ glass milk
- 4 Tbsp. melted butter
- 1¼ cups sifted flour
- 2 teasp. baking powder
- 2 Tbsp. sugar (omit if to be used with meat)
- ½ teasp. salt

MIX mashed potato, milk, and melted butter, and beat well. Sift and stir in the remaining ingredients. Turn on to a floured board, knead lightly and roll out to ½ in. thick. Cut into rounds, place on a greased baking sheet, and bake in a hot oven for 15–20 min. Serve as a tea biscuit, or omit sugar and use as a garnish for stews, etc.

The Creaming Method

165 STANDARD RECIPE FOR BUTTER SPONGE MIXTURE

1 egg	4 oz. (1 cup) flour
2 oz. (4 Tbsp.) shortening	1 teasp. baking powder
	Pinch salt
3 oz. (6 Tbsp.) sugar	½ teasp. vanilla essence
	Milk or water to mix

UNLESS sugar is already fine grind it with a rolling-pin. Cream (beat) sugar and butter together until white and creamy—use a wooden spoon or palette knife. Whisk eggs and gradually beat into sugar; if mixture begins to curdle add a little flour. Beat well. Sift flour and salt, and stir it lightly into the mixture, adding alternately with milk. Use enough milk or water to keep the mixture a soft "dropping consistency" (soft enough to drop from the spoon). Add baking powder and essence with the last third of flour. Turn into greased muffin tins or a small cake tin. Follow general rules for baking.

166 QUEEN CAKES

To standard Butter Sponge recipe (165) add:

2 oz. (3 Tbsp.) sultanas	1 oz. (5 Tbsp.) chopped peel, 1 egg

VARIATIONS

Add one of the following:

¼ cup grated coconut	2 oz. cherries
1–2 Tbsp. cocoa powder or 3–4 squares chocolate dissolved in milk	2 oz. chopped nuts
	½ teasp. ground ginger or other spice
	1 teasp. carraway seeds

167 BANANA CAKE

4 oz. (½ cup) shortening
12 oz. (1½ cups) sugar
2 eggs
1 cup mashed banana
1 teasp. lime juice
½ lb. (2 cups) flour
2 teasp. baking powder
¼ teasp. salt
Milk to mix
½ cup chopped nuts, if liked

MAKE in the same way as Butter Sponge (Recipe 165). Add banana pulp before stirring in the flour. Bake in a moderate oven (350° F.) for about 30 min.

N.B.—Egg white may be whisked till stiff and added separately if desired.

168 MADEIRA CAKE

8 oz. (2 cups) sifted flour
5 oz. (½–⅔ cup) shortening
5 oz. (½–⅔) sugar
Grated rind of 1 lime
4 eggs
2 teasp. baking powder
Large slice of citron for top of cake

LINE the cake pan. Make cake the same way as Butter Sponge (Recipe 165). Bake in a moderate oven for about 1½ hr. Place citron on top after the first 20 min. Follow general rules.

169 CORNSTARCH CAKE

6 oz. (1⅛ cups) cornstarch
2 oz. (½ cup) flour
6 oz. (¾ cup) shortening
6 oz. (¾ cup) sugar
3 eggs
2 teasp. baking powder
Vanilla essence to taste

MAKE in the same way as Madeira Cake (Recipe 168).

170 POUND CAKE OR CHRISTMAS CAKE

8 oz. ($1\frac{1}{3}$ cups) currants
8 oz. ($1\frac{1}{3}$ cups) sultanas
4 oz. ($\frac{2}{3}$ cup) raisins
4 oz. ($\frac{1}{2}$ cup) cherries
2 oz. (about $\frac{1}{2}$ cup) shredded peel
2 oz. (about $\frac{1}{4}$ cup) chopped nuts
2 teasp. allspice
2 teasp. cinnamon
$\frac{3}{4}$ teasp. ground mace
$\frac{1}{2}$ grated nutmeg
} or spice to taste

8 oz. (2 cups) flour
8 oz. (1 cup) butter
8 oz. (1 cup) sugar
4–6 eggs
$\frac{1}{2}$ cup molasses, if liked
$\frac{1}{4}$ pt. ($\frac{1}{2}$ nip) brandy or rum
$\frac{1}{8}$ teasp. soda

Pick and clean fruit, cut up or mince the raisins. If liked, soak the fruit in the rum or brandy. Prepare nuts and peel, and cut up cherries. Cream butter and work in sugar ; beat well. Whisk eggs thoroughly and beat into sugar mixture. Sift flour and spices and stir lightly into mixture. Add fruit and soda dissolved in a little warm water. Turn into a lined cake-pan and bake in a slow oven (275° F.) for about 3 hr.
Follow general rules.

N.B.—If prepared, mixture may be covered with greased paper and steamed for 2 hr., then baked in a slow oven (300° F.) for 1 hr.

171 SHREWSBURY BISCUITS

8 oz. (2 cups) flour
4 oz. ($\frac{1}{2}$ cup) shortening
4 oz. ($\frac{1}{2}$ cup) white sugar
1 egg
Grated rind of 1 lime

Make in the same way as Butter Sponge (Recipe 165), using only enough milk to mix to a firm dough (not a dropping consistency). Roll out thinly, prick all over and cut into fancy shapes. Place on a greased tin and bake in a moderate oven till pale gold colour—about 15 min.

N.B.—Any flavouring such as spice, nuts, chocolate, almond essence, etc., can be used.

172 CHEAP COFFEE AND MOLASSES BISCUITS

6 oz. (¾ cup) shortening
2 oz. (¼ cup) sugar
¼ cup molasses
¼ cup strong coffee
½ teasp. bicarbonate (baking) soda
¼ teasp. ground ginger } if liked
¼ teasp. ground clove } if liked

Make by the creaming method, but stiffer than Butter Sponge (Recipe 165), because the mixture must be firm enough to roll. Beat in molasses and coffee in place of eggs. Roll thinly and cut into fancy shapes. Bake in a moderate oven (375° F.) for about 10–15 min.

173 COCONUT COOKIES

2 oz. (¼ cup) shortening
4 oz. (½ cup) sugar
1 egg
½ teasp. lime juice
¼ pt. (½ glass) milk
6 oz. (1½ cups) sifted flour
1½ teasp. baking powder
⅛ teasp. salt
2 cups grated coconut

Make by the creaming method, but slightly stiffer than for ordinary Butter Sponge (Recipe 165). Add coconut with the flour. Drop small spoonfuls on to a greased baking sheet, leaving 1½ in. between each for spreading. Do not smooth. Bake in a moderate oven for 15–20 min.

174 AUSTRALIAN JACK

4 oz. ($\frac{1}{3}$ cup) brown sugar
4 oz. ($\frac{1}{2}$ cup) shortening
About $\frac{1}{2}$ lb. Quaker Oats
$1\frac{1}{2}$ teasp. water
$\frac{1}{4}$ teasp. bicarbonate (baking) soda
Flavouring *e.g.* lime juice, ground ginger, or essence

Cream butter and sugar. Dissolve soda in water and stir into butter. Stir in enough Quaker Oats to make a crumbly paste. Add flavouring. Knead lightly on a floured board. Press into a shallow greased tin—the mixture must not be more than $\frac{1}{2}$ in. thick. Bake in a very slow oven (250°–300° F.) until golden brown. While still warm mark in squares. The mixture will harden when cool.

The Whisking or Sponging Method

175 PLAIN SPONGE OR ANGEL CAKE

5 egg whites
5 egg yolks
$\frac{1}{2}$ lb. (1 cup) very fine sugar
$\frac{1}{4}$ lb. (1 cup) sifted flour
$\frac{1}{4}$ teasp. salt
1 Tbsp. juice and grated rind of 1 lime or $\frac{1}{2}$ orange

Whisk egg whites till stiff enough to form a peak, then gradually beat in half the sugar, adding about 1 teasp. at a time—the mixture should remain stiff. Beat egg yolks and orange juice with same beater until thick and pale, then beat in the rest of the sugar. Mix egg white and yolk. Sift flour and salt two or three times, then lightly fold (stir, not beat) flour into egg mixture. Pour at once into un ungreased pan—a special tube pan with a pipe up the centre is best. Bake in a moderate oven (325° F.) for 1 hr. if in a deep pan, or in a slightly hotter oven for 25–30 min. if in a shallow sandwich tin or small fancy tins.

176 CHOCOLATE SPONGE

Use ¾ cup flour and ¼ cup cocoa, and make in the same way as Plain Sponge (Recipe 175).

177 ECONOMICAL SPONGE ROLL

2 egg whites	Pinch salt
2 egg yolks	1 teasp. baking powder
½ lb. (1 cup) very fine sugar	4 Tbsp. cold water
¼ lb. (1 cup) sifted flour	Flavouring, *e.g.* ½ teasp. essence

Sift the baking powder with the flour and salt. Make in the same way as Plain Sponge (Recipe 175), using the water to keep the mixture to a pouring consistency. Pour into a shallow lined sandwich pan, spread thinly, otherwise it is difficult to roll when cooked. Bake on the top shelf of a quick oven for 7–10 min.—slow baking makes it crisp and difficult to roll. Tightly wring a clean towel out of very hot water. Sprinkle with plenty of sugar, and while the cloth is still steaming turn the sandwich on to it. Trim off any crusty edges. Spread at once with warm jam or jelly and roll up tightly. When cool remove cloth and sprinkle with fine sugar.

Miscellaneous

178 MERINGUES OR KISSES

4 egg whites	½ teasp. essence (if liked)
½ lb. (1 cup) very fine sugar (*e.g.* castor)	Chopped nuts (if liked)
(Grind the sugar if necessary)	Colouring (if liked)
	2 teasp. baking powder (if liked)

Whisk egg whites stiffly, and add $\frac{2}{3}$ of sugar very gradually, not more than 1 teasp. at a time. Continue to whisk until mixture will pull up to peaks (points). Lightly stir in remainder of sugar with baking powder, colouring, and essence or nuts if they are used. Shape with a spoon or an icing (fluting) pump on a baking sheet lined with greased paper. Bake in a *very* slow oven (about 250° F.) until firm—about 1–2 hr. Serve alone, or stick two merigues cases together with whipped-cream or ice-cream. If filled in this way decorate edges with chopped nut.

179 GROUND-NUT (PEANUT) MACAROONS

- 1 egg white
- 2 oz. ($\frac{1}{4}$ cup) fine sugar
- 5 Tbsp. finely chopped ground-nuts
- 1 teasp. essence
- 2 teasp. cornstarch, if liked

Parch and shell the nuts, then finely chop or pound them. Whisk egg white until very stiff, and gradually beat in sugar, 1 teasp. at a time. Lightly stir in nuts and essence, and cornstarch if a firmer macaroon is preferred. Drop small spoonfuls on a greased baking sheet, leaving at least $1\frac{1}{2}$ in. between them. Decorate each with half a nut. Bake in a slow oven (300° F.) till firm—about 20 min. They will harden as they cool.

CHAPTER 29

ICING FOR CAKES

THERE are four ways of mixing icing (or frosting) for cakes, and many different kinds can be made by changing the flavouring.

To Prepare a Cake for Icing

(1) See that the top is quite flat and not rounded. If necessary, cut it level and then turn it upside down, as the uncut surface will be less crumby.

(2) If overbaked, *grate* away any dark part.

(3) If no revolving icing table is obtainable, stand cake on an overturned plate, so that the rim of the plate will not be in the way when icing the sides. Stand this plate on a soup plate, so that you can turn it round more easily.

RULES FOR ICING

(1) Crush the sugar very finely, otherwise the icing may be lumpy.

(2) Beat icing thoroughly—this makes it smooth and glossy.

(3) See that the icing is thin enough to spread smoothly over the cake, but not so thin that it will run off. Test it on the back of a spoon—it should coat the spoon thickly and hardly drip at all.

(4) If the cake is needed quickly, use thicker icing—it will not take so long to dry.

(5) When necessary, smooth the icing with a large knife dipped in boiling water—smooth each place once only.

(6) Dry the icing in a warm place—if put in a slightly warm oven, leave the door open—too rapid drying cracks the icing.

(7) Put cherries, nuts, etc., in place before icing dries, otherwise they will not stick.

(8) When piping (fluting) a pattern on the sides of a cake, wait until the coating is quite dry, otherwise the pattern slips downward. Always squeeze evenly, but stop squeezing altogether before lifting the pipe at the end of a pattern. Hold the pipe absolutely upright when doing stars, dots, etc. Draw the pipe horizontally (sideways) for leaves, writing, etc.

If possible use a stainless steel pump and pipe. Tin ones are not good because they rust easily, and aluminium ones discolour the icing because of the lime juice or acetic acid in the icing. If nothing but an aluminium pump is obtainable, see that it is brightly polished before icing is put in.

People who have no pump at all sometimes use cones made from very stiff paper. The tip should be cut in fancy shapes. On the whole these are not very satisfactory.

180 GLACÉ OR UNCOOKED ICING

This is quickly made and cheap to use, but is less appetizing than the others.

½ lb. (1⅝ cups) icing (confectioners') sugar
About 2 Tbsps. water
Essence and Colouring to taste

crush sugar. Add flavouring, colouring, and enough water to mix to a thick coating consistency. Beat till smooth and glossy.

Variations.—Any flavouring such as orange juice, pineapple juice, coffee essence, etc., may be used. The icing takes its name accordingly.

181 CHOCOLATE GLACÉ ICING

- 2 oz. (2 squares) chocolate, or 2 Tbsp. cocoa powder
- 8 oz. ($1\frac{5}{8}$ cups) icing sugar
- $\frac{1}{2}$ teasp. vanilla essence
- $\frac{1}{2}$ teasp. butter

BOIL chocolate and butter in 1 Tbsp. water till creamy. Cool and continue as for Uncooked Glacé Icing.

182 BUTTER ICING

THIS should only be made by people who have a refrigerator, as it is not appetising unless firmly frozen.

- 3 oz. (or $\frac{1}{3}$ cup) unsalted butter
- $4\frac{1}{2}$ oz. (or 1 cup) icing sugar
- 1 egg yolk or white, Colouring } if liked

FLAVOURINGS

Use one of the following :

- 1 oz. (1 square) unsweetened chocolate melted over hot water
- $\frac{1}{2}$ teasp. vanilla essence
- $\frac{1}{2}$ teasp. almond or rose essence
- 2 Tbsp. orange juice and grated rind of 1 orange (add extra sugar if necessary)
- 2 teasp. coffee essence or add $\frac{1}{2}$ cup extra sugar and enough *strong* coffee to flavour

Beat butter until very creamy. Add egg yolk (if used) and gradually beat in finely crushed sugar. Colour and flavour to taste. If egg white is used, whisk it stiffly and beat it in *after* adding the sugar. This is sometimes called Japanese Icing.

183 AMERICAN OR BOILED ICING

Most people agree that this is the nicest kind to eat. It is not easy to use it for piping decoration because it dries very quickly.

For one half-pound cake use :

$\frac{3}{4}$ lb. ($1\frac{1}{2}$ cups) granulated (or No. 1) sugar	$\frac{1}{4}$ pt. ($\frac{1}{2}$ glass) water
	2 egg whites
	1 teasp. essence

Heat sugar and water and let sugar dissolve without stirring or boiling. Heat to boiling-point, and boil until syrup will spin a long thread when dropped from the spoon. Meanwhile, whisk egg whites stiffly. Gradually pour syrup on to eggs, whisking all the time. If icing seems too thin, place the bowl over a pan of boiling water and stir until mixture begins to get sugary round edge of bowl. Either spread smoothly over cake or roughen icing to give a frosty appearance.

184 COCONUT COFFEE BOILED ICING

1 cup granulated sugar	2 egg whites
$\frac{1}{2}$ cup brown sugar	$\frac{1}{2}$ cup grated coconut
$\frac{1}{2}$ cup coffee	Few grains salt

Make the syrup from the sugar and coffee. Continue as for American Icing (Recipe 183), and add coconut and salt after mixing syrup and egg white.

185 MOLASSES AND NUT BOILED ICING

1 lb. (2 cups) granulated sugar
3 Tbsp. molasses
¼ pt. (½ glass) water
2 egg whites
Few grains salt
1 teasp. essence or lime juice
1 cup chopped parched nuts

MAKE the syrup from the sugar, molasses, and water. Continue as for American Icing (Recipe 183), and add nuts and salt after mixing syrup and egg whites.

186 ROYAL ICING

THIS icing is very hard. It is the best kind for piping (fluting).

About ½ lb. (1⅝ cups) icing (confectioners') sugar
1 teasp. lime juice or 1–2 drops acetic acid—to break down the sugar and improve the icing
1–2 egg whites
Colouring, Flavouring } to taste

Lightly beat egg whites—they should not be frothy. Add about 2 Tbsp. finely crushed sugar and beat again. Gradually work in the lime juice and sugar until the icing is stiff enough for coating. Beat well and ice the cake. Prick any large bubbles with a darning needle, and leave the icing to dry. Reserve the remainder of the icing for piping, adding a little extra sugar as it must be stiff enough to pull up to points. Prevent it from hardening while the cake dries by covering the bowl with a damp cloth. Beat it again before using it.

187 ALMOND ICING

This is seldom used except on wedding or Christmas cakes, because ground almonds are expensive. When used it generally forms a foundation for Royal Icing.

½ lb. ground almonds	Flavouring of orange or lime juice, essence, brandy, or rum
½ lb. icing sugar	
1–2 eggs or 2–3 egg yolks	

N.B.—Egg yolks are often used rather than whole eggs where Almond Icing and Royal Icing are made together ; the egg whites can then be set aside for the latter.

Whisk egg and sugar over hot water till thick and frothy—the basin must not touch the water or the egg may curdle. This cooking makes the icing keep better—it need not be done if the icing is to be eaten within a few days. Brandy and rum also help to make the icing keep. Add flavourings and almonds and knead well. Sprinkle a pastry board with sugar and roll out icing to about ½ in. thick. Shape a strip for the sides and a round for the top. Cover the cake, doing the sides first. Smooth out any creases with a knife, and see that there is a sharp edge round the top. Leave to harden.

N.B.—Any surplus may be used up for marzipan fruit.

CHAPTER 30

PUDDINGS OR DESSERTS

COLD SWEETS OR PUDDINGS

188 MANGO FOOL

6 common mangoes, full but not ripe	$\frac{1}{4}$ pt. ($\frac{1}{2}$ glass) milk } for custard
About $\frac{1}{3}$ cup sugar	1 egg } for custard
	$\frac{1}{4}$ pt. ($\frac{1}{2}$ glass) water
	Cream if obtainable

WASH and peel mangoes and cut up roughly. Stew mango, sugar, and water to a pulp. Sieve or beat well. Heat milk and pour into lightly beaten egg; heat again without boiling until egg thickens. Stir all the time. Cool custard and then mix with mango purée and cream. Serve in ice-cream glasses. The mixture should be of the consistency of cream.

N.B.—Mashed bananas, stewed guavas, etc., can be used in place of mango.

189 MAMMY APPLE SNOW

1 large mammy apple	2 egg whites
2 oz. (4 Tbsp.) sugar	Cherries and angelica or citron to decorate
$\frac{1}{4}$ pt. ($\frac{1}{2}$ glass) water	

WASH and peel mammy apple, and cut up roughly. Stew mammy apple with sugar and water till soft, but not a pulp. Strain off all juice, and sieve or mash the fruit. Stiffly whisk egg whites, then lightly stir into the fruit pulp. Pile high in ice-cream cups and decorate.

190 GUAVA CREAM

About 1 pt. (2 glasses) guavas (pack tightly when measuring)
About 2 oz. (4 Tbsp.) sugar
1 pt. (½ glass) water
½ teasp. lime juice
½ pt. (1 glass) milk
½ oz. gelatine, *i.e.* 4 teasp. powdered or 4–5 sheets

N.B.—Use more gelatine if no ice is obtainable.

Wash and cut guavas in half. Stew them with sugar and water and rub through a sieve. Add lime juice. This amount should make ¾ pt. (1½ glasses) purée (do not use more than ¾ pt). Boil milk, add gelatine, and dissolve without further boiling. Chill purée and milk separately to prevent curdling. When cool mix the two, add more sugar if necessary, pour into a wet mould and leave on ice till set. Turn out and decorate with pieces of guava cut in a decorative way.

N.B.—Other fruit such as soursop, granadilla, or tinned peaches may be used in place of guava. These require no cooking.

191 COCONUT JELLY

1 pt. (2 glasses) milk
1–2 Tbsp. sugar
1 dried coconut
½ oz. (4 teasp. powdered or 4–5 sheets) gelatine

Grate the coconut. Heat milk and pour it over coconut. Leave to stand for about 5 min., then stir and squeeze coconut to extract full flavour and all the fat. Strain off coconut, pressing well. Re-heat the milk, add gelatine and sugar, and dissolve gelatine without boiling. Pour into a mould and leave on ice till set. Decorate with cherries, etc.

N.B.—If no ice is obtainable double the quantity of gelatine.

192 ORANGE SPONGE OR JELLY WHIP

Rind and juice of 2 oranges
2 oz. (4 Tbsp.) sugar
½ pt. (1 glass) water
½ oz. gelatine, *i.e.* 4 teasp. powdered or 4–5 sheets
2 egg whites

WASH and peel oranges very thinly. Add gelatine, sugar, and orange peel to water, and heat without boiling till gelatine dissolves. Strain, add orange juice, and cool. Add egg whites to mixture, place over a bowl of ice and whisk till stiff—about 15 min. Pile at once in a dish. Keep in a refrigerator till required. Decorate with cherries or sections of orange. If preferred pour into a mould after whisking. Set on ice, and turn out when firm.

N.B.—Packet jelly, which is already flavoured, may be used if liked. In this case use only half the packet, place in a measure and make up to ½ pt. with boiling water. Use no gelatine or orange. Add egg white, and proceed as above when jelly is cool.

193 FRUIT SALAD

1 banana
1 orange
1 grapefruit
1 apple
Piece of papaw
A few cherries
} or other fruit to taste

6 oz. (about ¾ cup) sugar
¾ pt. (1½ glasses) water
} syrup

BOIL sugar and water together till a thin syrup is formed. Set aside to cool. Wash and peel fruit, discard seeds, and cut all into neat pieces. Mix fruit in a glass dish. Pour on the syrup, of which there should be enough to float fruit. Chill before serving.

194 BLANCMANGE OR CORNSTARCH JELLY

2 oz. (6 Tbsp.) cornstarch
About 1 Tbsp. sugar
1 pt. (2 glasses) milk or milk and water

Flavouring

One of the following may be used:

Essence	Lime peel, Bay leaf, Spice } heated with the milk
1 stick chocolate or 1 Tbsp. cocoa powder	

Mix cornstarch and sugar (and cocoa powder if used) to a paste with a little milk. Boil the remainder of the milk and stir on to cornstarch. Pour back into pan, boil again for at least 7 min., stirring all the time. (If cooked for a shorter time, cornstarch is not digestible). When making larger quantities use a double cooker, and cook twice as long. Pour into a wet mould and leave till set. Turn out into a glass dish.

195 TRIFLE

5–6 sponge cakes or enough stale plain cake to fill a medium-sized glass dish	About 2 Tbsp. sherry, rum, or brandy
	½ cup milk or fruit juice
	½ pt. custard
Jam or tinned or stewed fruit	Cherries and angelica or citron to decorate

Slice sponge cakes, spread with jam, and pack into a glass dish. If fruit is used place between layers of sponge cake. Moisten with sherry or rum mixed with milk or fruit juice. Prepare either custard from powder (follow directions on tin) or egg custard.

To make egg custard lightly beat 2 eggs with 1 Tbsp. sugar. Heat ½ pt. (1 glass) milk and stir into eggs. Return to pan and cook until eggs thicken, but do not let mixture boil or it will curdle. Stir all the time. Cool custard and pour over sponge cakes. Decorate before serving. Use ice-cream glasses instead of one larger dish, if liked.

See also recipes :
178 Meringues
Ice-creams, pages 193-200

HOT SWEETS OR PUDDINGS

196 BREADFRUIT PIE OR SOUFFLÉ

2 cups breadfruit (cooked and strained)
½ cup sugar
½ teasp. salt
½ teasp. nutmeg
½ teasp. ground ginger
2–3 eggs
1 cup milk
½ cup cream, if obtainable

STEAM or boil breadfruit, strain, then sieve or mash. Mix all ingredients *except* egg white. Whisk egg white stiffly and fold lightly into mixture. Pour into a greased dish which may be lined with uncooked pastry, if liked. Bake in a moderate oven until well risen and golden brown—about 45 min. If pastry is used, have oven very hot for first 15 min.

197 SWEET POTATO PUDDING

3 cups freshly boiled sweet potatoes
¼ teasp. salt
2 teasp. honey or 1 Tbsp. sugar
3 Tbsp. butter
Juice of 1 large orange
2 eggs
Sherry or brandy, if liked
Cherries to decorate

IF possible crush potatoes through potato masher (ricer), otherwise use a fork. Measure after crushing.

Add all ingredients except egg whites and beat thoroughly. Whisk egg whites very stiffly and fold into mixture. Heap small moulds of the mixture on a greased baking sheet or turn into a greased pie-dish. Bake in a quick oven till golden brown. Decorate with cherries.

198 FRUIT CHARLOTTE

5–6 apples or other fruit, *e.g.* pomerac or banana
3 Tbsp. golden syrup
2 Tbsp. water
Grated rind and juice of 1 lime, or spice to taste
½ cup bread-crumbs
2 oz. (4 Tbsp.) brown sugar

WASH, peel, and slice fruit very thinly. Remove seeds, etc. Grease a pie-dish, and fill dish with alternate layers of fruit and bread-crumbs, packing tightly. Begin and end with bread-crumbs. Heat all other ingredients and pour over fruit. Bake 1¼ hr. in moderate oven.

N.B.—If no golden syrup is obtainable, use more sugar.

199 TROPICAL DELIGHT PUDDING

4–5 bananas
Juice of 1 orange
4 Tbsp. brown sugar
½ cup grated coconut

PEEL bananas, cut in half lengthways, and arrange in a greased pie-dish. Mix sugar and orange juice, and pour over bananas. Sprinkle thickly with coconut. Bake in a quick oven till bananas are soft and coconut is brown. Serve at once.

N.B.—Jam put between layers of banana may be used instead of sugar.

200 QUEEN OF PUDDINGS

¼ pt. (½ glass) bread-crumbs	1 Tbsp. sugar
½ pt. (1 glass) milk	1 oz. (2 Tbsp.) butter
Grated rind of 1 lime	2 egg yolks
	2 Tbsp. jam

MERINGUE

2 egg whites   4 Tbsp. *fine* sugar

HEAT milk, add crumbs, butter, lime rind, and sugar. Cover and leave to stand about 20 min. for crumbs to soften. Stir in egg yolks, pour into a greased dish, and bake in a moderate oven till set—about ¾ to 1 hr. Remove from oven and spread top with jam. Whisk egg whites very stiffly, then beat in very fine sugar, 1 teasp. at a time. Pile meringue on top of jam, sprinkle with sugar and bake in cool oven till crisp.

201 BREAD AND BUTTER PUDDING

3–4 slices bread and butter	1 Tbsp. sugar
1–2 Tbsp. currants and sultanas	Nutmeg or vanilla essence
	1 egg
	½ pt. (1 glass) milk

PICK and wash currants, prepare bread and butter. Arrange bread, currants, and sugar in layers in greased pie-dish, beginning and ending with bread. Lightly beat egg, add milk and flavouring, and pour over bread. Leave to soak 30 min. Bake in a moderate oven till set and brown on top—about 40 min.

202 RICE PUDDING

2 oz. (4 Tbsp.) rice	About 2 Tbsp. sugar
2 pt. (4 glasses) milk	Nutmeg

PICK and wash rice. Mix all ingredients in a greased pie-dish. Bake in a moderate oven till rice is soft and top is brown—about 1½–2 hr. Stir during the first half-hour.

N.B.—If pudding is required in a hurry boil rice in usual way, then mix with milk and sugar and brown in a quick oven. This method is not as good—the rice is not so nourishing or creamy, because it is swelled with water instead of milk.

203 CASSAVA PUDDING OR PONE

- 2 medium-sized sweet cassavas
- 1 small dried coconut
- 2 Tbsp. butter
- 1 teasp. baking powder
- 6 oz. (¾ cup) sugar
- ½ teasp. ground spice and clove
- ½ teasp. essence

PEEL, wash, grate, and mix cassava and coconut. Work in butter with a fork. Add sugar, baking powder, and flavouring, and enough water to bind stiffly. Put in a greased dripping-pan—the mixture should be about 1½ in. to 2 in. thick. Bake in a moderate oven till crisp and brown, about 1¼ hr. Cut into 2 in. to 2½ in. squares before serving.

N.B.—This mixture is always rather heavy. It is therefore filling but not very digestible. Some people cook and mash the cassava before using it.

204 CORNMEAL PUDDING

- 1 cup cornmeal or freshly grated corn
- 2 oz. (4 Tbsp.) butter
- 2 oz. (4 Tbsp.) sugar
- Pinch of salt
- 1½ pt. (3 glasses) milk or milk and water
- ¼ cup (4 Tbsp.) molasses
- ½ cup raisins
- Grated nutmeg and spice

CLEAN raisins. Heat milk and stir in the cornmeal. Mix all ingredients and beat well. Pour into a greased pie-dish, and bake about 2¼ hr. Serve hot or cold.

205 FARINE PUDDING

½ cup farine	½ pt. (1 glass) milk
Pinch salt	Spice or essence to flavour
¼ cup sugar	

Mix all ingredients in a greased pie-dish. Soak for ½ hr. Bake in a moderate oven till farine has softened and thickened milk, and till top of pudding is golden brown—about 2 hr. Serve hot or cold.

See also the following recipes :

69 Patriotic Pudding
68 Pineapple Pudding
131 Pumpkin Pie
133 Orange Puff Pie
135 Guava Tart
Etc.

CHAPTER 31

ICE-CREAMS

Both water ices or thickened ice-creams are most refreshing in a hot climate like ours. We have so many juicy fruits that there are many kinds of ice-creams that we can make.

GENERAL RULES

Allow about 1 qt. for 8–10 servings.
Flavour mixtures strongly, as freezing weakens the flavour.

Using a Freezer

(1) See that the freezer is clean and free from rust. After using it wash and dry metal parts thoroughly, but leave a little water in the wooden pail, otherwise the seams may open and make it leak.

(2) Do not fill container more than two-thirds full. The quantity of ice-cream always increases as it is beaten.

(3) Let the ice-cream mixture cool before you put it in the freezer or you will waste the ice.

(4) Use coarse freezing salt (1 part salt to 6 parts ice) in preference to kitchen salt which does not last so long.

(5) Pack freezer with alternate layers of ice and salt, beginning and ending with ice.

(6) Turn until mixture is stiff, then open container very carefully so that no salt gets into it. Remove beater, cover and pack tightly with newspaper and an ice-blanket or bag. Keep in a cool place till required.

Using a Refrigerator

(1) Beat or swizzle well before freezing—add stiffly beaten egg white if possible.

(2) Pour mixture into trays used for ice cubes and freeze in freezing cabinet (froster).

(3) When mixture is solid for 1 in. all round edge of tray, remove and beat it again, being as quick as possible. Put it back in the froster and finish the freezing.

N.B.—If you do not beat it, the ice-cream will freeze unevenly and be gritty.

Thickening Ice-creams

For three quarts liquid use one of the following :

(1) ¼ lb. (¾ cup) cornstarch or custard powder. Mix cornstarch to a paste with a little cold liquid. Boil remainder of liquid, then stir the two together. Boil in a double cooker for 15 min., otherwise cornstarch will not be digestible.

N.B.—Cornstarch may be cooked with only part of the liquid (*e.g.* water), and then combined with condensed milk, fruit juice, etc., after boiling.

(2) 1½ oz. (6 Tbsp.) flour. Prepare in the same way as cornstarch.

(3) ½ oz. (4 sheets or 4 teasp. powdered) gelatine. Dissolve gelatine in a little hot water and stir into mixture.

(4) 4 eggs. Beat eggs lightly. Boil 2 pints (4 glasses) of milk and pour into eggs. Return to pan and stir over fire till eggs thicken. Avoid boiling mixture or eggs will curdle.

N.B.—If cream or undiluted tinned milk is used, very little or no thickening is required.

206 COCONUT ICE-CREAM

(For a 3-quart freezer)

2 medium-sized coconuts
1 tin evaporated milk } or { 2 pt. (4 glasses) boiled
1 tin condensed milk } or { cow's milk
1 lb. (2 cups) sugar if fresh milk is used
Thickening in proportions given above

PEEL and grate coconut, and to it add 1½ pints (3 glasses) water. Mix well to extract milk, then strain through a fine cloth or sieve. Heat the milk, thickening, and sugar together, and add coconut mixture. Keep pouring this backwards and forwards from one vessel to another until cool; this emulsifies the globules of fat from the coconut and makes the mixture more appetising and digestible. Strain into freezer. Follow general rules for freezing.

207 GUAVA ICE-CREAM

(For a 3-quart freezer)

12 full guavas
1 tin evaporated milk } or { 2 pt. (4 glasses) boiled
1 tin condensed milk } or { cow's milk
About 1 lb. (2 cups) sugar if cow's milk is used
Thickening in proportions given above

WASH guavas and put to boil in an unchipped enamelled or brightly polished aluminium pan with 2 pints (4 glasses) water. (When boiled this should have reduced to about 1½ pints.) After boiling about 1 hr. strain, sweeten, and thicken guava juice. When quite cold (otherwise mixture will curdle) add milk. Follow general rules for freezing. When serving, decorate with pieces of red guava from which seeds have been removed.

208 SOURSOP ICE-CREAM

(For 3-quart freezer)

1 medium-sized soursop—full and ripe
A pinch of salt
1 tin evaporated milk } or { 2 pt. (4 glasses) boiled
1 tin condensed milk } { milk
About 1 lb. sugar if cow's milk is used
Thickening in proportions given above

PEEL soursop, mash in a bowl, and add 1 pint (2 glasses) water and a piece of lime peel. Mix throughly to extract flavour, then strain off the juice. Add another ½ pt. (1 glass) water to the pulp, squeeze and strain again to be sure that all the flavour is extracted. Add milk, sugar, thickening, and salt to juice. Strain into freezer and follow general rules.

209 GRANADILLA (OR BARBADEEN) ICE-CREAM

MAKE in the same way as Soursop Ice-cream

210 ORANGE ICE-CREAM

(For a 3-quart freezer)

Juice of 6 oranges—about 1 pt. (2 glasses)
1 tin evaporated milk } or 2 pt. boiled milk
1 tin condensed milk }
About 1 lb. sugar
Thickening in proportions given on page 194

HEAT milk, sugar, and thickening together. Prepare orange juice. Chill milk and juice separately. When both are quite cold, mix and freeze in the usual way. If mixed unchilled, the acidity of the orange will curdle the milk.

211 ORANGE WATER ICE

(Small quantity for a refrigerator)

3 Oranges	$\frac{1}{4}$ lb. ($\frac{1}{2}$ cup) sugar
Juice of 1 lime	1 pt. (2 glasses) water

(Sufficient for 4 to 6 people)

HEAT sugar and water to boiling-point and skim well. Wash and thinly peel the oranges and add peel to sugar and water. Simmer 5 min. Strain and add orange and lime juice. Follow general rules for freezing.

212 PINEAPPLE MILK SHERBET

(A small quantity for a refrigerator)

$1\frac{1}{4}$ cups chopped pine	$\frac{1}{2}$ lb. (1 cup) sugar
1 pt. (2 glasses) boiled milk	Juice of 1 lime
	Juice of $\frac{1}{2}$ orange

(Sufficient for 6 to 8 people)

PREPARE pine, reserving a few pieces for decoration. Mix fruit juice and pine. Dissolve sugar in the milk. Chill pine and milk separately to prevent curdling. When cold, beat the two together. Follow general rules for freezing.

N.B.—If a thickened mixture is preferred, dissolve 1 teasp. gelatine in the milk or make a custard using 1 egg.

213 BANANA ICE-CREAM

(A small quantity for a refrigerator)

2 crushed bananas	2 eggs
Juice of 1 lime	1 tin evaporated milk
$1\frac{1}{2}$ teasp. vanilla essence	$\frac{1}{2}$ pt. (1 glass) cow's milk
4 oz. ($\frac{1}{2}$ cup) sugar	Pinch of salt

(Sufficient for 6 to 8 people)

HEAT cow's milk and sugar together and pour on to beaten egg yolks. Stir over the fire until eggs thicken, but avoid boiling. Whisk egg whites stiffly. Mix all ingredients together, stirring in egg whites last of all. Follow general rules for freezing. Decorate with chopped nuts before serving.

214 MANGO ICE-CREAM

(Small quantity for a refrigerator)

½ pt. (1 glass) fresh mango pulp put through a sieve	1 egg or 1 teasp. powdered gelatine to thicken
1 pt. (2 glasses) cow's milk	¼ lb. (½ cup) sugar
	Few drops lime juice
1 tin evaporated milk	Colouring, if liked

(Sufficient for 8 to 10 people)

PREPARE mango pulp and chill. Prepare custard from egg and milk, or thicken with gelatine. Mix all ingredients and follow general rules for freezing.

215 VANILLA ICE-CREAM

1 pt. (2 glasses) cow's milk	2 eggs
	4 oz. (½ cup) sugar (less if condensed milk is used)
1 tin evaporated milk or condensed milk or 1 cup cream	Vanilla essence

HEAT milk and sugar and pour on to well-beaten egg yolks. Stir over fire till custard thickens. Whisk egg whites stiffly. Mix all ingredients, adding the egg whites last. Add nuts, etc., or serve with sweet hot sauce, if liked.

216 PEANUT ICE-CREAM

PREPARE a custard foundation. Sweeten to taste and add chopped parched nuts. Follow general rules for freezing.

N.B.—Cherries or stewed and chopped prunes may be used in the same way.

When small quantities of ice-cream are to be used as a sweet (dessert) they are often served with fresh or tinned fruit or with a hot sweet sauce.

217 PÊCHE MELBA

PUT half a peach in each ice-cream glass. Add a large spoonful of vanilla ice-cream. Decorate with very thick coloured fruit syrup and chopped nuts.

218 PEPPERMINT SAUCE

½ lb. (1 cup) sugar	Peppermint flavouring
¼ pt. (½ glass) water	Green colouring

BOIL sugar and water in an uncovered pan till a thick syrup is formed. Add colouring and flavouring. Pour while still hot over stiffly frozen ice-cream. Serve immediately.

219 AVOCADO PEAR ICE-CREAM

2 eggs	½ teasp. vanilla or almond essence, or other flavouring to taste
½ lb. (1 cup) sugar	2 medium avocado pears
1 pt. (2 glasses) milk	

(Sufficient to make 1 quart).

LIGHTLY beat eggs, add milk and half sugar, and cook in a double boiler until custard thickens. Add vanilla essence and cool mixture. Peel, stone, and mash pears (there should be about 1½ cups pulp) and add remaining sugar and almond essence. Thoroughly mix custard and pear purée. Follow general rules for freezing in a refrigerator.

220 CHOCOLATE SAUCE FOR ICE-CREAMS

4 oz. plain chocolate or ½ cup flaked breakfast chocolate	About ¼ glass milk
	½ Tbsp. thick sugar syrup, if liked

DISSOLVE chocolate in the milk. Add syrup if used. Serve very hot.

N.B.—The sauce should be thick.

CHAPTER 32

SWEETS, CANDIES, AND SUGAR CAKES

221 PINEAPPLE CHEESE OR FUDGE

1 pineapple	1 lb. (2 cups) granulated sugar

PEEL and grate pine, remove all eyes. Add sugar and heat slowly till sugar dissolves. Boil fast till syrup spins a strong thread. Beat for about 5 min., pour into a greased pie-dish or tin. Cut into squares when cool.

222 GUAVA CHEESE

WASH, peel, and rub ripe guavas through a sieve. Add 1 cup sugar to every cup pulp. Boil until mixture begins to shrink from the sides of the pan, stirring continuously. Test a little in cold water; if it forms a ball pour the mixture into a greased dish. When firm cut in squares and toss in fine sugar.

N.B.—The pulp left after making guava jelly can be used instead of fresh guavas, but neither taste nor colour is as good.

223 MOLASSES CAKES OR TULOONS

1 cup molasses	Flavouring, *e.g.* piece of
2 oz. ($\frac{1}{4}$ cup) sugar	orange peel, spice,
1½ cup grated coconut	ginger, or bay leaf

BOIL molasses, sugar, and flavouring until syrup spins a long thread when dropped from a spoon. Remove flavouring and add coconut. Beat well, and as it begins to thicken drop spoonfuls on a wet tin or banana leaf. Leave to cool.

N.B.—One cup parched ground-nuts or cashew nuts may be added. Remove skins from cashew nuts by scalding them. Tuloons made with nuts tend to spread; if necessary re-shape them before they are quite cold.

224 PULLED GROUND-NUT MOLASSES

½ lb. (1 cup) brown sugar	¼ glass water
1 oz. (2 Tbsp.) butter	Pinch cream of tartar or squeeze lime juice
2 Tbsp. chopped parched nuts	1 Tbsp. molasses

Boil all ingredients except nuts. Occasionally stir very gently. Test by dropping a small spoonful into cold water; when cooked it should form a hard ball. Pour the syrup into a greased tin and sprinkle the nuts over it. When the edges are a little firm, fold them in over the nuts. As soon as the mixture is cool enough to handle, oil the fingers, and lightly and evenly pull the candy for 8–10 min. Cut into pieces and leave to harden.

225 ORANGE OR LIME TOFFEE

1 lb. (2 cups) granulated or No. 1 sugar	2 oz. (4 Tbsp.) butter or margarine
	Juice of 1 lime or ½ orange

Melt butter, stir in sugar and juice. Boil for about 10 min., stirring gently. Test by dropping a little toffee in cold water; it should set and break with a snap. Pour into a greased tin. When half set mark in squares.

226 PLAIN VANILLA CARAMELS

1 lb. (2 cups) granulated or No. 1 sugar	1 oz. (2 Tbsp.) butter or margarine
3 Tbsp. condensed milk	2 in. piece vanilla bean
½ teasp. cream of tartar	¼ pt. (½ glass) water

Boil sugar, vanilla, cream of tartar, and water till it forms a hard ball when tested in cold water. Add milk, and butter in small quantities, letting each piece dissolve before adding the next. Boil again till it forms a hard ball when tested. Pour into a greased tin and mark in squares when half set.

227 COCONUT ICE OR SUGAR CAKE

1 lb. (2 cups) granulated or No. 1 sugar	1 cup grated coconut
¼ pt. (½ glass) water	Essence, Colouring } to taste

Boil sugar and water together. Test with a piece of twisted wire bent into a small ring; dip this into the syrup and blow through the ring; if small bubbles form, the syrup is ready. If no wire is obtainable drop a little syrup into cold water—it should form a *very soft* ball. Remove syrup from fire and beat until it begins to look "grainy." Stir in coconut, and as soon as the mixture begins to thicken pour half into a greased tin about 10 in. by 6 in. Colour the remainder and quickly pour over the first half. When cool, but not hard, cut into blocks.

228 CHOCOLATE FUDGE

1 lb. (2 cups) sugar (brown or white)	1 Tbsp. cocoa powder or 2 Tbsp. grated chocolate
¼ pt. (½ glass) fresh milk or 3 Tbsp. condensed milk, in about ¼ glass water	1 teasp. vanilla essence
	1 oz. (2 Tbsp.) butter or margarine

Melt sugar in the fresh milk or with just enough water to cover it. Add cocoa mixed to a paste with the condensed milk or with very little water. Boil for about 10 min. or until the mixture will set into a soft ball when tested in cold water. Stir occasionally. When cooked, add butter and essence, beat lightly, then pour into a greased tin. When cool, but not hard, cut into blocks.

N.B.—Chopped nuts, grated coconut or cherries, etc., may be used in place of chocolate.

229 MARSHMALLOWS

1 lb. (2 cups) granulated or No. 1 sugar	1 teasp. cream of tartar
1 oz. (8–10 sheets) gelatine	½ teasp. essence
¾ pt. (1½ glasses) water	1 egg white
	Colouring, if liked
	Icing sugar to coat

Melt sugar in 1 glass water. Mix cream of tartar to a paste with about 1 Tbsp. water, add to sugar and boil for about 20 min. or until the syrup forms a *hard* ball when tested in cold water. Break gelatine into small pieces and soak for 15 min. in the rest of the water (½ glass). Add to syrup and stir until dissolved. Set aside to cool slightly. Whisk egg white very stiffly and gradually beat in the syrup. Continue to beat until mixture is stiff. Add colouring. Pour into a tin lined with paper and thickly sprinkled with icing sugar. Sprinkle top with icing sugar, cover with paper, and press with a weight until set. Cut in squares and roll each piece in icing sugar.

N.B.—Chopped nuts, cherries, etc., may be added with the egg.

CHAPTER 33

DRINKS

Most doctors agree that everyone should drink at least 3 pt. (6 glasses) of non-alcoholic liquid every day. In the tropics we probably need more than this, because we lose much moisture from the body when we perspire.

Children, of course, should drink plenty of milk, boiled or pasteurized. Milk is also very good for adults.

Fruit drinks are good because they are rich in vitamins and mineral salts.

Tea and coffee are useful and refreshing. They are mild stimulants, and should not be taken too often or too strong.

230 TEA

Tea is made from the dried leaves of the tea bush. Buy a good quality, because cheap teas are often mixed with pieces of stalk or inferior leaves. Cheap tea will be weak and has a poor taste, so that extra tea has to be used. " Brick " or block tea is compressed tea made from inferior leaves, stalk, and tea dust. Although cheap it is hardly worth buying, because it has little taste and little strength.

To make tea for a few persons allow :

1 heaped teasp. good tea per person
1 heaped teasp. good tea for the pot
About 1 cup boiling water per person

For large numbers use less tea per person—for example, $\frac{1}{4}$ lb. tea will do for about 50 people.

The water *must* be boiling in order to draw out the full flavour of the tea, and it must be freshly boiled, otherwise it gives the tea a "flat" taste. Warm the teapot with a little boiling water. Pour off this water and put in tea. Carry teapot over to the fire and pour absolutely boiling water on to the leaves. Allow to stand about 4 min. and then use. (Some people strain the tea into a fresh warm pot at this stage.) Use the tea at once—long soaking of leaves extracts tannin, which causes indigestion and is definitely harmful. Serve tea hot with cold, boiled, or pasteurized milk, cream, or tinned milk. Serve sugar separately for those who like it.

231 ICED TEA

Make the tea in the usual way and strain after it has stood for 4 min. Chill thoroughly and just before serving add a lump of ice and a slice of lime.

232 COFFEE

Coffee made from the berries of the coffee bush must be freshly roasted and ground and kept in a tin with a tightly fitting cover or it will lose its flavour. The stimulating part of coffee, called caffeine, upsets some people, and for this reason a few firms now sell coffee from which caffeine has been removed.

Coffee can be made in several ways—using a jug, a saucepan, an ordinary percolator or a "drip" percolator. Whichever method is used, remember that fast or long boiling makes coffee bitter.

To make coffee for a few persons allow :

1 Tbsp. coffee per person
Pinch of salt
About $\frac{1}{3}$ of a pint of freshly boiled water
About $\frac{1}{3}$ of a pint of boiling milk

Use a smaller proportion of coffee for large numbers.

Where no percolator is available, measure coffee and salt into a hot fireproof jug or pan. Pour on boiling water, cover and infuse (draw) in a warm place for 10–15 min. Heat just to boiling-point, throw in a dash of cold water to settle the grounds, and strain into a hot coffee pot through a very fine strainer or a piece of muslin or flannel. Serve hot milk and sugar separately.

233 ICED COFFEE

CONDENSED milk or a mixture of milk and egg is sometimes used instead of boiled milk. Make coffee in the usual way, sweeten, add milk and chill thoroughly. Serve in small glasses.

234 COCOA

COCOA as well as being stimulating is a true food, because it contains some starch and fat. It is, therefore, a good drink for children or people doing hard work.

The amount of cocoa required per cup varies with the kind used. For one cup use :

1 stick cocoa or chocolate sold in the market, or 1 heaped teasp. cocoa powder	$\frac{1}{2}$–$\frac{3}{4}$ cup boiling water Boiled or condensed milk Sugar if necessary

Mix cocoa and sugar with boiling water, and boil it for 2–3 min. Most people forget to do this, and the starch in cocoa is then raw and causes indigestion. Add milk. Remember that the more milk and the less water you use, the better the cocoa will be.

Fruit Drinks, etc.

235 LIME SQUASH

4–6 limes according to size	3–4 Tbsp. sugar
	1 qt. (4 glasses) water

Wash limes and squeeze juice from them. Dissolve sugar in about 2–3 Tbsp. boiling water. Mix all ingredients and add ice just before serving. If limes are scarce use some of the peel to increase the flavour. Wash, peel very thinly, so that only green and no white skin is used; use 3–4 strips only and add to sugar. Pour on *boiling* water, cover, and infuse 10 min., then strain.

236 ORANGE OR GRAPEFRUIT SQUASH

These can be made in the same way as lime squash, but less sugar will be needed. Orange squash is improved by the addition of a little lime juice. Sour (Seville) oranges, which are so often left to rot on the tree, make a very refreshing drink—these need more sugar.

237 PINEAPPLE DRINK

Peelings from 1 pineapple	2 cloves
About 1 qt. (4 glasses) boiling water	Small piece dried orange peel, if liked
Sugar to taste	

Put peelings, cloves, and orange peel in a jug and pour on boiling water. Cover and leave for 1 day. Strain and sweeten. Use at once or bottle and keep 1–2 days.

N.B.—When pines are plentiful the pulp may be chopped and used with the peel.

238 COCONUT DRINK

THOROUGHLY chill the water from a green coconut. Add a little gin, if liked.

239 GUAVA DRINK

About 1 large handful guavas
1 qt. (4 glasses) boiling water
Sugar to taste
Small piece dried orange peel

WASH and cut up guavas. Prepare as for pine drink. Do not leave for more than 1–2 days in bottles, otherwise they will burst.

240 SOURSOP PUNCH

1 medium-sized soursop
About 1½ pt. (3 glasses) cold water
1 strip lime peel
Enough condensed milk or sugar to sweeten
Pinch of salt

WASH and peel soursop, mash in a bowl with lime peel. Gradually stir in 1 pt. water. Mix well and strain. Add another half pint water, and squeeze and strain again to be sure that all flavour is drawn out. Add salt and condensed milk or sugar. Chill before serving.

241 PONCHE DE CRÊME

Half tin condensed milk
¼ pt. (½ nip) rum
3 eggs
Sugar and essence to taste
Few drops lime juice

BEAT all ingredients lightly. Add crushed ice. Sprinkle a little angostura on top of mixture after filling glasses.

242 PONCHE DE CRÊME (Boiled)

6 eggs
1½–2 pt. cow's milk
½ lb. (1 cup) sugar
1½ pt. (3 nips) rum
2 oz. (6 Tbsp.) cornstarch
Vanilla essence to taste
Wine, if liked
Angostura bitters

Mix cornstarch with a little cold milk—boil the remainder and add to cornstarch. Stir the two together over the fire for 7 min. Cool and add beaten eggs. Swizzle and cook again until eggs thicken, but avoid boiling, otherwise mixture will curdle. Add rum and essence. Keep in a cool place till required. Add crushed ice and angostura before serving.

243 GINGER BEER

2 oz. green ginger
2 oz. cream of tartar
1 gallon boiling water
¼ cake yeast
Juice and rind of 2 small limes
1½ lb. sugar

Wash and pound ginger and add boiling water. Add juice and rind of limes, then cream of tartar. Cover but stir frequently. When lukewarm (tepid) add yeast dissolved in a little warm water. Mix well, cover, and leave to stand for 6 hours. Sweeten and bottle. Keep at least 3–4 days. Addition of a small quantity of rum makes it keep better.

244 MAWBY

1 heaped Tbsp. mawby bark
Small piece dried orange peel
½ in. piece of cinnamon
3–4 cloves
1 blade mace
6 pt. (12 glasses) cold water
2 heaped cups sugar

Boil mawby, orange peel, cinnamon, clove, and mace in 1 cup water till strong—about 5 min. Cool, and add 6 pt. cold water and sugar. Add plenty of sugar, as the sweetness goes off during fermentation. Strain into bottles, filling to the shoulder only, so that entire neck of bottle is left for froth. Screw down and leave for about 3 days.

245 SORREL

There are two kinds—red and white. The drink prepared from the white sorrel is more acid, therefore more water should be allowed.

- 3 cups sorrel (heaped) without seeds
- 3 pt. (6 glasses) boiling water
- A few grains rice or barley
- Piece of ginger ($\frac{1}{2}$ inch square)
- Piece of dried orange peel ($1\frac{1}{2}$ in. by $\frac{1}{2}$ in.)
- 6 cloves
- 1 lb. (2 cups) sugar

Wash sorrel, cut away seeds. Place in jar with ginger, orange peel, and cloves. Pour on boiling water, and allow to remain for 24 hr. Strain and sweeten. Pour into bottles, adding a few grains of barley or rice (this helps fermentation), and allow to remain for at least another day. Serve with ice.

For Barley Water, Carrot Water, Rice Water, Orange Punch, Egg Nog, see Chapter 43, Diets for Sick People.

CHAPTER 34

SAUCES

THERE are many different kinds of both sweet and savoury (salt) sauces—they are generally used for the following reasons :

(1) To make food more nourishing—*e.g.* butter sauce may be served with white fish which contains little fat.

(2) To moisten dry food—*e.g.* fried meat or steamed puddings are more tasty if served with sauce.

(3) To improve flavour and so make food more appetizing—*e.g.* a good tomato sauce can be served with re-heated food.

(4) To improve the appearance of food—*e.g.* steamed or boiled food which may be white and uninteresting looking is often coated with sauce.

Coating sauces must be made thicker than the flavouring sauces, which are poured from a sauce-boat.

246 CREOLE SAUCE OR GRAVY

1 ¢ (1 Tbsp.) fat pork
1 Tbsp. oil
1 Tbsp. cooking butter
1 tomato
1 small onion
2–3 blades chive
Sprig of thyme
½ Tbsp. vinegar
1 teasp. salt (less if salt butter is used)
Pepper to taste
½ Tbsp. flour
¼ pt. (½ glass) water

WASH and slice seasonings. Wash and cut up fat pork, heat on a slow fire to melt out fat. Add oil and fry seasonings lightly. Stir in flour, butter, and water. Boil up and add vinegar and salt.

N.B.—Flour and water are often omitted.

ORDINARY GRAVY

See Recipe 97.

247 BREADNUT SAUCE

1 doz. breadnuts	1 pt. (2 glasses) milk or white stock
1½ oz. (3 Tbsp.) butter	Pepper and salt to taste
½ oz. (2 Tbsp.) flour	

SCALD breadnuts, remove rind and skin, and pound them till smooth. Melt butter, add nuts, and fry to a pale brown. Stir in flour and stock and boil for 10 min., stirring all the time.

248 GROUND-NUT OR CASHEW-NUT SAUCE

2 oz. (or about 1 cup) nuts	1 pt. (2 glasses) stock
½ oz. (1 Tbsp.) butter	Pepper and salt to taste
½ oz. (2 Tbsp.) flour	Pinch of sugar, if liked

PARCH nuts, remove shell and brown skin, and pound or mince finely. (Nuts may be fried instead of parched, if preferred.) Melt butter, stir in flour, and fry to an even brown. Add nuts, and gradually stir in stock. Boil 5 min., and skim, if necessary.

249 MOCK APPLE SAUCE

(To serve with pork, sucking pig, and duck)

About 3 green common mangoes
Piece of lime peel
½ oz. (1 Tbsp.) butter
½ oz. (1 Tbsp.) sugar
¼ glass water

WASH, peel, and slice the mangoes. Cook them with the other ingredients till soft. Use a covered pan and stir occasionally. Take out the lime peel, and either sieve the mangoes or beat them with a wooden spoon. The sauce should be a thick purée. Serve hot.

250 WHITE SAUCE

For coating

1 oz. (4 Tbsp.) flour
1 oz. (2 Tbsp.) butter } to ½ pt. (1 glass) milk

Flowing (to pour)

¾ oz. (3 Tbsp.) flour
¾–1 oz. (1½–2 Tbsp.) butter } to ½ pt. (1 glass) milk

MELT butter in a small saucepan, add flour, and stir over the fire till butter is absorbed. (Don't let it turn brown.) Stir in milk, about one-third at a time. Boil up each time milk is added and stir all the time. Cook for not less than 5 min. Add pepper and salt to taste.

251 PARSLEY SAUCE

½ pt. white sauce
2 teasp. chopped parsley

STRIP parsley from stalk and wash thoroughly in Condy's Fluid. Dry it by squeezing tightly in a clean towel. Chop very finely. Make sauce and add parsley with salt, etc.

252 SHRIMP SAUCE

½ cup scalded shrimps
1½ oz. (3 Tbsp.) butter
¾ oz. (3 Tbsp.) flour
½ pt. (1 glass) milk
White pepper and salt to taste
Squeeze of lime juice

Scald shrimps ; remove skins and black cord down centre of back ; wash thoroughly ; cut up if very large. Heat butter, add shrimps, cover and cook until shrimps are tender—about 7 min. Take out shrimps and add flour. Continue as for white sauce. When sauce is ready add shrimps and lime juice with salt, etc.

253 BREAD SAUCE

(To serve with roast chicken or turkey, etc.)

½ glass bread-crumbs
½ pt. (1 glass) milk
1 small onion
2 cloves
4 black peppers (unground)
½ oz. (1 Tbsp.) butter
½ teasp. salt

Peel onion but leave it whole. Put all ingredients except bread-crumbs and butter into a saucepan. Heat to boiling-point, keep covered and allow to stand 15 min. to extract flavour of onion and clove. Strain. Add bread-crumbs and butter. Re-heat and serve in a hot sauce-boat.

254 MINT SAUCE

(To serve with mutton)

¼ pt. (½ glass) vinegar
3 heaped Tbsp. chopped mint
½ Tbsp. sugar
Pinch salt
2 Tbsp. boiling water

Wash mint in Condy's fluid. Dry well and remove stalks. Chop finely. Mix sugar, salt, and mint in a sauce boat. Add boiling water. When cold, add vinegar.

255 CREOLE PEPPER SAUCE—1

1 doz. red peppers
1 small *green* papaw
1 large onion
4 Tbsp. mustard
1–2 pegs garlic
2 Tbsp. salt
1½ pt. (3 glasses) vinegar
½ teasp. ground saffron
1 teasp. curry powder

Boil papaw in skin, then cut into small squares or strips. Scald, stone, and mince or chop peppers. Mince onion and garlic. Mix all solid ingredients, add vinegar, and simmer mixture gently for 20 min. Cool, bottle, and label.

N.B.—1 cup boiled salad beans may be added if liked. (Remove hard edges and cut in half.)

256 CREOLE PEPPER SAUCE—2

8 strong peppers
¼ bottle vinegar
3 ¢ mustard
1 onion (size of an egg)
1 teasp. salt
1 Tbsp. olive oil

Wash and cut up peppers. Take out seeds. Cut onion into small pieces. Put everything into a saucepan and let it boil for 20 min. This fills an ordinary sized bottle (about the size of a Fruit Salts bottle).

257 PEPPERS IN SHERRY

About 6–10 bird peppers
About ¼ pt. (½ nip) sherry

Wash and dry peppers and add to sherry. Keep in a stoppered bottle. Use with soup, etc.

258 MANGO CHUTNEY—1

25 green mangoes
½ lb. currants
¼ lb. raisins
½ lb. prunes or dates, if liked
¼ lb. green ginger
¼ lb. salt
1 whole garlic or garlic to taste
2 red peppers
2 pt. (4 glasses) vinegar

Clean and stone raisins, dates, and currants. Mince or chop them and mix with peppers and 1 pt. vinegar. Leave to infuse for 24 hr. Peel and slice mangoes and pound garlic. Mix all ingredients and boil to the desired consistency. Stir frequently. Bottle and label.

N.B.—Mangoes may be pounded with garlic if preferred.

259 MANGO CHUTNEY—2

1 doz. ripe mangoes
½ lb. raisins
¼ green ginger
1 whole garlic or garlic to taste
¼ lb. (about 1½ cups) tamarind
½ lb. (1 cup) salt
½ lb. (1 cup) sugar
1 qt. (4 glasses) vinegar

Wash and peel mangoes and cut flesh into strips. Wash and stone raisins. Peel and chop or pound garlic finely. Peel and cut ginger into dice. Scrape tamarind and discard seeds. Mix all solid ingredients. Boil vinegar, pour over mixture, and stir well. Bottle and label.

SWEET SAUCES

260 COCONUT CREAM

About 1 cup grated coconut	1 cup milk

HEAT the milk and pour it over the grated coconut. Let it stand for about 5 min. then stir and squeeze it to extract as much coconut fat and flavour as possible. Strain out the coconut, pressing it well. Chill the cream before serving.

261 BANANA SAUCE

2 medium-sized bananas	½ pt. (1 glass) water
1 clove and a small bay leaf	or other flavourings to taste
Pinch cayenne pepper	
½ teasp. guava jelly	

WASH and peel bananas and put all ingredients in a saucepan. Boil for 10 min., then sieve. Serve hot or cold.

262 CUSTARD SAUCE

1 egg yolk	¼ pt. (½ glass) milk
1 teasp. sugar	Flavouring to taste

HEAT milk. Mix egg yolk and sugar and stir in the milk. Strain into the saucepan and stir over a low fire until custard thickens. Do not boil or custard will curdle. Add flavouring. Serve hot or cold.

N.B.—This sauce can only be made thicker by adding more egg, longer cooking or boiling is useless.

263 JAM SAUCE

$\frac{1}{4}$ pt. ($\frac{1}{2}$ glass) water	1 heaped teasp. arrowroot or cornstarch
$\frac{1}{2}$ oz. (1 Tbsp.) sugar	Squeeze of lime juice
2 Tbsp. jam or jelly	Colouring, if liked
Piece of lime peel	

Boil sugar, water, jam, and lime peel for 7 min. Strain or simply remove peel. Mix arrowroot to a paste with a little cold water, add to sauce and boil again for 3 min., stirring all the time. Add lime juice and colouring.

Peppermint and Chocolate Sauce

See Ice-Creams, Chapter 31.

CHAPTER 35

USING UP SCRAPS; RE-HEATING FOOD

You will remember from what was said in the first part of this book that because heat destroys certain vitamins, raw food, or food only cooked for a short time, is more nourishing than food cooked twice, or for a long time. Heat also coagulates or hardens protein, and such things as meat may become dry with cooking because fat melts and water evaporates from it. Some vegetables are less nourishing after cooking, because boiling draws out the mineral salts. For these reasons the wise housewife tries to prepare just the right amount of food, so that no small pieces remain. Unfortunately this is not always possible, so we want to know the best way of using what is left over.

GENERAL RULES

(1) Make sure that the food is still fit to eat.

(2) Add nourishment in the form of egg, milk, butter, gravy, etc., to make up for any loss in the first cooking.

(3) Improve flavour with suitable seasonings or by adding some fresh food. Do not add any fresh food that requires long cooking.

(4) Re-moisten the food.

(5) Divide food into small pieces by mashing, mincing, or chopping, so that seasonings, moisture, etc., are well mixed up with the food, and so that it can be more easily made up into an attractive shape. While doing this, remove all pieces of skin, gristle, bone, etc.

(6) Never *re-cook* the food ; quickly *heat* it for as short a time as possible.

Suggestions for Using up Scraps

Dry Bread

Bake for rusks ; use for stuffing, bread and butter pudding, cabinet pudding, queen of puddings ; dry and crush for raspings, and use for coating fried foods, ham, etc.

Stale Cake

Use for puddings.

Dry Cheese

Toast or use for cheese pudding, macaroni cheese, cheese salad, etc.

Cooked Potato

Mix with meat for beef balls, shepherd's pie. Use in a salad, for stuffing, potato bread, etc.

Cooked Vegetables

Cooked vegetables, such as beans, peas, and carrots, can be used in a salad, or added to soup when it is cooked.

Boiled Rice

Make into cakes and fry. Use for milk pudding, etc.

Cooked Meat (Beef, Mutton, or Fowl)

Use for pies, rissoles, eggs in ambush, mince, curry, pelau, fritters, savoury pancakes, jelly, stuffed vegetables (*e.g.* tomato, melongene).

Cooked Fish

Use for fish balls, fritters, jelly (or cream), stuffed vegetables (*e.g.* christophine), Russian fish pie.

Bones

Use for stock, soup, or gravy.

264 MIXED RICE OR "COOK UP"

½ lb. cooked meat
¼ lb. salt meat, if liked
1 lb. (2 cups) rice
4½ cups water
1 onion
1–2 tomatoes
2–3 blades chive
Thyme and parsley
½ teasp. salt—more if no salt meat is used
½ teasp. pepper or piece green pepper
2 Tbsp. oil or dripping
1 heaped teasp. brown sugar

WASH and soak salt meat and prepare seasonings. Heat the oil, add sugar, and fry till it bubbles. Add seasonings, fry till golden brown. Cut salt meat into neat pieces, and add to seasonings with water, rice, and salt ; put to boil. Remove skin and bone from meat, cut into neat pieces, and add to rice when it is nearly cooked. If liked, add butter before dishing.

265 BEEF BALLS OR RISSOLES

½ lb. cooked meat
1–2 blades chive
Small piece onion, if liked
Parsley and thyme
1 small tomato
½ teasp. salt
¼ teasp. black pepper
½ lb. (2–3) cooked potatoes, or ¼ pt. or thick sauce or panada

THICK SAUCE OR PANADA

1 teasp. Worcester Sauce, if liked
2 Tbsp. flour
1 Tbsp. oil or butter
¼ pt. (½ nip) water or stock

PREPARE the seasonings and sauté (fry without browning) in a covered pot (this is because raw onion, etc., should not be mixed with cooked meat). If potatoes are used, mash and add salt if necessary. If a panada is used instead, melt the butter, add the flour, and gradually stir in the stock. Continue to stir and cook till smooth and very thick, so that it forms a ball in the pan. Cut away skin, gristle, and bone from the meat, and mince and chop it. Mix all ingredients, divide into required number of rissoles, and shape. Dip first in beaten egg or a thin batter, then coat with raspings or fresh bread-crumbs. Re-shape and press crumbs in place. Fry in smoking hot oil. Drain well. Serve on a plain d'oyley. Follow general rules for frying.

266 DURHAM CUTLETS

USE the same mixture as for beef balls, but shape them like small cutlets or chops. When fried put a 1 in. piece of uncooked macaroni in the thin end of each to look like a cutlet bone.

267 EGGS IN AMBUSH

4–5 eggs
½ onion
Small tomato
2–3 blades chive
Parsley and thyme
1 teasp. salt
½ teasp. black pepper

4–5 sausages
or
1 lb. cooked meat and panada
or
½ lb. cooked meat and
½ lb. boiled potatoes

HARD boil and shell the eggs. Prepare seasonings, meat, and potatoes or panada (made as in Recipe 265, but using 4 Tbsp. flour, 2 Tbsp. oil, ⅓ pt. stock or water). If sausages are used, skin them. Divide mixture into 4–5 equal parts, and using a little flour, flatten out to a circle about ½ in. thick. Use one part to enclose each egg, flatten slightly at each end. Coat and fry in the same way as beef balls. Cut in half and stand each piece with cut side upwards on a small circle of toast or fried bread. Serve hot or cold.

268 SHEPHERD'S PIE

½ lb. cooked meat
About ½ cup gravy or stock
½ teasp. salt
¼ teasp. black pepper or piece of green pepper
1 onion
1–2 blades chive
1 small tomato
Parsley and thyme
1 lb. (about 4–5) cooked Irish potatoes
1–2 Tbsp. oil or butter or dripping
1–2 Tbsp. milk

PREPARE seasonings and sauté (fry without browning) in a covered pan. Cut skin and bone from meat, and mince or chop it. Mix meat, seasonings, and gravy and place in a greased pie-dish. Mash potatoes, add milk, butter, and if necessary a little salt and pepper. Pile potato mixture over meat to form a crust. Smooth with a wet knife, then decorate. Brown quickly in a *hot* oven or under hot coals—no real cooking is needed.

N.B.—Some of the potato may be used to line the pie-dish, if liked.

269 FISH PIE

MAKE in the same way as Shepherd's Pie, using cooked fish instead of meat.

270 CURRY OF COLD MEAT OR FISH

½ pt. (1 nip) stock or coconut milk
1 onion
1 apple or mango or christophine
2 Tbsp. flour
About 1 Tbsp. curry or massala
1 Tbsp. oil or dripping
½ teasp. salt
½ teasp. lime juice
1 teasp. chutney
1 lb. cooked meat or fish
Rice
Hot peppers to decorate

PREPARE seasonings, fruit, and coconut milk. Heat oil, lightly fry curry and then seasonings. Add flour, christophine, chutney, lime juice, and coconut milk. Boil up and skim well. Remove skin and bone from meat or fish, and cut into neat pieces. Add it to the sauce and heat it quickly without re-cooking. Serve on large dish surrounded with a border of boiled rice and decorate with pieces of red pepper.

271 STUFFED MELONGENE

About 1 cup cooked meat, minced or chopped
1 large melongene
1–2 tomatoes
3 Tbsp. butter or dripping
⅔ cup bread-crumbs
1 teasp. salt
½ teasp. pepper
2–3 Tbsp. raspings (dried crumbs)

WASH melongene and cut off a slice. Scoop out the pulp, leaving a thin shell. Dice pulp and cook in butter or dripping in a covered pan over low heat till soft. Chive and onion may be cooked with the melongene, if liked. Mix all ingredients except raspings and fill the shell. Sprinkle top with raspings, add dabs of butter. Brown quickly in a hot oven or under hot coals—do not re-cook.

272 COOKED FISH OR SALMON CAKE

2 cups flaked cooked fish or dried salmon
1 cup bread-crumbs
1 cup milk
1 egg
2 Tbsp. melted butter
1 teasp. lime juice
1 teasp. salt (less if salmon is used)
½ teasp. pepper

REMOVE skin and bone from fish, flake and measure it. Beat egg lightly and add milk. Mix all ingredients.

Turn into a greased pie-dish. Bake in a quick oven till set. Serve hot or cold.

273 RICE CAKES

2–3 cups boiled rice 1 egg Salt or sugar to taste

LIGHTLY beat egg, and stir into the rice. Flavour to taste. Form into neat cakes and fry till golden brown in smoking hot oil. Drain well.

274 SALAD OF COOKED VEGETABLES

USE such things as cooked salad beans, carrot, Irish potato, christophine, etc. These may be mixed with lettuce and cress (after thorough washing), sliced banana, chopped nuts, chopped raw onion.

Cut all ingredients into neat pieces and arrange in an attractive way. Serve with Mayonnaise or French Dressing, see Chapter 11, Green Vegetables.

See also the following recipes:

85 Fish Fritters
139 Beef Pies
139 Stuffed Breadfruit
139 Fish Jelly
142 Russian Fish Pie
142 Savoury Custard

CHAPTER 36

PRESERVATION OF FOODS

IT sometimes happens when there is a very good fruit crop, or plenty of game or fish about, that we can buy these foods very cheaply, or that we have more food than we can use at the time. When this happens we must prevent the food from going bad by protecting it from little moulds, yeasts, or bacteria that are floating about in the air (see Chapter 15, Storage of Food). We must therefore destroy these little moulds, etc., or stop them growing and prevent fresh ones from getting at the food. This can be done in several ways :

(1) By heating the food—either partly cooking it or smoking it.

(2) By freezing it.

(3) By drying it—either over fires or in the sun.

(4) By shutting out air—as when tinning (canning) or covering jam, etc.

(5) By adding preservatives such as salt, nitre (saltpetre), vinegar, spices, etc.

Two or three of these methods are often used together. It should be remembered that preserved food is not as nourishing as fresh food. Long storage, great heat, and in some cases the use of chemicals destroy vitamins, and may harden food and make it less digestible.

PRESERVED EGGS

See Chapter 8, Eggs.

275 SALTED FISH (TASA SALLÉ)

1 medium fish, *e.g.* king fish or mackerel. About 10 Tbsp. salt

REMOVE head and bone the fish by cutting from the back and separating flesh from the backbone. Do not cut along the under-side (belly), as fish should remain in one large piece. Remove bone and entrails. Wipe with a wet cloth instead of washing. Using a sharp knife, make slits lengthways on inner side of fish. Rub all over with salt, working it *well* into the slits—use extra salt if necessary. Place on a large dish and leave for one day. Pour off brine solution which forms as fish stands. Wipe with a clean cloth and dry in the sun—for several days if necessary.

Keep in a clean dry place till required, and then scald before using.

276 SOUSED MACKEREL OR RED FISH

1 large red fish	About $\frac{1}{4}$ pt. ($\frac{1}{2}$ nip) water
2–3 cloves	3 or 4 unground black peppers or piece red pepper
2 bay leaves	
1 teasp. salt	About $\frac{1}{4}$ pt. ($\frac{1}{2}$ nip) vinegar

N.B.—This will only keep 4 to 5 days.

SCALE and bone the fish—cut into 2 or 4 fillets. Add salt and roll fillets from head to tail. Place in a pie-dish, add all other ingredients, making certain that there is enough vinegar and water to cover the fish. Cover the dish and bake slowly for $\frac{3}{4}$ hr.

N.B.—*No* onion, chive, or tomato should be used, otherwise the fish will not keep.

277 SMOKED MEAT

This method is best for fairly small pieces of meat. Unfortunately it makes it rather dry and tough. Clean meat and rub it well with plenty of salt. Hang it over a slow fire made from green wood ; turn constantly until all sides are smoked. Leave it hanging over the place where a wood fire is used daily. When using part of the meat, cut from the lower end, so that the cut surface is quickly dried by the smoke.

To Preserve Mangoes, Peppers, Tomatoes, etc.

See recipes for Chutney, Hot Sauce, etc., in Chapter 34, Sauces.

278 CRYSTALLIZED SHADDOCK

Wash, dry, and grate off some of the green peel. Cut into strips about 1½ in. at the widest part. Soak in cold water for 12 hr., changing the water several times, or better still leave under a slowly running tap—this removes bitter flavour. Put into fresh water and boil until soft. Colour during this stage if liked. Squeeze out all the water by twisting the strips.

Prepare a syrup by slowly dissolving 1½ lb. (3 cups) white sugar in ¾ pt. (1½ nips) water (do not stir). Simmer the peel in the syrup until it has all dried up (do not let it brown).

Prepare a second syrup using 1½ lb. (3 cups) sugar in ½ pt. (1 nip) water. Pour this hot over the peel, cover, and leave for a week or ten days. If syrup does not entirely cover peel, turn it daily, otherwise the exposed part will go mouldy. Drain and dry peel in the sun.

279 CANDIED PEEL

NEATLY cut peel from about 6 oranges or lemons. Soak for 3–4 days in salt water made by dissolving ½ cup salt in 2 pt. (4 glasses) water. Drain well and boil until soft. Soak 12 hr. in cold water to extract any salt that remains ; change water two or three times.

Make a syrup by dissolving 3 lb. sugar in 1 pt. (2 glasses) water, then boil the peel in this until the syrup candies. Take out peel, sprinkle with fine sugar and dry before a fire, in a cool oven, or in the sun.

For Jams, Jellies, and Marmalades see Chapter 37.

CHAPTER 37

JAMS AND JELLIES

EVERYONE should know how to make jam and jelly, because quite often people have a large crop of fruit, such as guavas, plums, etc., which it is difficult to use up in any other way.

Choice of Pan

(1) Use a wide shallow pan. The jam will boil quickly and much steam will evaporate, so that the jam will jell (thicken) quickly without turning brown.

(2) Use a thick pan : jam burns easily if the pan is thin.

(3) Choose a suitable sized pan as jam boils over if the pan is too small.

(4) Buy a stainless steel pan if you can afford it. Otherwise use enamelled iron (being certain that it is free from chips) or aluminium *brightly polished* before the fruit is put in.

Choice of Sugar

Buy as good sugar as you can afford. Cheap sugar makes a lot of scum which has to be removed, and is therefore wasteful and non-labour-saving.

Choice of Fruit

(1) Use full but not ripe fruit. Slightly under-ripe fruit contains a gummy substance called pectin which

helps the jam to jell. When ripe this pectin turns into a sugar called pectose.

(2) Use sound, unbruised fruit.

(3) Gather fruit on a dry day if possible : damp fruit may cause jam to go mouldy.

Preparation of Fruit

(1) Wash and drain, or wipe the fruit.

(2) Discard any bruised or over-ripe fruit and remove stems, thick skins, etc.

(3) Soak very acid fruit, *e.g.* tamarind, overnight. Next day cover with fresh cold water, heat to boiling-point, then throw away the water. Add a pinch bicarbonate (baking) soda, if liked.

(4) Cut fruit into suitable sized pieces.

GENERAL RULES FOR JAM

(1) Do not let jam boil until all sugar has dissolved.

(2) Stir occasionally while boiling.

(3) Skim when necessary.

(4) Boil steadily : too fast boiling breaks the fruit, while too long boiling turns sugar brown.

(5) When jam looks thick test it by putting a teaspoonful on a cold dry plate. Leave about 5 min. in a cool place, and if jam sets it is ready.

(6) Bottle at once in clean dry warm jam jars (bottles). If warm they are less likely to crack and more likely to be dry. Stand them on something wooden while filling.

(7) Cover at once with circles of clean waxed or grease-proof paper. Cut a larger piece of paper or cellophane to cover not only the top but the rim of bottle. Damp *one* side of this and stretch over bottle with damp side outwards. Tie down with fine twine. As the paper dries it tightens. If liked, brush over paper with white of egg or melted wax.

N.B.—The old idea was to cool jam before covering. This is bad as it allows germs, moulds, and dust to enter. Cover jam while it is still steaming.

(8) Label bottles stating kind of jam and date of making. Store in a cool dry place.

Proportions and Method for Different Fruits

Soft Fruit (*e.g.* tomato)

Use no water. Allow 1 lb. sugar to every lb. fruit. Flavour with spice. Place fruit in a wet pan and heat gently for about 15 min. to extract a little juice. Add sugar and follow general rules.

Firm fruit (papaw, pomme cythère, pomerac, plums, mammy apple, etc.)

Flavour with ginger or spice. Break a few of the stones and put back the kernel.
Allow half a pint of water to 6 lb. fruit, $\frac{3}{4}$ lb. sugar to every lb. fruit. Dissolve sugar and water slowly. Add fruit and follow general rules.

Hard fruit (pumpkin, googe, pineapple, etc.)

Flavour with the spice, ginger, or vanilla bean. Allow about half as much water as fruit, $\frac{3}{4}$ lb. sugar to every lb. fruit. Boil fruit gently without sugar until nearly soft. Add sugar and follow general rules.

280 ORANGE MARMALADE

8 sour oranges
Juice of 2 limes
Juice of 2 sweet oranges
8 lb. sugar
8 pt. water

WASH and peel oranges. Save peel and shred it finely. Slice fruit, remove seeds (pips), and soak them in half a pint of water. Soak fruit and peel overnight in remainder of the water. Strain water from seeds and add to fruit with lime and orange juice. Using the water in which fruit soaked, boil fruit and peel until the liquid has reduced to half. Add sugar and follow general rules for jam.

281 GRAPEFRUIT MARMALADE

1 large grapefruit
1 orange
1 lemon
5 lb. sugar

WASH fruit and slice thinly, discarding all seeds. Cover with 3 qt. of cold water and let stand until next day. Bring to boil slowly and boil 5 min. Remove from fire, add 5 lb. sugar, stirring until sugar is dissolved. Allow to stand in pan until next day. Boil slowly, and stir occasionally, until marmalade is thick and rich. This makes 7 lb. of marmalade.

GENERAL RULES FOR JELLY

(1) Wash fruit and cut it up roughly—skins, seeds, etc. should not be removed as these all make jelly, and will easily be removed while straining.

(2) Cover fruit with water and boil till it has reduced to half.

(3) Strain through a cloth. This should be tied to the legs of a chair or stool turned upside down on a table. If a really clear jelly is required let the juice drip, but if quantity rather than clearness is required squeeze the jelly cloth.

(4) Allow 1 lb. sugar to every pint (2 glasses) strained juice.

(5) Boil fast to preserve the colour.

(6) Test and bottle in the same way as jam.

282 GUAVA JELLY

10 lb. guavas to make 4–5 pt. juice
4–5 lb. sugar
½ in. piece of alum to clear jelly and make it thicken quickly

283 TOMATO JELLY

Use less water Add flavouring

284 APPLE JELLY

Add grated rind of 1 lime

CHAPTER 38

THE EARLY MORNING MEAL

SOME people for lack of money, time, or inclination eat very little or no breakfast (or "tea" as the first meal of the day is usually called in the West Indies). This is a bad plan, because our bodies need food to stimulate them and to provide energy, and without food we are more likely to tire easily and do work of a low standard.

The amount and kind of food people eat will naturally vary, but in all cases it is wise to start the day with some kind of fruit or fruit juice, which will act as a laxative, and so help the bowels to work regularly.

Other suitable foods are : cereals—*e.g.* corn flakes, cream of wheat, etc. ; bread or toast (wholewheat is best), with butter and honey or marmalade, or cheese if no other protein food can be afforded ; scrambled, poached, or fried egg ; fried bacon or sausage ; tea, coffee, or cocoa (see Chapter 33, Drinks).

285 TOAST

USE up stale bread cut into neat slices.

Toast over a glowing fire. Toast cooked too slowly is inclined to be very hard. Watch toast ; any which has burnt and been scraped is never so nice. When ready, stand two pieces of toast together or prop against a clean vessel ; any which lies flat will steam and go flabby. Serve in a toast rack. To be correct, toast for this meal should be served dry, but some West Indians prefer it buttered while hot.

286 FRIED EGG AND BACON

4 slices bacon	1 or 2 slices bread cut in neat fingers
2 eggs	

REMOVE rind from bacon and fry slowly in its own fat till clear and slightly brown. (Some people prefer it fried till crisp and dry). Turn slices when necessary. Dish and keep hot. Break eggs one at a time into a cup without spoiling shape of yolk, slip into slightly cooled bacon fat. Tilt pan to keep white from spreading, and fry very gently till white is set. Fast frying makes white bubbly-looking and very tough and indigestible. Serve eggs on top of bacon. Soak up fat with bread and fry till crisp and brown.

CHAPTER 39

AFTERNOON TEA

MANY doctors agree that this is an unnecessary meal, because three good meals a day (early tea, breakfast or luncheon, and dinner) are as much as the body needs and can readily digest. Those of us who get thirsty and enjoy afternoon tea must therefore remember that it should be a dainty but light meal.

Serving Tea

A small table and embroidered cloth is used, as people generally sit in comfortable chairs about the room or on the gallery, rather than round a dining table.

For each person provide :

Cup and saucer and teaspoon. These should be grouped round the teapot so that the hostess may fill and hand them to each guest ; or they may be partly filled with tea and handed on a tray by the butler to the guests who will help themselves to milk and sugar.
Small tea knife for spreading jam, etc.
Small tea fork if rich creamy cakes are served
Small fancy napkin, if liked—these should match the cloth

For general use provide :

Plates and d'oyleys for cakes and sandwiches
Sugar-bowl and tongs or spoon
Slop basin for dregs of tea when a second cup of tea is served

Strainer for tea
Milk jug
Teapot
Hot-water jug
Stand, tray, or mat to protect table from heat of teapot, etc.

Suitable Food

Tea, iced or hot. (See Chapter 33, Drinks.)
Sugar. If it can be afforded use lump (loaf) sugar. This looks well though it is not so sweet.
Milk or cream.
Cakes and scones. (See Chapter 28, Cakes.)
Bread and butter. Cut very thinly and remove crusts, if liked. Arrange on a plate in slices or rolls.
Small sandwiches with sweet or savoury fillings. Use a sharp knife, cut bread very thinly, remove crusts, and spread with butter and filling. Keep sweet and savoury sandwiches apart, and garnish the latter with a little well-washed parsley or cress.

Suitable Fillings for Sandwiches

Jam
Honey or honey and chopped nut
Chopped dates flavoured with lime juice
Chopped raisins, brown sugar, and lime juice
Grated or thinly sliced cucumber, or sardine, flavoured with vinegar, salt, and pepper
Sliced tomato
Potted meat or fish
Pea-nut butter
Crushed avocado pear flavoured with Worcester Sauce and salt
Grated cheese mixed with mustard and enough butter to make it of a spreading consistency

CHAPTER 40

FEEDING BABIES

A CHILD's digestion may be ruined and his health seriously affected if he is wrongly fed, and it is therefore most important that babies have the proper food from birth.

GENERAL RULES

(1) Breast feeding is the best whenever it is possible.

(2) Whatever kind of milk is given to baby it must be absolutely clean, pure, and fresh.

(3) Hours of feeding must be regular and punctual. The baby's stomach then gets used to receiving food at certain times, and the food will be better digested.

(4) Babies weighing less than 10 lb. (or under 5 months if the weight is unknown) sometimes need as many as six feeds between 6 a.m. and 10 p.m. In this case there should be 3 hr. between each feed.
Babies weighing over 10 lb. (or *healthy* ones who weigh less than this) should have 5 longer feeds with 4 hr. between each. Three-hourly feeding is only necessary if the child has a weak digestion or is a poor sucker, or if the mother has not got much milk.

(5) No night feeds should be given after the one at 10 p.m. Mother and child both need a long undisturbed sleep. Irregular feeding to quieten a restless baby is bad for the child's digestion and character, and will increase, and not cure, the restlessness. Good habits must be formed from the start.

(6) During hot weather when baby is thirsty, tepid boiled *unsweetened* water should be given as often as possible. Let baby take as much as he likes—he cannot have too much as long as it is unsweetened. The boiled water can be kept in an "icyhot."

(7) Baby needs a balanced diet—the necessary food factors (see pages 6–7) are found in milk :

Protein (in the form of casein) for muscles and flesh

Mineral salts (especially calcium and iron) for bones, teeth, and blood

Carbohydrates (in the form of lactose or milk sugar) for heat and energy

Fats (in the form of cream) for heat and energy

Vitamins to help growth and protect from disease

Water to carry away impurities and help digestion

Special Note.—Babies under 5–6 months cannot digest starch. The common practice of giving them arrow-root pap, sago, or flour and water paste is definitely dangerous, as the undigested starch ferments inside the baby's digestive organs and will cause diarrhœa, dysentery, etc. All the carbohydrate given to baby should be in the form of sugar.

(8) The quantity of food given to baby must be carefully *measured.*

(9) Baby must not be allowed to fall asleep while feeding, otherwise he will not have enough milk and will be hungry before the next feed is due. Also baby might choke.

BREAST FEEDING

If a mother is healthy and clean in her habits this is the ideal way of feeding a baby because :

(1) The milk is the correct temperature, it contains all the food factors in exactly the right amounts, and is pure.

(2) It is an economical way of feeding.

(3) It seems to have some emotional effect on mother and child, drawing them more closely together, and making both happy and contented.

(4) The mother will more quickly regain her normal health and figure. The uterus (or womb) contracts more rapidly when the extra supply of blood to the lower part of the body is drawn to the breasts.

Before feeding her baby, the mother must thoroughly wash her nipples with soap and boiled water.

For one complete feed the baby should be put to the breast for 15–20 min.

The quantity of milk received should be enough to make the baby gain 4–6 oz. a week. Mothers should take their babies to the Clinic or Infant Welfare Centre to have them weighed weekly.

Supplementary Feeds

Supplementary Feeds (from tinned or fresh milk or a prepared food) may be necessary if the mother is weak or has to go out to work. She should continue to breast feed her baby part of the time, only giving a bottle when necessary. The supplementary feeds should not be made too sweet, otherwise baby may prefer them to the better breast milk.

Strained orange, prune, or tomato juice

These should be given to a healthy baby from the time he is 1 month old. Begin with ½ teasp. juice mixed with ½ teasp. boiled water, and gradually increase the amount until at 6 months baby is taking the juice of an orange unmixed with water. Give the juice once a day, 1 hr. before a feed, as orange and milk taken together may curdle. Do not add sugar to the juice unless it is *very* sour.

FEEDS FROM FRESH MILK

When breast feeding is impossible a mother can take animals' milk (cow's, goat's, buffalo's, etc.) and make it as much like human milk as possible by adding water, sugar, fat, etc.

The following table should give some idea of what changes will be necessary :

	Protein	Fat	Sugar	Mineral Salts	Water
Human Milk	2·29	3·18	6·20	0·30	88·03
Cow's Milk	3·55	3·69	4·88	0·71	87·17
Goat's Milk	4·30	4·78	4·46	0·75	85·71
Buffalo's Milk	6·11	7·45	4·17	0·87	81·40
Ass's Milk	2·25	1·65	6·00	0·50	89·60

Goat's milk is thought to be the best substitute for human milk because it is not likely to contain tubercle bacilli (tuberculosis germs) ; it is rich in iron, and it is more easily digested than cow's milk.

Cow's milk turns acid in the stomach, and so barley water is sometimes used instead of boiled tap water. To make goat's or cow's milk suitable for a baby, it is necessary to add boiled water, otherwise there would be too much protein. Fat and sugar must then be added, as when reducing the protein the fat and sugar are reduced at the same time.

To make Barley Water see Recipe 311.

The milk must, of course, be purified by boiling.

To prepare 20 fluid oz. (1 pt.) cow's or goat's milk for a baby mix :

10 fluid oz. (½ pt. or 1 glass) boiled milk
1 oz. (2 level Tbsp.) sugar
1 oz. (2 Tbsp.) butter or ghee
Enough boiled water or barley water to make mixture up to 20 fluid oz. (1 pt.)
Instead of adding the butter or ghee, 1 teasp. cod-liver oil before any 3 feeds, *i.e.* 3 teasp. per day. This is better than mixing it with the milk as, if some of the milk is left, baby would not get his full share of cod-liver oil. It also helps to make him used to a spoon

When ready the milk should be warm ; blood heat (98·4° F.) is best.

The amount of milk given to the baby must depend on his weight rather than his age. Multiply the child's weight in pounds by 2½. The number obtained will be the number of fluid ounces of prepared milk he needs in 24 hr.

Examples :

An 8 lb. baby requires 8 × 2½ = 20 fluid oz. (1 pt.) of prepared milk
Six 3-hourly feeds of 3½ fluid oz. (7 Tbsp.) each; or
Five 4-hourly feeds of 4 fluid oz. (8 Tbsp.) each
A 12 lb. baby requires 12 × 2½ = 30 fluid oz. of prepared milk
Five 4-hourly feeds of 6 fluid oz. (12 Tbsp.) each

FEEDS FROM TINNED MILK

If there is any doubt about fresh milk being pure, it is wiser to use tinned milk.

Sweetened condensed milk contains more sugar than baby really needs, but some people recommend it because it keeps better than unsweetened evaporated milk. Mix the milk with boiled tap water or barley water and add fat, *e.g.* butter, ghee, or give cod-liver oil before the feed.

The amount to be given is as follows. To every pound of baby's weight allow :

2 teasp. milk
1 teasp. butter or ghee (or cod-liver oil, as above)
5 Tbsp. boiled water
This is enough for the whole 24 hours

Examples :

For a 7-lb. baby allow :

$7 \times 2 = 14$ teasp. milk
$7 \times 1 = 7$ teasp. (just over 1 oz.) fat
$7 \times 5 = 35$ Tbsp. ($17\frac{1}{2}$ fluid oz.) boiled water

A baby of this weight should have 6 feeds in 24 hr., therefore for 1 feed allow :

$2\frac{2}{3}$ teasp. milk
1 teasp. fat
6 Tbsp. boiled water

For an 11-lb. baby allow :

$11 \times 2 = 22$ teasp. milk
$11 \times 1 = 11$ teasp. fat
$11 \times 5 = 55$ ($27\frac{1}{2}$ fluid oz.) boiled water

A baby of this weight should have 5 feeds in 24 hr., therefore for 1 feed give :

$4\frac{1}{2}$ teasp. milk
2 teasp. fat
11 Tbsp. boiled water

It is specially important to give strained fruit juice to babies who are fed on tinned milk. This will make up for the vitamins which are destroyed when milk is tinned.

Feeds from Patent Foods—Lactogen, Chocolate, etc.

These are safe, but some are expensive.
Follow carefully all the directions given on the tin.
Always use boiled water for mixing them.

FEEDING BOTTLES

Special bottles can be bought ; those that have only one opening (which is for the teat) are best. Boat-shaped bottles that have two openings are bad. They often cause wind (gas), as the baby may suck in air, and the valve, besides being an extra thing to clean, is an unnecessary expense.

Feeding bottles

When money is short choose an ordinary white glass bottle, with sloping rather than square shoulders—these are easier to clean.
See that the rubber teat is in good condition—if the hole is large, baby will get the milk too quickly and will have wind. If the hole is too small, baby will get tired out by sucking and may not finish his milk.
Scald the bottle and teat at least once a day. Place them in a pan of cold water and heat slowly to boiling-point. Cover and leave them soaking in boiled water till required.
Wash in cold boiled water immediately after each feed and before milk dries. Cover and leave soaking in boiled water till required again.

Teats may be scoured with salt. Although boiling water will make them perish more quickly, it is necessary to scald them, because this is the only thorough way of purifying them.

WEANING

In the tropics it is wise to *start* weaning baby when he is about 7 months old.

Begin by giving him 2 teasp. oat jelly or baked flour porridge, then gradually start him on :

Sieved fruit, *e.g.* prune, papaw, sapodilla (after removing seeds), banana, mango
Sieved bharji (spinach purée)
Custard—baked or steamed
Scalded and scraped beef, etc.
Biscuits, well crisped—*never* soaked
Hard baked crusts or rusks

Hard crusts and biscuits help baby to cut his teeth. The other food should be sieved, so that it is in a semi-liquid state, because baby has not yet cut enough teeth to chew his food.

For further help on weaning see Chapter 41, Meals for Toddlers.

287 BAKED FLOUR (DEXTRINISED FLOUR)

Tie some flour in a clean cloth and boil it for 4–5 min. Take flour from the cloth, place it in a shallow pan and bake until crisp right through.

While still hot, crush to a powder with a rolling-pin.

Store in a covered tin or bottle till required.

288 BAKED FLOUR PORRIDGE

Mix 2 teasp. baked flour to a paste with a little cold water. Add 8 oz. (about ¾ glass) of boiling milk, stirring all the time. Put porridge back in the saucepan and boil for 5 min., stirring all the time.

289 OAT JELLY

Take ¼ cup well cooked quaker oat porridge and ¼ cup boiling water—boil them together for 5–7 min.
Strain and serve warm *without* sugar.
Pour a little of baby's milk over the jelly.

N.B.—This is good for constipation.

EFFECTS OF BAD FEEDING

Too much milk	Indigestion (wind) Sickness (vomiting) Diarrhœa Distended abdomen Flabby flesh
Too little milk	Thinness Slow growth Wasting diseases, *e.g.* anæmia, etc. Sleeplessness Nervousness Wind (gas)
Irregular or unpunctual feeding	Restlessness Vomiting Wind
Using starch when baby is too young	Vomiting Wind Thinness Distended abdomen

Lack of vitamins	Poor teeth and bones Deficiency diseases (see Chapter 3, Vitamins)
Impure milk or dirty bottles	Thrush (a fungus affecting the mouth) Diarrhœa Dysentery Tuberculosis or other diseases Eczema

CHAPTER 41

MEALS FOR TODDLERS

THE food for the toddler (a child of 1–5 years) needs just as much care as that of his baby brother—carelessness or neglect may have serious lasting effects on his health and his character.

Remember these rules when planning his meals :

(1) His diet must be plentiful and nourishing, because children grow very fast during these years and because they never seem to be still and so use up much energy. Re-heated food, which is less nourishing than fresh food, should not be given.

(2) The food should be light and easily digested to bring about a gradual change from a milk diet to a solid one. All solid food should be sieved up to the age of 15 months, as the child has too few teeth for proper chewing. Leave off sieving gradually.

(3) Meals must be at regular times : the food will be better digested.

(4) The food must be fresh and pure, and must be attractively cooked and served. It is important that during this habit-forming time in his life the toddler grows to like those foods which are good for him.

(5) Condiments, hot sauces, etc., are not good—a healthy appetite is the best " sauce."

(6) Titbits or snacks should not be given between meals as they spoil the child's appetite.

QUANTITIES FOR TODDLERS OF DIFFERENT AGES

Food	8–9 Months	10 Months	1 Year	2 Years
Purée of steamed spinach (bharji) or carrot or lettuce	1 teasp. daily,	gradually increased to	1 or 2 Tbsp.	2–3 Tbsp.
Quaker oats jelly or barley jelly	4 teasp. daily,	gradually increased to	3 Tbsp.	½ cup
Purée of prune or baked apple	—	2 teasp. increased to	1 or 2 Tbsp.	
Milk pudding (rice or cornstarch)	—	2 teasp. increased to	3 Tbsp.	1 cup, or according to appetite
Sieved vegetable soups	—	2 teasp. increased to	3 Tbsp.	1 cup, increased according to appetite
Potato (baked or boiled in its skin)	—	1 teasp. increased to	1 Tbsp.	2 Tbsp. do.
Eggs	—	2 teasp. increased to	1 whole egg (not more than twice a week). Mix with baked bread-crumbs to make it lighter and more digestible	
Red gravy	—	2 teasp.	1 Tbsp.	
Scraped beef	—	1 teasp.	½ Tbsp. } Mix with baked bread-crumbs	
Fish	—	—	2 Tbsp. } Mix with baked bread-crumbs	2 Tbsp.
Porridge	—	—	3–4 Tbsp.	½ cup
Dried cereals	—	—	3–4 Tbsp. from 15 months or earlier if child has enough teeth	
Jelly (fruit or chicken, etc.)	—	—	1 Tbsp.	½ cup
Custard	—	—	1 Tbsp.	½ cup, or according to appetite

(7) Never give sweets, candies, sugar cake, etc., last thing at night after the teeth have been cleaned.

(8) Provide a balanced diet. If a child has a craving for odd things such as coal, plaster, soil, etc., it often means that he is not getting enough mineral salts ; a craving for sweets, etc., may mean lack of sugar.

Protein

Protein for building good muscles should be in the form of :

Milk. From 1–5 years a child needs 1 pt. (2 glasses or 3 teacups) pure boiled milk a day. If tinned milk is used give extra fruit to make up for the shortage of vitamins.

Eggs. Cook them lightly. Coddled, poached, or scrambled eggs are best ; fried egg is very indigestible.

Gravy, Meat Juice, from a roast, etc.

Soup, from marrow bones, beef, lentils, etc., is good.

Fish. Fresh fish is better than salt fish. Steamed or stewed fish should be given rather than fried fish.

Meat. A little scraped or minced scalded beef is sometimes given from 9 months, depending on the number of teeth and child's health.

Minced chicken and tripe are digestible.

Pork should never be given.

Carbohydrates

Carbohydrates (starch and sugar), for heat and energy, must not be given in very large quantities. Because these foods are so cheap, many mothers fill the child with them and give too little protein and fat. The child may look plump and healthy for a time, but he will probably grow pot-bellied. His flesh is flabby instead of being firm and muscular, and he is easily affected by disease germs.

Starch obtained from *coarse* cereals or provisions is best.

Honey, which is a form of glucose, is the most digestible of all sugars.

For Fats, Mineral Salts, Vitamins, Water, see Chapters 2 and 3.

A DAY'S MEAL FOR A TODDLER OF TWO YEARS

Give the juice of 1 orange when the child wakes.

Early Morning Meal

1 cup milk
$\frac{1}{2}$–1 cup porridge or cereal
1–2 pieces brown bread and butter with honey

Midday Meal

2 Tbsp. fish
2 Tbsp. potato
2–3 Tbsp. carrot
} or $\frac{1}{2}$–1 cup vegetable soup, baked bread-crumbs
Pudding made from 1 cup milk
2 Tbsp. prunes or other fruit

Evening Meal

1 cup milk
Brown bread and butter with honey or seedless jam
Plain cake or biscuit

290 CODDLED EGG

Place a new-laid egg in boiling water. Cover and stand aside for from 5–8 min. (do *not* boil). The white should not be set but should look like a jelly.

291 POTATO SURPRISE

Bake a large potato in its skin. Cut off the top, scoop out and mash the inside and add a pinch of salt and ½ teasp. butter. Refill the skin, leaving a hollow in the middle. Break an egg carefully into this hollow and bake again just long enough for the egg to set lightly.

292 CARROT PURÉE

Boil or steam one carrot until tender. Peel and press through a sieve or coarse strainer. Add a pinch of salt and serve with white sauce.

293 CREAMED SPINACH (PURÉE)

Thoroughly wash and strip spinach. Scald or steam it and press through a sieve. Add a little butter and salt.

294 POACHED FISH

1 small slice fish
½ cup milk
¼ teasp. salt
1 teasp. butter

Prepare fish as for steaming ; place in a small greased pie-dish, add milk, and cover with greased paper. Bake in a moderate oven for about 15 min. or until fish is set and white in appearance.

N.B.—This method is convenient if the oven is already in use—no nourishment is lost, as the milk is used instead of gravy.

295 STEWED TRIPE

2 oz. tripe
$\frac{1}{4}$ oz. ($\frac{1}{2}$ Tbsp.) butter
$\frac{1}{8}$ oz. ($\frac{1}{2}$ Tbsp.) flour
$\frac{1}{4}$ pt. ($\frac{1}{2}$ glass) milk
Small piece onion
$\frac{1}{4}$ teasp. salt
Lime juice

WASH tripe thoroughly. Place in small enamelled or aluminium pan, cover with cold water, heat to boiling-point, and throw away this water. This whitens and purifies the tripe. Mince or cut tripe into small pieces, season with salt, chopped onion, and lime juice. Cover with cold water and stew gently for 2 hr. or until tender. When cooked, add butter and flour mixed to a paste with the milk. Boil 5 min. to cook flour, and serve hot.

296 SALAD DRESSING FOR CHILDREN

1 Tbsp. melted butter
1 Tbsp. orange juice
1 teasp. honey or sugar
Squeeze of lime

MELT and partly cool butter. Add all other ingredients. Prepare just before use, otherwise butter will harden and form lumps.

Other suitable recipes for toddlers will be found as follows :

315 Scrambled egg
314 Poached egg
70 Steamed fish
29 Stewed fish
40-47 Broth
48-59 Cream soups
305 Chicken jelly
306 Milk jelly
307 Egg jelly
308 Orange jelly
66 Steamed custard
200-205 Milk puddings

CHAPTER 42

DIETS FOR MOTHERS

WHEN a mother is pregnant (*i.e.* " making a baby ") or when she is feeding her baby, she should be specially careful about her food, otherwise both she and her child will suffer.

As a baby grows he will need all the food factors (protein, fat, carbohydrate, mineral salts, water, and vitamins), and as he can only receive his food through his mother, she must have a properly balanced diet.

In order that the baby may be strong he must have plenty of calcium for building bones and teeth, iron for his blood, and a good supply of vitamins, not only for growth but to protect him from disease. Nature, when looking after the baby's health, arranges that if there is a shortage of any of these things, it is the mother who will go without and not the child. For example, if there is a little but not enough calcium in the mother's food, it will all go to the baby, and the mother may find that her teeth suddenly decay badly, and in some cases even her bones become weak.

We therefore see that a mother must have a plentiful balanced diet, rich in foods containing vitamins and mineral salts.

Examples

Vitamins A and D, milk, butter, ghee, oily fish (cavalli), liver, mangoes, avocado pears, carrots.

Vitamins B_1 and B_2, wholewheat or bran bread, porridge, brown rice, liver, egg yolk, yeast, cabbage.

Vitamin C, milk, pineapple, mango, papaw, tomato, lettuce, and cress.

Mineral salts—milk, wholewheat, green vegetables (ochroes, spinach, green figs).

See Chapter 3, Vitamins.

Meals should be at regular times, and a light meal at night is better than a heavy dinner.

The food must be carefully cooked, otherwise it may cause indigestion and upset both mother and child. Steamed, stewed, or baked food is more digestible than fried food.

It is wise to eat less rather than more *solid* food at this time. Except for liver (which is rich in vitamins) only a little red meat should be eaten. White meat (*e.g.* chicken) or fish is more digestible.

" Plenty to drink " is one of the most important rules for expectant and nursing mothers. The following drinks are specially good :

Boiled cow's or goat's milk—this contains all the food factors, including a good supply of calcium ; coconut water (milk)—this helps to keep the kidneys in proper order and, as it is so easy to get, all mothers should take it every day. Fruit juice (*e.g.* orange squash) —this is rich in vitamins and mineral salts.

Pure water—all mothers should drink at least 2 pt. (4 glasses) daily ; this will help both mother and child to keep well, as it helps digestion and the removal of waste from the body.

No alcohol should be taken at this time as it is bad for the baby.

CHAPTER 43

DIETS FOR SICK PEOPLE

Sometimes, when people are sick, poisons (or toxins) collect in the body. They may be due to something going wrong, like appendicitis, or they may be the work of germs. The blood fights these poisons, and in doing so it may become overheated, in which case the sick person will have a fever with raised temperature. Ordinary food is difficult to digest when this happens, and the appetite is poor. Some special rules for planning diets for sick people are :

(1) Follow carefully any instructions given by the doctor.

(2) Give light and easily digested food ; it will often have to be liquid or semi-liquid.

(3) The patient will not eat much, therefore as only a little food can be given, it must be specially nourishing.

(4) Prepare only a little of each food, so that there can be as many changes as possible, and the food will not be stale. Food which has been offered to a sick person should never be served to anyone else.

(5) Do not use much seasoning, especially pepper.

(6) Serve food in a dainty and attractive way ; this helps the appetite.

Sickness or weakness may be due to a number of causes, some of them are :

The attack of germs, *e.g.* typhoid, malaria.

An operation, *e.g.* removal of tonsils or a kidney.

An accident, *e.g.* broken leg.
Childbirth, etc., etc.

It is easy to see that the food we prepare for sick people will be of different kinds, and for this reason the recipes are arranged in groups.

DIETS DURING FEVER

Give *liquid or semi-liquid* foods because they are easier to take and digest, and they will help to make up for all the water lost when perspiring freely.

During fever the body loses much nitrogen, so protein is required. Several of the usual sources of protein cannot be obtained as liquids, so it is wise to use some "protein sparers." These are obtained by buying jelly or gelatine, or by boiling down cow-heel, chicken bones, sea-moss, etc.

Liquid foods are grouped as follows :

(1) Cooling drinks—orange or lime squash, coconut, carrot, or barley water. They are often left by the patient's bedside for him to drink as he pleases.

(2) Nourishing foods—milk, egg nog, albumen water, arrowroot drink.

(3) Stimulating drinks—beef or chicken tea, fish tea, coffee, tea. These, although useful to give a feeling of well-being, cannot be used to replace the true nourishing drinks.

297 MILK PUNCH

½ pt. (1 glass) boiled or pasteurised milk
Sugar and flavouring to taste
Colouring, if liked

SWEETEN milk and flavour with essence, spice, or if to be iced, with fruit syrup. Add colouring, if liked—it often helps in the case of children. Swizzle well. Serve warm or iced. Provide straws if iced.

298 ORANGE AND MILK PUNCH

½ glass orange juice
Sugar, if liked
½ glass boiled or pasteurized milk

FREEZE orange juice and milk *separately*. When thoroughly chilled swizzle the two together. Sweeten to taste and serve at once.

299 EGG NOG (EGG FLIP)

1 cup or 1 glass boiled or pasteurized milk
1 egg
Sugar and flavouring to taste

BEAT egg and sugar *lightly*—if frothy it is difficult to drink, and even if taken through a straw nearly all the egg white is left in the glass. Add milk and flavouring. Brandy or rum is sometimes used if allowed by the doctor. Serve hot or iced.

300 ORANGE NOG

1 egg
Juice of 1 or 2 oranges
Sugar to taste

LIGHTLY beat egg, add orange and sugar. Serve iced.

301 ALBUMEN WATER

1 egg white
7 Tbsp. cold boiled water
Sugar or salt to taste

LIGHTLY beat egg white, add water, and leave to stand half an hour. Strain and add sugar or salt.

302 ARROWROOT DRINK (OR PORRIDGE)

1 *heaped* teasp. arrowroot
½ pt. (1 glass) milk
Sugar and flavouring to taste

Mix arrowroot to a smooth paste with a little cold milk. Boil remainder of milk with sugar. Stir in arrowroot. Continue to stir and boil for 7 min., by which time mixture will have boiled down to a cupful. (Less boiling will not make the starch in the arrowroot really digestible). Serve at once, otherwise it will become thick and unappetising.

N.B.—Cornflour (cornstarch) is sometimes used instead of the arrowroot.

303 SEA-MOSS JELLY

About a handful (2 ȼ) sea-moss
2 pt. (4 glasses) water
½ Tbsp. sugar
¼ pt. (½ glass) boiled or pasteurized milk
½ teasp. essence
Colouring, if liked

Pick and wash sea-moss thoroughly and soak it overnight. Cover with cold water, heat to boiling-point and discard water. Rinse well and pick over again, discarding discoloured parts. Add 2 pts. water and simmer till reduced to about one-third original amount —about 1½–2 hr. or longer if sea-moss is fibrous. Strain, add milk, sugar, and flavouring. Pour into cup or small mould. Place on ice and turn out when set.

304 COW-HEEL JELLY

For stock: 1 cow-heel and cold water to cover

For every pint of jelly:
1–2 teasp. lime juice
2 cloves
piece cinnamon } if liked
1 teasp. sugar }

Sherry or brandy if allowed by the doctor

Cut cow-heel into pieces and remove all marrow and fat. Wash well in warm water and scrape thoroughly. Place in deep pan covered with cold water, heat to boiling-point, then pour away water and rinse well. Return to pan, cover with cold water, and boil. Skim when necessary, and simmer till cow-heel is tender and begins to come away from the bone. Add more water if required. Remove from fire, take meat from bone and complete cooking—about 7 hr. in all. Strain, cover and stand on a grid to cool (air should be able to pass under the bowl). Next day remove all fat from the top, and re-heat with cloves, etc., for about 5 min. Strain and set on ice.

305 CHICKEN JELLY

1 chicken carcass
Cold water to cover
1 onion
2–3 cloves

Cut up the bones, add water and simmer till reduced to about one-third the original amount liquid—this takes about 4 hr. Strain, cover, and cool on a grid. Remove all fat, season lightly and set on ice.

306 MILK JELLY

½ pt. (1 glass) milk
1 Tbsp. sugar
Flavouring to taste
¼ oz. gelatine (*i.e.* 2 teasp. powdered or 3 sheets gelatine)

Boil milk and sugar and pour on to gelatine. Stir well, heat again if all gelatine does not dissolve, but avoid boiling as this spoils the taste. Add flavouring. Strain and leave on ice till set.

N.B.—If no ice can be obtained add extra gelatine (half as much again).

307 EGG JELLY

1 egg
3 oz. (6 Tbsp.) sugar
Rind and juice of 1 large lime
Sherry, if allowed
$\frac{1}{4}$ oz. gelatine (2 teasp. powdered or 3 sheets)
Cold water

WASH lime and peel very thinly. Squeeze juice and make up to $\frac{1}{2}$ pt. (1 glass) with sherry and cold water. Put into a pan with peel, sugar, and gelatine, and heat without boiling till gelatine dissolves. Cover and stand for 10 min. to draw out flavour of lime, then strain. Beat egg lightly, stir into gelatine mixture and heat without boiling till egg thickens. Stir all the time. Cool, pour into wet mould or cup, and set on ice.

N.B.—Use more gelatine if no ice is obtainable.

308 ORANGE JELLY

Rind and juice of 1 orange
Juice of 1 lime
$\frac{1}{4}$ pt. ($\frac{1}{2}$ glass) water
$1\frac{1}{2}$ oz. (3 Tbsp.) sugar
$\frac{1}{4}$ oz. gelatine (*i.e.* 2 teasp. powdered or 3 sheets gelatine)

WASH orange and peel very thinly. Heat water, sugar, and orange peel in an enamelled pan. Add gelatine and stir till dissolved, but do not boil. Cover and stand 10 min. to draw out flavour. Strain and add juice. Pour into mould or cup and set on ice.

309 BEEF TEA

1 lb. lean beef
Pinch of salt
1 pt. (2 glasses) cold water

CLEAN meat and remove skin and fat. Chop or mince finely. Add water and salt, cover, and allow to stand half an hour. Simmer for 3 hr. in a double cooker, stirring occasionally. Strain and remove all traces of fat—this may be done by passing pieces of clean absorbent paper over the surface of the beef tea. Serve hot.

310 RAW BEEF TEA OR LIVER DRINK

¼ lb. lean beef or liver
¼ pt. (½ glass) cold water
Juice of 1 lime
¼ pt. (½ glass) fruit juice, *e.g.* mixture of orange and grapefruit
1 teasp. sugar, if necessary

Quickly wash and scald the meat, remove fat, and chop finely. Add cold water and a pinch of salt, and soak for 2 hr. in a cool place. Pass through a fine strainer or cloth. Add fruit juice and sugar, if necessary. Ice and serve in a coloured glass with a slice of lime. Use at once—being uncooked, raw beef tea will not keep for any length of time.

311 BARLEY WATER

2 oz. (4 Tbsp.) pearl barley
2 pt. (4 glasses) water
Juice of 1 lime
Sugar, if liked

Pick and wash barley. Cover with cold water, heat to boiling-point and discard this water. Simmer barley and 2 pt. water for 2 hr., using a double cooker if possible. Strain and add lime juice and sugar. Ice before serving. Barley water may be mixed with an equal quantity of milk; in this case omit the lime juice.

312 CARROT WATER

2–3 carrots
1 pt. (2 glasses) water
½ teasp. salt

Scrape or peel and wash and chop carrots. Add water and salt. Simmer for ¾–1 hr. Strain and serve cold.

313 RICE WATER

½ oz. (1 Tbsp.) rice 1 pt. (2 glasses) cold water

PICK and wash rice. Add water, and boil half an hour. Strain and serve cold.

Coconut Water
Lime Squash
Coffee
} See Chapter 33, Drinks.

DIETS FOR SICK PEOPLE WITH NO FEVER e.g. CONVALESCENTS

Just as much care should be taken in planning these meals. All the general rules for invalids must be remembered, but some solid food may be given. The food should be stimulating to give a feeling of well-being and increase the appetite, and very nourishing and plentiful to build up the patient's strength and make up for loss of flesh, etc.

Suitable Foods :

Milk and egg dishes, as given in the following recipes:

66 Custard
306 Milk Jelly
307 Egg Jelly
191 Coconut Jelly (or Cream)
194 Blancmange (Cornstarch Jelly)
188 Mango Fool
189 Mammy Apple Snow
190 Guava Cream
215 Ice-cream
Porridge or Corn Flakes with milk

Egg dishes :

Lightly boiled egg with bread and butter or toast
314 Poached Egg
315 Scrambled Egg
316 Omelette

Soups :

44 Fish Broth
43 Mutton Broth
42 Cow-heel Soup
48–59 Cream Soups

Meat :

317 Sweetbread Stewed with milk
Breast of Chicken, Cream of Chicken
Minced Liver

Fish :

Steamed or boiled rather than fried, served with white (milk) sauce
318 Fish Cream

314 POACHED EGG

1 egg
1 round hot buttered toast
½ teasp. salt
1 teasp. vinegar or lime juice, if liked (this helps to set egg quickly)

PREPARE toast and keep it hot. Half fill a *shallow* pan (*e.g.* frying pan) with water and add salt and vinegar or lime. Break egg into a cup and slip it into water just before water boils. Tilt pan so that egg does not spread, or slip egg into a greased circular cutter placed in pan. Gently baste top of egg with water and cook till *white* is set—about 2–3 min. Drain and serve on toast.

315 SCRAMBLED EGG

1 egg
1 Tbsp. milk
¼ teasp. salt
Pinch white pepper
½ Tbsp. butter
Washed and chopped parsley
Round of buttered toast

PREPARE toast and keep it hot. Beat egg lightly, add milk, salt, and pepper. Melt butter in a small saucepan and stir in egg. Cook till creamy, pile on toast, and garnish with parsley.

316 OMELETTE

2 eggs
1 Tbsp. butter
2 teasp. chopped parsley, if liked
Salt and pepper

THOROUGHLY beat eggs with parsley, pepper, and salt. Heat butter in a small frying pan. Pour in eggs and stir till mixture begins to thicken. Smooth top. While still creamy, fold or roll omelette, brown underside, then place with browned side upwards on a hot dish. Avoid overcooking as this makes it harder to digest. Serve at once.

317 STEWED SWEETBREAD

1 small sweetbread (calf's) about 3–4 oz.
¼ teasp. salt
Pinch white pepper
About ½ pt. (1 glass) stock or water
Toast or cooked mashed potato

SAUCE

¼ glass milk
¼ glass stock
1 Tbsp. flour or arrowroot
½ Tbsp. butter

SOAK sweetbread in cold salted water for 1 hr. Cover with clean cold water, heat to boiling-point and throw away the water. Remove any gristle or fat. Cover with stock, add salt and pepper and stew till tender—about 1 hr. Place sweetbread on a piece of buttered toast or small heap of mashed potato and keep hot. Melt the butter, stir in flour, milk, and stock. Boil and stir the sauce for 5 min. Pour it over sweetbread. Garnish with parsley.

N.B.—Parsley, like cress, should be washed in Condy's fluid.

318 FISH CREAM

¼ lb. white fish
½ oz. (2 Tbsp.) flour
½ oz. (1 Tbsp.) butter
1 egg
¼ pt. (½ glass) milk
¼ teasp. salt
Pinch of white pepper

CLEAN, bone, and cut up or pound fish. Melt butter, add flour, and stir in milk. Cook until very thick, stirring all the time. Beat all ingredients together. Pour into a buttered mould or cup, cover with greased paper, and steam till set—about 40–45 min. When cooked turn out and serve with sauce.

N.B.—Chicken may be used instead of fish.

319 FISH SOUFFLÉ OR PUDDING

USE same ingredients and method as for Fish Cream, but whisk egg white very stiffly before adding. Steam or bake in a buttered pie-dish till set and well risen. Serve at once without turning out.

FOOD FOR PEOPLE WHO HAVE CONSTIPATION

Constipation is very common among people of all kinds and ages, and is one of the great causes of ill-health. It means that the bowels are not cleared of waste matter. It may be due to the wrong kind of food, to the want of air and exercise, or to irregular habits of clearing the bowels daily.

Food collected in the large intestine :

(1) Hinders the digestion of fresh food.

(2) May bring on appendicitis.

(3) Causes pains in the stomach, specially at the menstrual period.

(4) May cause a stoppage, and then the body instead of getting rid of the waste matter absorbs it into the blood. This waste is a form of poison and may cause headaches, want of energy, bad breath, a furred tongue, skin eruptions or spots, etc.

The careful choice of foods will relieve or prevent constipation. Here are some useful hints:

(1) Use foods which

(*a*) contain cellulose or roughage : *e.g.* cabbage, farine, mango. These stimulate the intestine.

(*b*) have a laxative effect, that is, make the bowels work easily : *e.g.* organic acid in prunes, oranges, etc., or oils such as sweet oil, etc.

(*c*) set up slight fermentation : *e.g.* honey, molasses, etc.

(2) Eat a reasonable amount of food ; either too much or too little may cause constipation.

(3) Drink plenty of water. A glass last thing at night and first thing in the morning is specially good.

Suitable Foods

The following recipes are suitable:

116 Wholewheat Bread
117 Bran Bread
123 Cassava Bread
174 Australian Jack
160 Bran Muffins
80 Tannia Fritters
199 Tropical Delight Pudding
Farine used for coating fried food
Raw fruit
Salads of all sorts
Cooked green vegetables of all sorts

CHAPTER 44

DIETS FOR VEGETARIANS

IN the first part of this book we discussed the fact that everyone needs a balanced diet containing plenty of protein. Some of the best protein foods are meat, fish, and eggs. Meat and fish are expensive, and for this reason some people become partial vegetarians. Other people are vegetarians because they dislike the idea of animals being killed for food, or because their religion does not allow them to eat any animal food.

Special care is needed in planning a balanced diet for these people, because large quantities of vegetable food are bulky but not stimulating, and they may distend and overwork the digestive organs without providing enough protein food.

The following foods are rich in protein and should be used plentifully :

Cheese	30–33	per cent.	protein
Peanuts (ground-nuts)	25·8	,,	,,
Dried beans	22·5	,,	,,
Split peas	21·0	,,	,,
Eggs	13·0	,,	,,
Prunes and dates . . .	4·3	,,	,,
Milk	3·5	,,	,,

320 GROUND-NUT CUTLETS

- 4 oz. (or about 2 ¢) nuts
- 4 Tbsp. bread-crumbs
- Small piece onion
- 1 small tomato
- 1 blade chive
- ½ teasp. chopped parsley
- Few drops lime juice
- ¼ teasp. salt
- Pepper to taste
- ¼ glass milk, 1 Tbsp. butter, 2 Tbsp. flour } to bind
- Tomato or Creole Butter Sauce

(Sufficient to make 4 small cutlets)

PARCH and shell nuts, then mince or pound them. Prepare seasonings and lightly fry them in about 1 Tbsp. butter. Remove seasonings from butter and add flour. Stir in the milk, thus making a panada or very thick sauce for binding the ingredients together. Mix all ingredients, divide into four equal parts and shape as cutlets or rolls. Coat with egg and bread-crumbs or raspings. Fry in smoking hot oil till golden brown.

N.B.—Cooked mashed potato may be used instead of the panada. The mixture may be made sweet instead of savoury.

321 LENTIL SOUFFLÉ

- 1 gill (½ glass) lentils or other legume (split peas, gubgub, etc.)
- 2 eggs
- 2 Tbsp. butter
- Seasonings to taste
- Cream, if available

PICK, wash, and soak lentils in about one and a half glasses water. Stew or steam them in the same water until soft, then sieve or beat them to a thick purée. Lightly fry any seasonings in a covered pot. Add butter, seasonings, cream, and egg yolks to lentils. Whisk egg whites very stiffly and fold them lightly into mixture. Pour into a greased pie-dish and bake in a moderate oven till set and well risen—about 20 min. Sprinkle with pepper. Serve at once before soufflé falls.

322 CURRIED EGGS

½ pt. (1 glass) coconut milk
1 onion
1–2 blades chive
1 mango or piece of googe
2 Tbsp. flour
About 1 Tbsp. curry or massala
2 Tbsp. butter or oil
½ teasp. salt
½ teasp. lime juice
1 teasp. chutney or hot sauce
3–4 hard-boiled eggs
Rice
Red peppers to decorate

PREPARE seasonings, coconut milk, and eggs. Cut googe or mango into neat pieces. Heat oil, lightly fry curry and then seasonings. Add flour, googe, chutney, lime juice, and coconut milk, boil up and skim well. Shell eggs and re-heat in the sauce. (Eggs may be cut in half lengthways if liked.) Place eggs on a hot dish. Coat with sauce and arrange a border of rice.

N.B.—Curried bananas may be prepared in the same way.

323 STUFFED EGGS

3 eggs
2 Tbsp. butter
Pepper and salt to taste
Flavourings, *e.g.* one of the following :

- 2–3 sardines or anchovies
- 1 teasp. curry powder
- ½ teasp. marmite
- 1 Tbsp. finely grated cheese and ½ teasp. mustard, etc.

Raspings
6 very small rounds bread and butter
6 slices tomato
} if liked

BOIL eggs hard, turning them constantly at the start, so that yolks do not set on one side. Shell eggs, cut in half, and remove yolk. Wipe out these white cups of egg, cut a small piece from the bottom so that they will stand firmly, and decorate edge. Sieve or mash yolk, add butter, pepper, salt, and prepared flavouring, and mix thoroughly. Fill white cups using a fluting (icing) pipe or teaspoon; pile mixture high. Add raspings if liked. Serve on a bed of well washed salad, or decorate with parsley or cress and stand on a slice of tomato on top of a small round of bread and butter.

324 SAVOURY CUSTARD

2–3 eggs
1 pt. (2 glasses) milk
1 teasp. salt
Pepper
1 teasp. chopped parsley, 1 boiled onion } or 2 Tbsp. grated cheese

PREPARE seasonings or cheese. Lightly beat eggs. Mix all ingredients and pour into a greased pie-dish. Bake or steam gently till set—about 45 min. Do not let custard boil otherwise it will curdle (see Custard, recipe 66).

N.B.—When not intended for a vegetarian, add about half-cup flaked cooked or salted fish, or small pieces of bacon or ham.

325 CHEESE PUDDING

½ glass fine bread-crumbs (with no crusts)
½ pt. (1 glass) milk
About 4 Tbsp. grated cheese
2 Tbsp. butter
1–2 eggs
Salt and pepper to taste
½ teasp. dry mustard

WARM milk, add all ingredients *except* egg white. Whisk egg white very stiffly, and fold lightly into mixture. Pour into a greased pie-dish. Bake on the top shelf of a moderate oven till set, well risen, and golden brown—about 20–30 min. Serve at once before mixture falls.

326 MACARONI CHEESE

3 oz. macaroni (or enough to cover the bottom of a 1 pt. pie-dish
3 oz. (or about ½ cup) grated cheese
1 Tbsp. butter
2 Tbsp. flour
½ pt. (1 glass) milk, or ½ glass milk and ½ glass macaroni water
½ teasp. mustard
½ teasp. salt
¼ teasp. pepper
Slices of tomato or hard-boiled egg to decorate

BREAK macaroni into about 1½ in. pieces, wash and cook in boiling salted water till soft—about 20–30 min. Strain off water. Melt butter, add flour, and stir in milk, about one-third at a time. Boil up, stirring well. Add macaroni, salt, pepper, mustard, and about two-thirds of cheese. Pour into a greased pie-dish and sprinkle remainder of cheese on top. Brown in a hot oven as quickly as possible, decorate with tomato or hard-boiled egg.

327 CHEESE TARTLETS

2–3 oz. shortcrust pastry
¼ pt. (½ glass) milk
½ oz. (2 Tbsp.) flour
½ oz. (1 Tbsp.) shortening
1–2 oz. (2–4 Tbsp.) grated cheese
Pepper and salt to taste
1 egg

MAKE pastry, roll out thinly, and line about 10–12 pie-pans. Prick bottom of each and set aside on ice. Grate cheese. Melt butter in a small saucepan and stir in flour without browning. Gradually beat in the milk and boil up, stirring all the time. Add cheese, pepper and salt, and egg yolk. Whisk egg white stiffly and fold lightly into cheese mixture. *Half* fill pastry cases and bake in a steady oven till well risen and golden brown—about 20 min. Serve at once before mixture falls.

See also the following recipes :

73 Rice and Peas
35 Curried Breadnuts
34 Pigeon Pea Stew
40 Pea Soup
53 Lentil Soup
58 Ground-nut Soup

CHAPTER 45

SOME EAST INDIAN RECIPES

MOST East Indians eat very little meat, and many eat none at all. What meat they do have must have been killed by one of themselves. The fats they use are mostly in the form of ghee (butter) or coconut oil (see Chapter 23, Frying).

Indian foods are usually served rather dry and are very peppery, so it is necessary to know how to make good massala (curry paste).

328 MASSALA

- 6 Tbsp. dhania (coriander)
- 1 heaped teasp. souǹp (anise seed)
- 1 heaped teasp. wuǹg (cloves)
- 1 heaped teasp. hàrdi (or colouring) saffron
- 1 heaped teasp. jira
- 1 heaped teasp. méthi
- 1 heaped teasp. gol mirich (black pepper)
- 1 teasp. sarso (mustard seed)—if to be used for beef use double quantity
- 3 grains (pegs) lesun (garlic)
- 1 large onion (piyaj)
- Lal mircha (red pepper) to taste

GRIND on a *stone*. Grind saffron first, adding enough water to make a stiff paste. Add all other ingredients by degrees, grinding very finely. Omit onion, garlic, and red pepper if it is to be kept overnight.

329 KALOUNJI

- 3 caraili (these are like knobby cucumbers)
- 2 Tbsp. massala
- 6 Tbsp. oil

Wash caraili and cut along concave edge. Cut across if very large and remove seeds and tips. Heat oil in a deep pot till smoking and fry massala till brown. Use massala to stuff cavity in caraili. Fry caraili in a covered pot till soft and brown. Turn as required, being careful that stuffing does not fall out. Serve with rice, roti (bread), or bara (salt cake).

330 CARAILI CHOKA

Wash and slice caraili. Cover with salt for about half an hour. Squeeze well to extract salt and bitterness. Fry in smoking oil till soft and brown. Serve with roti, salt fish, etc.

331 BAIGAN (MELONGENE) CHOKA

Prepare as Caraili Choka (Recipe 330).

332 ALU (POTATO) TALKARI

1 lb. (about 5 medium) potatoes
1 teasp. salt
1 Tbsp. massala
2 Tbsp. coconut oil
1 teasp. méthi
¼ pt. (½ glass) water

Put oil to burn with méthi, strain and fry massala till light brown. Peel, wash, and slice potatoes, and add to massala with water and salt. Cover and simmer until potatoes are soft.

333 CHANA (CHICK PEAS OR GRAM)

2 lb. (1 seer) chana peas
2 Tbsp. massala
4 Tbsp. oil
½ onion and a piece of red pepper
2 teasp. salt

Soak peas overnight, then remove outer skin. Put in a bowl and sprinkle with salt. Grind onion and pepper with massala and fry lightly in smoking hot oil. Add peas, cover, and fry till fairly soft, stirring constantly. Drain and serve with roti or rice.

334 BHAJI (SPINACH)

2–3 bundles spinach
2 Tbsp. coconut oil
1 clove garlic
1 onion and a piece of red pepper
1 teasp. salt

THOROUGHLY wash and strip spinach. Pound or chop onion, garlic, and pepper. Burn oil, then brown onion, etc. Add spinach and salt—stir thoroughly. Cover and allow to steam in its own water. When nearly soft, open pot and allow water to dry off.

335 URDI OR WOOLLY PYROL WITH SAHINA (DASHEEN LEAVES)

2 bunches dasheen leaves
½ lb. (1 cup) urdi (small greenish black peas)
1 Tbsp. massala
2 Tbsp. ghee

SOAK urdi overnight, then grind. Add massala. Wash and strip mid-ribs from leaves. Dry with a towel. Thinly spread back of leaf with urdi mixture, pack seven layers and roll. Slice into ¾ in. strips and fry. Drain and serve.

N.B.—Use a special towel for wiping dasheen leaves as it will be stained.

336 DAL (OR DHOLL)

½ lb. (1 cup) split peas (matar ke dal)
Small piece of saffron (about 1 in. long)
½ medium-sized onion
1 peg garlic or ½ teasp. jira
¾ pt. (1½ glasses) water
½ teasp. salt
1 Tbsp. coconut oil

Pick, wash, and soak peas overnight. Next day boil with saffron until soft. Add salt and chopped onion, then swizzle and remove from fire. Burn the garlic or jira in the coconut oil. Strain, add to peas, stir well, and cover. After a few minutes when the flavour of the burnt jira or garlic becomes pronounced, serve with boiled rice. The dal should be of a medium consistency.

337 MURGI TALKARI (CURRIED CHICKEN)

1 young chicken	2 Tbsp. flour (or añta)
1½ Tbsp. massala	3½ Tbsp. ghee or oil
2 teasp. salt	¼ pt. (½ glass) water

Pluck, singe, clean, and joint chicken. Burn oil (if used) with a peg of garlic and brown the massala. Coat joints of chicken with flour and brown. Add rest of ingredients, cover, and simmer until tender—about 45 min. Stir frequently. Enough water must be left to be served as gravy.

338 MACHHALI KA TALKARI (STEWED FISH)

1 lb. fish—or 1 medium-sized fish	3–4 blades chive
1 Tbsp. massala	1–2 tomatoes
½ onion	1 teasp. salt
Piece of red pepper	3 Tbsp. oil
2 Tbsp. flour	¼ pt. (½ glass) water

Grind massala, onion, and pepper. Wash and cut up chive and tomato. Trim, clean, and cut up fish. Sprinkle salt on fish and press on a mixture of flour and massala. Burn oil with a peg of garlic, remove the garlic and lightly fry seasonings, then the fish. Add water and simmer until soft—about 10–15 min.

339 GOS (MEAT)

COOK in the same way as fish, adding 1 teasp. parched, ground jira seeds to gravy just before serving. Stew for an hour and a half.

340 PHULOURI

½ cup dal (or dholl) flour	2 teasp. salt
1 Tbsp. massala	Water to mix
	3 Tbsp. oil

PREPARE flour by washing and soaking split peas. Dry them and grind on a massala stone. Mix dal flour, salt, and massala with enough water to make a stiff dough. Knead lightly, shape into small balls, and fry in smoking hot oil. Drain well.

341 DAL PURI

½ lb. (1 cup) split peas	Piece of red pepper
Small piece saffron	1 lb. (4 cups) flour
1 teasp. jira	½ teasp. bicarbonate (baking) soda
1 peg garlic	
½ onion	½ teasp. salt

(Sufficient to make 6–7)

PICK and soak peas overnight. Next day boil with saffron till fairly soft. Parch and grind jira, add onion, garlic, pepper, and finally peas. Grind well. Sift flour, salt, and soda. Add enough water to mix to a stiff dough. Form into balls about the size of an orange, roll out to ¼ in. thick, and put about 2–3 Tbsp. dal mixture in the centre of each circle. Fold over edges to cover dal and roll out to ¼ in. again. Place on hot greased baking-stone, daub with ghee or paper saturated with oil. Turn constantly. Cook till brown and puffy —about 10 min.

342 PARATHA (ROTI WITH GHEE)

½ lb. (2 cups) flour	¼ teasp. salt
¼ teasp. bicarbonate (baking) soda	Milk to mix

SIFT flour, soda, and salt together. Add enough milk to mix to a stiff dough. Form into balls about the size of a small egg—flatten each with a rolling-pin or bottle. Daub with ghee, then fold into a ball again. Roll out, cook on a hot baking-stone. (Baking-stone should be previously heated and tested by sprinkling with flour which should brown within a few seconds.) Turn constantly while cooking and spread plentifully with butter.

343 BARA (INDIAN SALT CAKE)

4 Tbsp. dal flour	Pinch bicarbonate (baking) soda
2 Tbsp. white flour	½ teasp. salt
1 Tbsp. massala	Water to mix

PREPARE dal flour as for Phulouri. Sift all dry ingredients together, add massala and mix to a stiff dough with water. Shape into a ball and roll out to a circle about 5 in. across and ¼ in. thick. Fry in smoking hot oil till golden brown. Drain well.

344 MOHAN BHOG (SWEET CAKE)

½ lb. (2 cups) flour	4 Tbsp. munaka (raisins)
¼ teasp.bicarbonate (baking) soda, or 2 teasp. baking powder	¼ lb. (½ cup) sugar
1 teasp. ground spice and clove mixed	Goat's milk or water to mix
	3–4 Tbsp. ghee

PARCH flour in a dry iron pot till pale gold colour, turning constantly. Pick and wash raisins. Sift flour, soda, and spice ; add sugar and raisins. Using a wooden spoon, mix to a dropping consistency with goat's milk. Heat ghee till smoking, stir in mixture, and cook until ghee is absorbed—about 5 min. Cool slightly, mould, and when cold, cut in slices.

N.B.—For special cakes use equal parts rice flour and white flour. To make rice flour, steam white rice, dry thoroughly and grind finely.

345 GULGULA

1 lb. (4 cups) flour	About $\frac{1}{2}$ cup milk
1 teasp. dal chini (ground spice)	4 teasp. baking powder
2–3 eggs (anda)	About 6 oz. (1 cup) raisins
	1 lb. (2 cups) sugar

Sift flour and spice into a bowl, add eggs and enough milk to mix to a stiff paste. Beat thoroughly. Add raisins, baking powder, and *half* sugar, and mix well. Form into a roll on a flour board, cut off 1 in. slices and dip each in remaining sugar. Fry in smoking hot oil till golden brown and cooked through. Sugar again or soak for a short time in thick syrup.

346 JILEBI (FRIED YEAST MIXTURE)

1 lb. (4 cups) flour	About $\frac{1}{2}$ pt. (1 glass) warm water
$\frac{1}{4}$ oz. yeast or 2 ȼ piece of baker's dough (leaven)	Thick sugar syrup made by boiling 1 lb. (2 cups) sugar, $\frac{1}{2}$ pt. (1 glass) water and spice
2 teasp. sugar for yeast	
Spice, if liked	

Mix yeast and sugar. Sift flour and add to yeast with enough warm water to make a thick batter. Leave to rise overnight. Next day beat lightly and add enough water to make it of a pouring consistency. Prepare a pot of smoking hot ghee or oil. Pour mixture into ghee through a funnel or tin cup with a small hole in the bottom. Form rings by circling pan 3 or 4 times. Fry till golden brown. Drain and soak in hot syrup for 5–7 min. When cool the syrup must not remain sticky, but dry with a sugary coating.

347 THE IDEAL CHAPATTI (DIET)

Taken from an Indian paper

Nutrition Research : One Anna Recipe.

A recipe for a nutritious chapatti suitable for outdoor workers in India has been evolved by the Nutrition Research Laboratories at Coonoor. A manual labourer needs at least two good meals a day. It is often impossible for him to return home to consume his midday meal, and he cannot afford to eat it in a hotel even if one were available. The meal, therefore, which he takes with him, should be sufficient in quantity and well balanced—that is, it should contain the essential nutritive elements in correct proportions. It should be cheap, made of easily obtainable foods, and be simple to prepare. It should be easy to carry, that is, it should be solid to avoid the possibility of spilling, small in bulk, and not require a special utensil to contain it, and should also remain fresh and palatable for a number of hours.

The Ingredients

Such a missi chapatti fulfilling all these conditions may be made from the following ingredients : Wholewheat, 10 oz. or 5 chataks, Bengal gram flour (chana pea flour), 2½ oz. or 1¼ chataks, onions, ¾ oz. or ⅜ chatak ; fenugreek leaves (or any other green edible leaves), ½ oz. or ¼ chatak, milk, 1 oz. or ½ chatak ; salt, ½ oz. or ¼ chatak, and ghee or butter, ¼ oz. or ⅛ chatak.

These constituents, except ghee, are mixed, water being added and the whole kneaded into a dough. Chapattis are made from the dough in the ordinary way, good thick chapattis being recommended, since these remain fresh longer than the thin ones. Subsequently ghee is smeared on the chapattis. The weight of this meal is about 1 lb. or half a seer ; it will supply about 1,300 to 1,400 calories, which is approximately half the daily requirement of a labourer, and about 50 grammes of protein.

The mixture contained in the chapattis is rich in vitamin and mineral salts. If fresh milk cannot be obtained, khoa or skimmed milk powder can be used. For those who can afford it, the addition of a greater quantity of milk or an egg to the dough is recommended.

CHAPTER 46

CHINESE DISHES

Some general hints

(1) Use soya bean oil except for noodles, which require lard. Soya bean oil is a good source of vitamin.

(2) Use cornflour (cornstarch) for thickening in the proportion of ½ oz. (1½ Tbsp.) to ½ pt. (1 large cup) water.

(3) Season with Shee Yow instead of salt—a special quality may be bought for table use.

(4) Soak all dried vegetables :

Mushrooms—cold water 1 hour, then remove stems
Gum choy (lily petals)—hot water 15 min.
Wun Yee (cuplike fungus)—hot water 15 min.
Chungchow (parsnip)—hot water 10 min.
Lin ny yow koy (lotus roots)—hot water 20 min.

(5) Serve food straight from the fire—people often wait while it is being cooked.

N.B.—A particular point about Chinese food is its long preparation and very short cooking ; this should make it nourishing as there is little loss of vitamin.

348 PORK SOUP WITH CHINESE VEGETABLES

1 lb. lean pork
2 oz. foo chook (dried bean curd)
2 oz. dried mushrooms
1 onion
2–3 blades chive
1 teasp. pepper
1 Tbsp. shee yow
1 teasp. ve tsin (gourmet powder)
3½ pt. (7 glasses) cold water
2 young see quar (quiquee)

Soak bean curd 30 min. if fresh, overnight if dark and old. Soak mushrooms 1 hr. Clean, cut up (1 in. long, $\frac{1}{4}$ in. thick), and season pork, using shee yow instead of salt. Simmer pork, bean curd, and mushrooms $1\frac{1}{2}$ hr. Wash and peel see quar (it should not strip along the edges for this shows that it is old). Cut in half lengthways, then across diagonally in 1 in. blocks. Add it to soup 5 min. before removing from fire.

349 JAN SIN YU (STEAMED FISH WITH MIXED VEGETABLE DRESSING)

1 lb. fish (grouper is best)
$\frac{1}{2}$ oz. gum choy (lily petals)
$\frac{1}{2}$ large onion or $\frac{1}{2}$ oz. spring onions
$\frac{1}{2}$ oz. fresh ginger
$\frac{1}{4}$ oz. chung choy (dried parsnip leaves)
2 large mushrooms (dried)
} cut into fine pieces
1 Tbsp. shee yow
1 teasp. salt
1 Tbsp. cornflour water

Soak lily petals, mushrooms, and parsnip in the usual way. Remove hard ends from lily petals and chop vegetables finely. Clean fish, wash with lime juice, and place in a steamer with a piece of greaseproof paper or a dish at the bottom. Mix vegetables with remaining ingredients except ginger and put over fish. Steam until firm—about 20–30 min. Add peeled and sliced ginger half way through the steaming. Serve at once.

N.B.—$1\frac{1}{2}$ oz. pork cut into fine slices can also be added.

350 STEAMED CHICKEN

1 fat chicken, about 3 lb.
6 pegs garlic
3 teasp. salt
2 Tbsp. shee yow
1 teasp. ng heung foon (spice powder)

Pluck, singe, and clean chicken in the usual way, but do not cut it up. Pound garlic and salt to paste, add shee yow and spice powder. Rub chicken well with this mixture both inside and out. Turn wings underneath, and place chicken breast upwards in a steamer or in a tightly covered pan containing very little water. Steam till tender—about 1½–2 hr. Serve with mixed vegetables, which may be cooked at the same time :

1½ oz. bamboo shoots (could be obtained canned)
2 oz. water chestnuts
1 oz. mushrooms
¼ oz. wun yee (lichen)
½ oz. chung choy (preserved parsnips in bundles)
¼ oz. ginger (fresh)
½ oz. gum choy (lily petals)
4 hung jo (jujube fruits)

Cut all ingredients into very fine pieces. Mix together with a little salt, pepper, sugar, sesame oil, cooking sherry, soya sauce, and cornflour water. Place on top of the chicken (20 min. before serving).

351 NG HEUNG JA GAI (FRIED SPICED CHICKEN)

1 young chicken, about 4 lb.
½ teasp. salt
½ teasp. ng heung foon (Chinese spice)
¼ teasp. pepper
4 Tbsp. gin

Pluck, singe, and clean chicken in usual way. Remove head and lower leg and wing joints. Cut into four pieces, *i.e.* cut in half each way. Mix all ingredients and leave to soak with chicken for 12 hr. Half-fill a deep pot with oil. Fry chicken in smoking hot oil till golden brown and tender—about 30 min. (allow 1 hr. if chicken is whole). Use a slow fire and avoid over-heating oil. Baste chicken if not covered with oil. When cooked cut chicken into pieces about 1 in. long and ½ in. wide. Place in a dish and sprinkle spicery salt on the top.

352 PORK WITH FOO CHOOK AND KIM CHIM

2 oz. foo chook (dried bean curd)
2 oz. kim chim (dried lily)
3 Tbsp. soya bean oil
1 lb. pork or chicken
1 Tbsp. shee yow (salt sauce)
½ teasp. salt
½ teasp. pepper

Soak bean curd overnight in cold water or for 20 min. in boiling water. Soak dried lily ½ hr. in boiling water. Clean and cut pork into neat pieces—about 1 in. cubes. Season with salt, pepper, and shee yow. Brown pork in hot oil and add about ½ pt. (1 glass) water. Add bean curd, cover, and simmer 1 hr. Add dried lily, cook for another ½ hr., when all ingredients should be tender.

353 CHOP SUEY

Ingredients	
6 oz. chicken meat 3 oz. onions ½ oz. mushrooms	cut into fine slices
½ oz. bamboo shoots ½ oz. celery	cut into fine slices

4 oz. bean sprouts
8 oz. tomatoes
1 egg well beaten

Scald tomatoes and remove skins. Soak mushrooms, remove stalks, and slice finely. Wash and pick bean sprouts. Place chicken in a hot oiled pan and cook for 1 min. Add bamboo shoots, bean sprouts, onions, celery, mushrooms, and salt to taste. Cook for 1 min. Add tomatoes and cook for 2 min. Add a little cornflour water, a few drops of sesame oil and soya sauce (shee yow) and a ¼ teasp. sugar (add noodles if desired), and cook all together for 1 min. Add a dash of rum or Worcester Sauce, if liked. Place in dish and keep hot. Put beaten egg in a hot oiled pan and cook for 2 min. Place omelette over the Chop Suey and serve.

N.B.—Lobster meat or pork may be substituted for chicken, and ½ oz. fun si (corn noodles) may be added to recipe. To prepare the latter, place corn noodles in a saucepan of boiling oil and cook for 3 min., then take out and add to chop suey with the cornflour water. 1 or 2 carrots, cristophines, or cabbage leaves may also be added, if liked.

354 SEY FOO GNAR CHOY (BEAN SPROUTS WITH TOMATOES)

- 2 portions (4 ¢) gnar choy (bean sprouts)
- ¾ lb. (about 4 good sized) tomatoes
- ½ onion (or ½ oz. spring onions) cut into 1½ in. slices
- 1 teasp. salt
- 3 Tbsp. stock or water
- 2 Tbsp. cornflour (cornstarch) water
- ¼ lb. pork if liked (cut in very thin slices)
- About 4 Tbsp. oil

Scald and skin tomatoes, and cut in half. Remove roots from bean sprouts, and wash thoroughly. Slice onion. Clean and chop pork. Heat oil in a deep pot; when smoking pour off all except for about ½ Tbsp. Brown pork. Add bean sprouts and toss for 1 min.

Add stock or water, cover, and steam 2 min. Add salt, onion, and tomatoes, and toss again for 1 min. Add cornflour water and cook 3 min. Serve at once.

N.B.—Good bean sprouts are pale and short. Sprouted peas may be used instead. Celery may be added, if liked.

355 STEAMED EGGS WITH HAM MI

4 eggs
3 oz. ham mi (dried shrimps)
1 cup water
½ teasp. pepper
½ Tbsp. shee yow
½ oz. spring onions

WASH dried shrimps and soak for ½ hr.; chop finely. Beat eggs and add all other ingredients. Pour into a greased bowl and steam till set—about ½ hr.

356 POW CHOY AND WUN YEE (CABBAGE AND WUN YEE)

6 Tbsp. oil
1 lb. cabbage
2 oz. wun yee
1 oz. pork
¼ cup cornstarch water
1 Tbsp. shee yow

SOAK cabbage 15 min. in salted water. Throw away discoloured parts and stalk. Cut into ½ in. slices, then across so that it is more or less in squares. Soak wun yee in hot water for 15 min., then pick off woody pieces. Chop the pork in very thin slices. Heat oil in deep pot. Pour off all except for ½ Tbsp. Toss cabbage and wun yee in pot for about 2 min. Add all other ingredients, cover, and steam in its own water for 5 min.

N.B.—More pork can be added as in previous recipe, if liked.

357 CRISTOPHINE AND WUN YEE

2 cristophines
½ lb. pork
1½ Tbsp. shee yow
1 oz. wun yee
¼ teasp. pepper
2 Tbsp. soya bean oil
½ cup cornflour water

SOAK and thoroughly pick wun yee. Peel and cut cristophine into straws. Clean, chop, and season pork with 1 Tbsp. shee yow and pepper. Heat oil and brown pork quickly. Add cornflour water, remaining ½ Tbsp. shee yow and wun yee. Simmer 10 min., stirring often. Add cristophine and cook again for 15 min.

CHAPTER 47

MISCELLANEOUS RECIPES

358 CONQUINTAY FLOUR

TAKE full green plantains, peel and slice thinly lengthways. Lay slices on a board and dry in the sun, turning occasionally. When quite dry and crisp—about 4–5 days—pound while warm from the sun and sift through muslin. Use for bakes, coo-coo, etc.

359 FOO FOO OR POUND PLANTAIN

BOIL 4–5 green plantains without salt. When soft, cool, peel, and pound them in a wooden mortar. Dip pestle in cold water frequently, otherwise plantain will stick. When plantain forms a smooth ball, re-heat, season, and serve it with Creole soups.

360 STUFFING OR FORCEMEAT

½ cup Fresh bread-crumbs
Cracker crumbs
Cooked mashed potato
Cooked mashed chatigne
Farine
} Use one of these or a mixture of two of them

2 Tbsp. butter or chopped suet or fat pork
2 teasp. chopped parsley
2–3 sprigs of thyme
1 Tbsp. chopped onion or chive } if liked
1 chopped tomato } if liked
¼ teasp. pepper or piece of red pepper
½ teasp. salt
Beaten egg or milk to bind

This can be used for chicken, turkey, fish, etc.

Prepare all ingredients, removing stalks from parsley and thyme. Mix all dry ingredients. Add enough egg, milk, or water to bind them firmly together—use as required.

361 CHOW CHOW

Wash, peel, and slice full but unripe mangoes. Sprinkle with pepper and salt and add about 1 Tbsp. vinegar to every 2–3 mangoes. Serve with meat or fish.

362 VANILLA ESSENCE

Soak 2–3 vanilla pods in ½ pt. (1 nip) rum.

A strong essence is more economical as less will be required for flavouring.

363 HOME-MADE VINEGAR

Plain " acid water " made from acetic acid and water is not a good substitute for vinegar. Used regularly it is definitely harmful.

(1) *Cane juice vinegar.* Allow juice to ferment for 4–5 weeks. Strain and colour with a little burnt sugar.

(2) *Gingerbeer and Mawby vinegar.* Ferment liquid for 1–2 weeks.

(3) *Molasses vinegar.* 4 pt. (8 glasses) molasses
6 gallons soft water
1 pkt. (½ oz.) yeast

Stand mixture in a warm place for 3 weeks. Strain and bottle.

INDEX

PAGES FOR ADDITIONAL RECIPES

ADDITIONAL RECIPES

ADDITIONAL RECIPES

ADDITIONAL RECIPES

ADDITIONAL RECIPES

ADDITIONAL RECIPES

ADDITIONAL RECIPES

ADDITIONAL RECIPES

ADDITIONAL RECIPES

ADDITIONAL RECIPES